TOURISM IN INDIA

Challenges and Opportunities

TOURISM IN INDIA

Challenges and Opportunities

Editors

Dr. Ruchi Ramesh

Dr. Sudhir Kumar Singh

Association with

SOCIETY FOR SOCIAL EMPOWERMENT, NEW DELHI

PENTAGON PRESS

Tourism in India: Challenges and Opportunities
Dr Ruchi Ramesh, Dr. Sudhir Kumar Singh (Eds.)

First Published in 2012

Published by

PENTAGON PRESS
206, Peacock Lane, Shahpur Jat,
New Delhi-110049
Phones: 011-64706243, 26491568
Telefax: 011-26490600
email: rajan@pentagonpress.in
website: www.pentagonpress.in

Cataloging in Publication Data—DK
Courtesy: D.K. Agencies (P) Ltd. <docinfo@dkagencies.com>

Tourism in India : challenges and opportunities / editors, Ruchi Ramesh, Sudhir Kumar Singh.
p. cm.
Contributed articles.
Includes bibliographical references (p.) and index.
ISBN 9788182746022

1. Tourism—India. I. Ruchi Ramesh. II. Singh, Sudhir Kumar. III. Society for Social Empowerment.

DDC 338.479154 23

Printed at New Elegant Printers, New Delhi.

Contents

Contributors

1. **Alokka Dutta**, Department of Political Science, Bhagini Nivedita College University of Delhi.
2. **Aamnayi Mishra**, D.A.V. College, Titilagarh Dist: Bolangir, Odisha.
3. **Amulya K. Tripathy**, teaches Political Science at D.A.V. College, Titilagarh Dist. Bolangir, Odisha.
4. **Bindi Varghese**, Asst. Prof Department of Tourism Studies, Christ University Bangalore.
5. **Krishan Gopal**, Deputy Librarian, Jawaharlal Nehru University. New Delhi.
6. **Lakhvir Suneja**, S.O.S.T.T.M. Jiwaji University Gwalior.
7. **Mondira Dutta**, Convener, Central Asian Area Studies Programme Centre for South, Central, South East Asian and South West Pacific Studies School of International Studies Jawaharlal Nehru University New Delhi.
8. **M. Thilakavathy**, Associate Professor, Department of History and Tourism, Ethiraj College Chennai.
9. **N.C. Jana**, Reader, Department of Geography, The University of Burdwan, Burdwan, W.B.
10. **Ruchi Ramesh**, Associate Professor, Department of Sociology, R.K.M.V. Shimla (H.P.)

11. **S. Prabhakar**, Joint Director Lok Sabha, New Delhi.

12. **Sudhir Kumar Singh**, Assistant Professor, Dyal Singh College, University of Delhi, New Delhi.

13. **Suresh, R.**, Associate Professor, Post Graduate & Research Department of Political Science, Sree Narayana College, University of Kerala, Kollam, Kerala.

14. **Syfujjaman Tarafder**, M.Phil Student, Department of Geography, The University of Burdwan, Burdwan, W.B.

Introduction

Tourism has emerged today as an engine of economic growth and an instrument of eliminating poverty, solving unemployment problem, opening up new fields of activity and the uplifting status of women.[1] Tourism has direct as well as indirect social and economic impact on the host country as tourist have higher disposable income and greater leisure time and they are also better educated. The primary reason for the growth of tourism industry can be attributed to the easy accessibility of information, development of technology and improved transport infrastructure. The World Tourism Organization defines tourists as people "who travels and stay in places outside their usual environment for not more for one consecutive year for leisure, business and other purposes are not related to the exercise of an activity renumated from the place within visited."[2] For better understanding, tourism can be categorized into three categories. The first type is domestic tourism, which includes the residents of a given country traveling only within this country. The second type is inbound tourism, involving non resident involving in the given country. The third and final is outbound tourism, involving residents traveling in another country.

Tourism industry has been propelled by the growing pace of globalization and realization of freedom. Rapidly connected transportation and communication system has further aggravated the flow of the tourists from one part of the globe to another part. Tourism represents one of the world's largest industries with rapidly growing numbers of visitors. In 1995 the global tourist flow was 534 million which rose to 920 million in 2009.[3] However the ongoing worst economic recession after 1929, global economy growth have been obstructed and it has shed negative impact of the flow of tourists particularly from the resourceful Developed countries towards Developing and under Developing countries of the globe. Against this backdrop UNWTO forecasts a growth in international tourist arrivals of between 5 per cent and 6 per cent in 2011. It is expected that by 2020 it will reach 1.5 billion people. The top ten destinations in worldwide travel did not experience major changes for the year of 2009-10, even in terms of receipts and arrivals. The United States, France, and Spain are considered the top three leaders in both arrivals and receipts, though order and rankings change. The United States was the first in receipts, but second in arrivals; France was the continued leader in tourism arrivals, and was third in receipts; Spain, while third in arrivals, was the second biggest tourism earner worldwide. Germany and Turkey both climbed in 2009 rankings, respectively, to eighth and seventh place. China has done tremendous development despite non cooperative international economic regime. Few decades earlier it was not a prominent figure on the map of the international tourism. But it has done extremely hard work to ensure firm and steady development in this sector and accordingly China's international tourism spending grew quickly in 2009-10, overtaking France as the fourth largest in terms of global tourism expenditures. It has been opined by the pundits of the international system that Asia will dominate the international system in 21st century. The way Asia is growing it could be said that it seems to be possible provided it could be translated into strategic and political level of bi-lateral and multi-lateral relationship. However the pace of economic development and its sustainability in Asia has put the continent as the harbinger of global tourism map. International tourism growth during 2010, led by Asia, was positive in all regions globally and it has been continued even in first two months of 2011. The UNWTO World Tourism Barometer indicated a 7 per cent increase in arrivals for international tourism. This continues an upward trend that began in the last quarter of 2009, after negative results spanning 14 consecutive months. Of the 77 global tourism destinations, 60 of these (or 78%) showed positive results in 2010. Twenty four destinations reporting data showed growth in the double digits during the same period. This is encouraging news, especially from countries like Egypt, Japan, the US Virgin Islands, Israel, India, and Kenya.[4] Tourism is one of the world's largest industries, generating an estimated 11 per cent of global Gross Domestic Product (GDP), employing 200 million people and transporting nearly 900 million international travelers per year —a figure that is expected to double by 2020. Developing countries currently have only a minority share of the international tourism market (approximately 30%) but this is growing. International tourism arrivals in developing countries have grown by an average of 9.5 per cent per year since 1990, compared to 4.6 per cent worldwide.[5] [WTTC Report] The tourism industry makes important contributions to the economies of developing countries, particularly to foreign exchange earnings, employment, and GDP.

Many researches have been carried out to establish link between tourism and poverty elimination. The findings of these research have vindicated that tourism could be an asset to eliminate poverty and promote culture as well as peace and development throughout the world in general and developing countries in particular. It could be a panacea of many curses against humanity and establish a peaceful global society.

Being a democratic country India has done well in previous decades to provide basic amenities to the poorest of the poor. But a sizable number of people are still languishing below the poverty line and lives a life which is by all interpretations is at par with the animals. For an ideal democracy it is a big embarrassment. Welfare of its citizens is the life blood of democracy particularly to provide all kinds of amenities to the common people with exclusive provisions for destitute. Kautilaya, the great Indian Philosopher has insisted in his famous book *Arthsastra* that a king must nurture their subject as a new born baby is nurtured by his/her parents. One could trace the origins of democracy, good governance and human rights from his writing. He was the prime minister of the greatest Indian empire called Mauryan Empire. We are aware about the fact that monarchy was not accountable for the people, s welfare because merely it was of the opinion that it derives its legitimacy of rule from the almighty god therefore it is only accountable to god. In democracy, people are the custodian therefore the elected ruler must be accountable for the people and people are most benefited element by all theoretical frameworks. But in reality prevalence of chronic poverty across the globe particularly in less developed and developing countries exclusively in those countries which have adopted democracy as a mode of governance is a blatant denial of the fundamental rights of the common people. In many developing countries it is matter of governance but in majority of them lack of resources and rampant corruption is denying the basic tenets of democracy to the common people. Tourism could be facilitators of human virtues in this direction. Needles to say that unattended problem of poverty and our lop-sided developmental process have stalled the real growth of our great country. Due to this issues 1/3 of the country remains under the controls of the Naxals, where the writ of the state is not existed. It is one of the most turbulent problems for India in 21st century. Since tourism has just started to take off in India therefore there is ample opportunity to develop it in foreseeable future in a phenomenal way. The 11th Five Year Plan (2007-12) is in operation and has declared Inclusive Growth as the target of development. The billion questions is that how far we are able to ensure inclusive growth without incorporation 1/3 of our poorest of the poor populace into the mainstreaming process of development. This population is equivalent to the entire population of United States of America.

India is a developing country and recently World Bank has announced that within next two years, India will be surpassing China in GDP growth.[6] Despite being a newly emerged country, India has done tremendous progress in all round development. Today after six decades of our independence, one of the biggest concerns remains and that is inclusion of the marginalized into the mainstreaming process of development. It is one of the most crucial factors, which sustains a kind of unrest in our society. Poverty is a great denial of democracy and fundamental human rights. It is true that since last few decades we have been able to upgrade the life standard of 300 million people. But according to the Planning Commission still around 35 per cent people lives below the poverty line. According to the 2011 census, India has 121 crore population and still existing gender gap vindicates the point that gender has been discriminated despite growing literacy, awareness and prosperity. Currently 11th Five Year Plan (2007-12) is in operation. According to the Approach Paper of the 11th Plan, "The 11th Plan provides an opportunity to restructure policies to achieve a new vision of growth that would be much broader based and inclusive, bringing about a faster reduction in poverty and helping bridge the divides that is currently the focus of so much attention. The first steps_in this direction were initiated in the middle of the Tenth Plan based on the National Common Minimum Programs adopted by the UPA-1 government (2004-09). These steps must be further strengthened and consolidated into a strategy for the 11th Plan."

The fact of the matter is that huge unemployment has triggered much malice within our society and for their mitigation we need to go to the root cause of the problem instead of paying lip services. We have to provide basic facilities to all people including the have notes. State is unable to provide them employment and private sector boom due to the process of globalization has only been able to provide employment to the skilled people at certain extent. But what about unskilled people, how they will earn their bread. It is a Himalayan question before us at the outset of the 21st century. Arjun Sengupta committee was appointed by the UPA-1 governmnet and according to the report of that committee the state of unskilled people is extremely worse. Even onslaught of globalization and changing life style has reduced their traditional ways to earn bread and nurture their family.

Tourism could be a great facilitator for the employment of the unskilled sector. There is hardly any actual estimate of their number but according to certain concrete estimates it could be more than 100 million. Tourism sector did not require skilled people in bunch. Unskilled people required in a big number to facilitate the smoothness of the industry . Another benefit is that we are confronting the menace of migration and if not prevented properly Indian villages could be vintage villages after 4-5 decades. The growing pace of migration from rural areas to urban areas has devastated the existing infrastructure in the urban sectors. It has created a major threat to the urban governance. We have initiated many methods to contain it but it is growing without any interruption. Our villages are enormous sources of cultural diversity and great protector of environment. Majority of western tourists are fed up with their material life and want peace and for that purpose we must use our village as points of obsession for outside tourists. Promotion of tourism sector could be a great help in this direction. Since we have not developed tourism sector at par with South East Asian countries despite last one decade's unprecedented growth. The promotion of village or rural tourism will be a great help for the overall tourism and industry. The growing pace of tourism sector will involve unskilled poorest of the poor working class. It could provide them ample opportunity to earn their bread and remains back to their place of origin. It will serve the twin purpose of providing employment to the unskilled poorest of the poor and prevent the rapidly increasing migration from villages to urban sectors.

Another turbulent contemporary problem we are confronting is threat on our culture. With the growing pace of the process of globalization, our culture is under threat. Fortunately tourism sector could be a big protector in this direction also. The foreign tourists are coming to India for many reasons but one of the important among them is our cultural beauty and diversity. We have numerous varieties of songs, Gazals and many modes of indigenous cultural heritage. When unpredicted number of foreign tourists will pour in than our policy planners will be compelled to preserve it. Common people will also witness the fact that our culture is so great that foreigners are getting obsessed with this and needles to say that it will promote our culture in a phenomenal manner. It will also impart a new lease of hope and self confidence within our youth about our acceptance to the outside world and thus will be helpful to preserve our plural identity. Degradation of the environment has put a big question mark on the future of the humanity. Ozone layer has been damaged and in result unpredicted weather condition has just started to prevail, which will be much worse after 2020. More destruction's are on the cards due to degradation of environment. For this we need to keep in mind that it is a global problem therefore global efforts are required for the resolution of the problem. We have to initiate also some concrete measures to correct the system. We need to adopt the notion of *Eco-Tourism* for the preservation of our precious environment. Governments have initiated many schemes for the pursuance of the cause but no tangible results have been achieved yet. This cause could be a strong component to our tourism promotion policy. We need to incorporate it as an integral part of our tourism policy. For that purpose community based tourism need to be promoted. Villages and local communities need to be engaged into the process. In border terms decentralization in this field is the requirement of the time. Tribals who live in the forest since millennia need also to be taken into confidence. Likewise protection and promotion of rivers, wild animals and many things affiliated with the system of tourism could be protected in a sustainable manner. Now the billion dollar question is how it could be realized. Following methods could be facilitator in this direction.

Making Sustainable Tourism more Pro-poor

Tourism could be a great mechanism for the mitigation of poverty. India is engulfed with chronic poverty despite marvelous development since last six decades after independence. Moving the sustainable tourism agenda to tackle poverty alleviation requires action on a number of fronts:

- Expanding the focus of mainstream tourism initiatives beyond mainstream destinations, to destinations where many of the world's poor live and/or recognizing that many of the world's poor live alongside mainstream destinations and their voices need to be heard.
- Putting the poor and poverty (including the environmental dimensions of poverty) at the centre of the sustainability debate, rather than *just* the environment.
- Moving beyond a community tourism focus to developing mechanisms that unlock opportunities for the poor at all levels and scales of operation.
- The key distinctive feature of pro-poor tourism is that it puts poor people and poverty at the centre. Starting from there, it sees tourism as one component of the household, local and national economies and environment that affects them. The current sustainable tourism debate starts with mainstream destinations as a priority and targets environmental concerns with social issues towards the periphery.

Poor people of the developing and under developed countries are thus at the edge of the picture. The current approach to 'sustainable tourism' fails to take into account the links between poverty, environment and development. In a world of growing inequality, there can be no doubt that attacking poverty is a critical component of sustainable development. Global stability depends upon this recognition. Since its inception, India has been committed to establish justice based international order. For that purpose all round development of the developing and under developed countries is badly required. Tourism has the potential to play a harbinger role in this direction. India being a leading developing country must set an example in this direction which could be emulated in poor countries. Poverty is the root cause of the global anarchy and promotion of tourism could be extremely useful to the global efforts of poverty alleviation. India must take the lead, which will be followed by other countries.

Strategies for Pro-poor Tourism

Pro-poor Tourism (PPT) is defined as *tourism that generates net benefits for the poor.* Benefits may be economic, but they may also be social, environmental or cultural. Pro-poor tourism is not a specific product or sector of tourism, but an approach to the industry. Strategies for making tourism pro-poor focus specifically on *unlocking opportunities* for the poor within tourism, rather than expanding the overall size of the sector. Three core areas of focus include: increased economic benefits, enhancing non-economic impacts, and policy/process reform. In each area, following methods can be identified. [Capacity Building]

Strategies focused on economic benefits

(i) **Expanding business opportunities for the poor:** Small enterprises, particularly in the informal sector, often provide the greatest opportunities for the poor.

(ii) **Expanding employment opportunities for the poor:** Unskilled jobs may be limited and low-paid by international standards, but are much sought after by the poor.

(iii) **Enhancing collective benefits:** collective community income from tourism can be a new source of income, and can spread benefits well beyond the direct earners.

India has done tremendous development in last few decades and it has been estimated by gamut of the pundits of the international economics that India will keep its pace in foreseeable future too. For the sustainability of this growth and make democracy genuine, we need to accommodate aspirations of have notes into the mainstreaming process of development. Since a huge number of haves not are unable to earn their bread from any available sources therefore it is high time to develop tourism as a sacred industry. Tourism sector has not been developed in our country at par with our South East Asian brethren. In 2010 we had excellent progress. In 2010 India welcomed 17.9 million foreign visitors compared to 14.4 million in 2009, making a 24 per cent increase. Footfalls at domestic tourist destinations witnessed a 10.7 per cent surge, touching 740 million as against 669 million in 2009.[7] We have the potential to bring tourism sector at par with the leading European countries like Spain and France. The present surge is just a drop into the ocean. There are many huge areas of tourist obsession which has not even started. But it needs missionary zeal and determination. World class infrastructure is also required for ensuring smooth movement of tourists. We have all varieties of tourist obsession and it is the time to utilize it. All round development of tourism sector will be extremely important for inclusive growth of the country. This book deals with pertinent issues related for the promotion of tourism sector of our country.

Dr. Ruchi Ramesh
Dr. Sudhir Kumar Singh

REFERENCES

1. www.ica.coop/tica/cartagenverma.pdf
2. World Tourism Organisation [http;/www.world.tourism.org], a global forum for tourism policy issues and a practical of tourism know how
3. World Trade Organization (WTO), 2010 Report.
4. *Source : http://www.undpi.am/node/17.*
5. This figure is commonly quoted by the World Travel and Tourism Council (WTTC) although the World Tourism Organization (WTO) puts the figure much lower. The difference reflects the difficulty in defining what is and is not included within the tourism 'industry' and whether services such as transport are included in the calculation. The WTTC figure also incorporates the multiplier effect of tourism spending and so reflects the wider 'tourism economy' rather than just the industry itself.
6. *Times of India*, New Delhi, 13 January 2011.
7. In Incredible India, Tourism Tool The Highway in 2010, *The Times of India*, New Delhi, July 21, 2011.

1

Role of Women in Tourism: Various Aspects

Alokka Dutta

Tourism has become the world's largest industry, according to the World Tourism Organization; no surprise when one considers that it incorporates the world's oldest profession. In some developing regions, such as the Caribbean or the South Pacific, tourism is the primary sector in which significant economic growth takes place. In other regions, including areas of Latin America, Africa, the Middle East, and formerly communist eastern Europe, tourism is just beginning to take off. In all of these areas, tourism's impact has been decidedly mixed. Nowhere is this more visible than in the context of women's roles in tourism.

The tourism industry positions itself as a major employer of women globally and an industry that is women friendly—opening doors for women—as the UNWTO proudly claims! However research and the stories of women engaged in tourism around the world has shown repeatedly that it is an industry that is far from being gender just...

Continuing world prosperity has clearly been the main driver behind this boom. Asia and the Pacific stand out as the motors of international tourism expansion and the tourism juggernaut continues to move notwithstanding man made and natural crises. Emerging markets and developing economies especially in Asia, tourism promotion by national governments especially in developing regions, increased investment in infrastructure, marketing and advertising, development of domestic markets, liberalisation of air transport, are key factors in this expansion in the tourism business

Women's Empowerment

So what does this growth mean for women—particularly for women in destinations of the global south? To what extent do they benefit from this phenomenon? Has tourism opened doors for women? Has its unstoppable growth contributed to women's empowerment?

The advancement of women and the achievement of equality between women and men is a matter of human rights and a condition for social justice. These are essential to build a sustainable, just, secure and developed society. For decades now, women have placed issues of violence, race, caste and other forms of discrimination that hit them the hardest; and the need for equality and human rights of women—including social, economic, political, legal, sexual and reproductive rights—at the center-stage of this struggle.

World wide seminars from Rio, Copenhagen, Vienna, Cairo and Beijing to Durban, particularly the CEDAW (Convention for Elimination of all forms of Discrimination against Women), the UN Fourth World Conference on Women and its subsequent Beijing Platform for Action, have set out critical concerns and strategic action points, and with the same intensity but leaving one with little sense of progress on substantive issues.[2] There has been enormous frustration at the lack of government commitment and accountability to development goals in general and gender equality commitments in particular.

So, what is the role that tourism has played and can play in this important struggle for equality, equity and empowerment of women?

Margaret Swain argues that tourism is built on attractions to sameness and differences. "Is the world's largest industry willing to be feminist?" she asks.[3] It explains phenomena in terms of women's as well as men's experiences. It is political when asking how to promote equity among women and men, based in understandings of the cultural and social positions of women and their subordination in relationship to men. It asks the question "does this work for women?" and seeks the perspective of women as well in interrogating data, frameworks, experiences and policies.

Regarding this it can be explained that international, national and state level policies on tourism do state a general commitment to women's empowerment but rarely go beyond that to understand and evolve specific measures. The UNWTO's Global Code of Ethics for Tourism, for instance, does not specifically address the gendered aspects of tourism although Articles 2, 6 and 9 are linked to some of the issues being debated. Article 2 calls to respect equality between men and women and promote human rights particularly individual rights for marginalised and vulnerable groups. It disapproves of exploitation of human beings, such as sexual exploitation. Article 6 concerns travel-related press material and other media and states that these should contain truthful and balanced information on travel destinations that could influence the flow of tourists. These media should not in any way promote sex tourism, it asserts. Article 9 on Rights of the workers and entrepreneurs in the tourism industry, focuses on the protection of legal rights of workers, their salaries and working conditions and argues that these should be guaranteed under the supervision of the national and local administrations. It also suggests that workers should be given sufficient social protection. Despite these clauses, it seems critical that the Global Code address issues of the empowerment and exploitation of women more directly, given the significant role that women play in tourism..

Often women are exhorted to subscribe to an individual empowerment ethics—overcome what's in your mind and you can do it! In celebration of World Tourism Day 2007 a leading travel and tourism magazine[4] ran a lead feature on India's

"Incredible Women in Tourism"—profiling a series of urban upper/middle class women who worked in up-market travel agencies, hotels and the government in the sector. Most subscribed heavily to the individual empowerment ethic. Most felt they were not disadvantaged being a woman and the key to success was hard work and the individual will to achieve. If the magazine had featured local women in tourism destinations struggling in the sector; their perspectives, experiences and realities would have been very different. But apparently, these masses of women do not count. This attitude that policy makers, governments and the industry of tourism have adopted of viewing women's empowerment as an individual's challenge can prove to be very dangerous as it diverts focus away from the need to deal with institutionalized gender discrimination in tourism.

Policies and budgets have the potential both to perpetuate gender bias and blindness, and to transform them. Gender disaggregated data, gender-sensitive policies and indicators are essential to building up a picture of the nature and extent of gender inequality. We need to understand the way institutions with their gendered rules work and we need to develop the political will, processes and tools to challenge and change them. Gender audits and gender budgeting are tools that could be employed meaningfully—particularly at community levels. These in turn will impact women's political participation and decision making on the forms, impacts, models and pace of tourism in their communities. It is time tourism recognised women's agency and heard their voices in its development.

Women's—Participation in Decision Making

In India, women have been viewed by governments and policy makers merely as extensions of the traditional roles they play in families and society—that of nurturers and caregivers. The focus was on promoting the welfare of women and thereby, children rather than empowering women to acquire their rights. Schemes and policies for women, therefore, were limited in both vision and approach. Rural India, where two-third of India's population resides, faces enormous challenges in health, education, nutrition, employment and environment. Women bear primary responsibility in every one of these areas—day after day. India's rural women have been systematically denied the freedom, resources, information and decision-making power they need to carry out these responsibilities and have been kept in an almost unimaginable state of powerlessness, illiteracy, isolation and malnutrition. The 73rd Amendment of the Indian Constitution mandated an unprecedented transfer of decision-making power and resources in the rural areas to local democratic councils—the panchayat. Most revolutionary of all, one-third of all panchayat seats are reserved for women—guaranteeing them a role in determining the future of their communities. If fully implemented, women potentially have a voice in the decisions that affect their lives.

Early advocates of tourism viewed tourism employment as a positive way of integrating under-privileged subgroups of society into mainstream economy. However, these have tended largely to reinforce an existing sexist, ethnic and caste-based system of social stratification. In tourism particularly, women's roles in economic production cannot be understood without reference to the cultural context of women's structural position in society and the home. Kinnaird and Hall[5] cite the example of tourism-dependent areas of Britain and Ireland to make this point. They argue that innovations like the 'bed and breakfast accommodation' in tourism ghettoize women in ways of work that are an extension of their domestic activities. This is particularly interesting in the context of India's Ministry of Tourism (headed in succession by two very articulate women as Tourism Ministers) showcasing bed and breakfast accommodation schemes as a policy intervention towards women's empowerment. Similarly the Rural Tourism Project of the Ministry, while having the laudable aim of women's empowerment among other aims, has largely conceptualised empowerment in economic terms without taking into account the social patriarchal structures and roles that their lives are embedded in. These policy initiatives reveal the naiveté of the government in offering simplistic solutions to the need for genuine empowerment of women in tourism.

Often women's economic empowerment programmes, particularly those for poor rural women, focus on micro-credit and self-help groups. This in some ways only increases the burden on women and limits their capacity to leverage productive and scaled up micro-enterprise. An evaluation report of the Rural Tourism Project of the Ministry of Tourism[6] has more or less equated gender sensitisation to the formation of women's self help groups and seems to believe that this is an adequate indicator of women's empowerment. The focus instead should be on collective enterprise with women's ownership and to ensure its success requires significant capacity building and market linkages.

The Nature of Employment

A very strong argument in favour of tourism development is that it generates employment at different levels due to the wide range of services and products it requires. Undoubtedly, there is truth and merit in this argument. However, it is important to understand what kind of employment local women have access to in tourism and what happens to men and women employed in tourism.

Tourism does provide a range of activities where women can participate and also creates opportunities for entrepreneurship development. Global data on number of women and men working in tourism-related professions suggests that the organised tourism sector is a particularly important sector where 46 percent of the workforce comprises women (in general, 30-40 percent of the workforce is women) (ILO, 2007). Of the data available for the years between 1988 and 2005, it appears that there has been a broad increase in the participation of women in the tourism industry at a global level.

However apart from their overall presence in the industry, other factors indicate that women do not seem to benefit and be empowered particularly from tourism. As in many other sectors, there is significant horizontal and vertical gender segregation of the labour market in tourism. Vertically, the typical "gender pyramid" is prevalent—lower levels and occupations with few career development opportunities being dominated by women and key managerial positions being dominated by men. In India too, women in the organised sector in tourism are relegated to relatively low skill, low paying or stereotypical jobs like front-desk and reception, housekeeping, catering and laundry services. They face very high risks of sexual harassment and exploitation and are discouraged from forming unions or associations to consolidate their strength and influence. The proportion of women's to men's wages is less. Women feature significantly more in part time and/or temporary employment and are typically paid less than men for the same work done.

The feminisation and informalisation of the workforce in tourism, particularly in developing countries, is a matter of concern. Unfortunately, few research studies focus on the gender dimension resulting in little quantitative data on this trend. Women are seen, and hence favoured, as a passive, compliant and sometime invisible workforce that will accept low wages without demanding for their labour and human rights. What remains constant is the low economic value accorded to work performed by women in conditions of exploitation, no job security and violations of human rights. This occurs both directly through prohibitions on labour organisation and indirectly through further abuses where women have claimed rights such as to organise or to be free from sexual harassment.

Many women workers face difficult, often exploitative conditions. India's national newspapers carried a horrifying story of a woman working in an ayurvedic massage parlour in Kerala who was allegedly set on fire by her employer after she refused sexual favours to clients. The International Labour Organisation published a report highlighting the high levels of violence, stress and sexual harassment in hotels, catering and tourism. Unsurprisingly, it is mostly women in junior positions who experience these problems, but unlike in other sectors, women face harassment not only from colleagues and managers but also from clients. Factors such as late working hours, service of alcohol, dress codes, racism, negative attitudes towards service staff and the uninhibited, sexualised nature of tourism and tourism promotion contribute to a high-risk environment for women and younger workers, as well as ethnic minority, migrant and part-time workers.[7] That these attitudes and difficulties prevail primarily in small scale enterprises is another myth that needs to be exposed. As the case below (see box) highlights it took India's national airline six decades to acknowledge that women can supervise cabin crew as ably as men. Sexist and gendered attitudes abound, making it difficult for women at all levels to claim equality and equity. The Chief Justice of Karnataka High Court Cyriac Joseph, speaking to an all-woman audience at the Asia Women Lawyers' Conference[8] on the theme "Women's rights are human rights' declared "there was no point in women trying to be men and do all that a man is expected to do." Cautioning women, he said, "Once you lose your womanhood, there is nothing left to be protected."

Women's Representation

The ideological constructs of the advertising industry have infused the tourism, aviation and hospitality industry. In tourism marketing, women are the 'face' of the sector, being the most widely-used objects in tourism promotion after natural beauty and cultural heritage. Women have been objectified and depicted as pleasure providers[9]—their images often exoticised, patronising and misleading.

There is also a strong case for eliminating sexual objectification of women working in the tourism industry. With sex tourism being the most negative and prominent example, there is a significant amount of sexual objectification of women working in the tourism industry. Women are expected to dress in an "attractive" manner, to look beautiful (i.e. slim, young, and pretty) and to "play along" with sexual harassment by customers.[10] Stereotypical and sexist images of women are often part of tourism promotion in brochures and advertisements. Friendly, smiling and pliant women fitting certain standards of attractiveness, attired in traditional costumes, waiting to submissively serve the customer's every wish is the typical portrayal of women in tourism material. The industry however has chosen not to be particularly disturbed by this view of women, of seeing it as a gross violation of their dignity and rights, and believes it to be justified in the sale of a product. It is time the global tourism industry takes responsibility for the way women are used in the selling of tourism and also addresses this in its code of ethics.

Tourism modifies local cultural practices in ways that affect men and women differentially. For example, in Kumarakom, increased houseboat tourism severely restricted privacy of local women who used the same backwaters to bathe and to meet with other women socially. When tourism makes products of culture, it tends to commodify women in particular—although both men and women are impacted by the insensitive selling of culture. Jane Henrici[11] gives an interesting example of women in Peru—"Before the tourists came, when a woman wore flowers in her hair in public, it meant she was available to enter into a dating relationship. Once the tourists arrived they liked to take pictures of the photogenic women wearing flowers. Soon the pressure built for all women in the market to wear flowers—detaching it from its cultural meaning and becoming a pure aesthetic signifier in a touristic frame."

Focus on Women in Conferences

At the historic World Women's Conference at Beijing in September 1995, Nina Rao led a workshop on 'International Tourism' at the NGO forum on Women. Following that an important workshop in collaboration with Institute of Management in Governance in Kerala widened the debate on of tourism development and its effects on women—in relation to change in land use pattern, changes in job opportunities, pressure on women when natural resources like water and common property resources were privatised by tourism.

> In 1997 Nina Rao initiated a study on gender issues at the workplace—a survey of organised workplaces linked to the tourism industry—airlines, travel agents, hotels. In 1998, a workshop on Women and Tourism in Salem, Tamil Nadu on World tourism Day, organised jointly with Tamil Nadu Environmental Council and other partners drew enthusiastic participation. A workshop for elected women members of Panchayats on Women and Tourism in collaboration with Institute for Management in Government, Trivandrum was another important milestone.

In 2007, the UNWTO's theme for the World Tourism Day was "Tourism Opens Doors for Women." This was an opportunity to take the debate further on whether women really benefit from tourism, as well as to confront the rhetoric and propaganda of the UNWTO. A fortuitous invitation from the UNWTO to participate in a high level think tank of about 20 people from around the world helped us in this task. We influenced the UNWTO to include aspects of exploitation of women in its statement on ethics, to substantiate its generalised statements through research, to bring out a status report on the status of women in tourism and to ensure that women from all sections (particularly informal sector) had a role in influencing tourism policy and practise. Two round tables on the theme in Goa and Kerala received media attention. In Kerala the government announced its policy of ensuring that women are not commoditised in the advertisements for tourism.

Women and Natural Resources

There is a direct correlation between the depletion of natural resources and increased burden on women in daily work in any region of the world. When tourism restricts community access to or contributes to the depletion of natural resources, it is women not only as homemakers, but also as community members, who suffer the most.[12] Women's access to and control over forest produce and water comes into sharp conflict when tourism usurps these very resources needed to fulfil their life and livelihood needs. The daily burden on women of finding water for the household or firewood for cooking is oftentimes doubled or tripled.

When tourism displaces people from traditional livelihoods or worse still physically displaces them, the worst affected are women who are engaged in the bulk of ancillary occupations like tobacco cultivation, coconut harvesting, fish sorting and processing which are jeopardised through such displacement. Transition from certain activities to others, for example away from agriculture, could have implications for food security. Certain traditional occupations risk being crowded out that could have an effect on the society as a whole. A study in Kumarakom in Kerala shows that women moved out of agriculture to tourism linked construction work as it paid them better daily wages.[13] But having neglected the fields, they ended up losing on both counts as the construction work was only short-term but they could not return to cultivate fields overgrown with weeds. It becomes the prerogative of governments and the industry to ensure that rather than displace them, tourism should build and bolster supplementary livelihood options that women can choose from. The demand for water by hotels can mean less local water for nearby farmers, which can affect food production and increase the workload of women in collecting water from other sources. The establishment of golf courses and special tourism zones or enclaves can also put severe constraints on land and water resources for communities burdening the women the most. The incriminating links between tourism and climate change will unfortunately add to the burden women already bear.

Severe Abuse of Human Rights

The gross violation of human rights due to sex tourism and trafficking of women are the shadow side of the booming tourism industry. Migration and trafficking of women, both from within developing countries and cross border to service the tourist trade is commonplace. Russian women to Thailand and the Philippines and Goa, eastern European women to European countries and women from Nepal and Bangladesh are trafficked to India to service the sex trade. The reports of the Special Rapporteur on Violence against Women (UNCHR) have highlighted the linkages between countries in economic transition and the increase in trafficking and forced prostitution of women.

There is also a strong case for eliminating sexual objectification of women working in the tourism industry. With sex tourism being the most negative and prominent example, there is a significant amount of sexual objectification of women working in the tourism industry. Women are expected to dress in an "attractive" manner, to look beautiful. Though there are efforts by few tourism service providers to condemn child sex tourism and actively participate in campaigns that combat it, tourism industry bodies have not taken serious action against the exploitation of women in trafficking. There is also a strong case for eliminating sexual objectification of women working in the tourism industry. With sex tourism being the most negative and prominent example, there is a significant amount of sexual objectification of women working in the tourism industry. Women are expected to dress in an "attractive" manner, to look beautiful. In fact while tourism is celebrated as a globalised and modernised form of development—it is global tourism, globalised crime and technology like the internet that have also given the sex industry new means of exploiting, marketing and supplying women and children as commodities to buyers.[14]

The Challenges Ahead

The tourism industry and stewards of tourism development face many serious social and human challenges in the years ahead. The growing links between migration—both voluntary and forced—and tourism needs to take into account the gender dimensions of this global phenomenon. HIV/AIDS is not only driven by gender inequality but entrenches it. Tourism is increasingly seen to have a role in this entrenchment in its links to trafficking, prostitution and sex tourism.

A categorical position condemning the blatant and inhuman exploitation of women in tourism through trafficking and the sex industry is a moral challenge that the global tourism industry needs to respond to. Declaring that the tourism product will not be promoted at the expense of women's dignity, respect and rights is the other position that the industry needs to endorse and practice.

The increasing trend of promoting tourism in conflict zones and the consequent impacts it has on women who are already battling for survival is another matter of serious concern. Disasters and epidemics have an uneasy relationship with tourism—but gender dimensions are rarely integrated into assistance and reconstruction efforts with the focus being largely on the safety of tourists and revival of tourism infrastructure.

Engendering tourism policy and understanding tourism's impacts on women will be key steps to combating the feminization and informalisation of the workforce in tourism, particularly in developing countries. Research that focuses on the gender dimension of this process could lead to policy and interventions that can work to the advantage of women. Most policies today focus on and favour large and medium enterprise in tourism. Shifting the focus to privilege small and micro-enterprise will not only lead to sustainable options, but create more viable spaces for women's engagement in tourism.

Poverty, and in particular urban poverty, which threatens to be an issue of growing magnitude has deep roots in gender injustice. Tourism often wipes out the existence and means of livelihood of the urban poor in an overt manner while continuing to depend covertly on cheap labour and exploitative relationships in order to flourish. Ensuring basic protection in terms of social security, access to information and credit and market linkages will be critical to enable larger numbers of women in the informal economy—both in rural and urban areas—to gain from tourism.

Women's engagement to assert their rights as stakeholders in all aspects of tourism development (planning, implementation, participation, ownership and monitoring) is also determined by their informed participation in decision making spaces. Facilitating an understanding of tourism and its patterns among women would not only enable them to raise questions about the course of tourism development but also make claims on its outcomes.

REFERENCES

1. The experiences of women as tourists is increasingly a topic for study and research. This paper however focuses on women who live in tourism destinations, particularly destinations in the Global South.
2. *Tourism Management*, Vol. 17, No. 2, 1996.
3. Gender/Tourism/Fun (?) Eds. Swain and Momsen CCC 2002. Swain (1995) offered the following definition of Gender in tourism:
   A system of culturally constructed identities, expressed in ideologies of masculinity and feminity, interacting with socially structured relationships in divisions of labour and leisure, sexuality, and power between women and men.
4. Express Travel World September 2007.
5. Kinnard and Hall, 1996, ibid.
6. Evaluation study Rural Tourism Scheme Mott MacDonald MoT June 2007.
7. Gender, Globalisation and Tourism Cultures, Presented by Dr. Annette Pritchard at the Special Meeting of Women Ministers of Culture, 2005. http://womenministers.government.is/Programme//nr/3269
8. Women must not try to be men: Cyriac Joseph23/09/2007 URL: http://www.thehindu.com/2007/09/23/stories/2007092354980500.htm
9. 'Tourism—Its Effects on Women in Goa, a report to the People', Bailancho Saad; Goa, 1987.
10. Gruetter, K. and Pluess, Ch. (Hg.), 1996. Herrliche Aussichten! Frauen im Tourismus. Zuerich: Rotpunktverlag (Splendid Views! Women in Tourism)
11. Calling to the Money: Gender and Tourism in Peru Jane Henrici Gender/Tourism/Fun (?) Eds Swain and Momsen CCC 2002.
12. Minke Valkh (ed) "Natural resources Management and Gender". Paradigm Publisher, London, 1996.
13. Dr A.K. Jaiasree, "Tourism and Women: Lessons from Kovalam". www.thrani.org.
14. Hughes, M.D., "The Internet and Sex Industries: Partners in Global Sexual Exploitation," Technology and Society Magazine, Spring 2000.

2

Tourism A Development Syndrome: Study on Orissa

Amulya K. Tripathy and Aamnayi Mishra

Introduction

It is difficult to pin-point in all the problems which will determine the direction of tourism's development in the twenty-first century. This difficulty results from dynamic transformations which are in our modern civilization. Twenty years ago in his book entitled "The Third Wave", A. Toffler wrote that humanity will stand in the face of new challenges, and it appears that these processes are in the future. According to the author the title "The Third Wave", like the previous two indicate, "...will squeeze out previous cultures and civilizations bringing it's morals into effect, which was inconceivable for people who had been born earlier."

The speed of our everyday life was considerably slower, as the first wave, the agricultural revolution, needed one thousand years to run its course. The Industrial revolution, or the second wave, needed only three hundred years from the beginning to the end. However, these prior transformations are incomparable to the speed and progress of our modern civilization. This third wave has been dubbed the technological revolution is now in process.

Some of the more visible processes in our modern life include; the quick development of the technology, the revolution in genetics, the conquest of outer space, the rapid development of cities, and the changes in our jobs and lifestyles. With this information we can state that A. Toffler was correct in saying "The third wave will burst us, we will feel the effects of the third wave in our lifetime". Toffler's vision of radical changes in economics accompanied by worldviews of new "liberal opportunities" will create the disintegration of the industrial society. Traditional industries will be replaced with new industries based on modern technology, causing transformation between the relationships of our home and work place, working time and free time, and prosperity versus poverty. The meaning of the natural environment will become more important as the world will be seeking new values resulting in changes of cultures and ideologies. Lifestyles and family functions will change, taking on new meaning with concepts such as science, careers, and employment. However, the question remains, what impact will these new changes have on tourism? Will tourism use these opportunities, or will it be an enclave in which we can rest from civilization. Tourism is a dynamic discipline and is affected by these processes previously said. The analysis of trends in the modern tourist market show there are many changes suggesting that tourism in the future will differ from present day affairs. The complexity of tourism will bring about many difficulties throughout its development. J. Krippendorf stated, "it is possible that tourism, an antidote for the industrial world, has become an industry and predacious devourer of the environment". The more difficult challenge of the twenty-first century will be the protection of the environment. Fortunately the tourism industry has begun using modern technology in the fields of computer science, communications, and the building of transportation to preserve the environment. The development of tourism is also known to be an asset to social economics; however, there tends to be strong speculations to the overall benefits in this aspect. Tourism transfers cultures, which will lead to the composite cultures of World and ultimately a unified World.

The Conditions and Prognosis in the Development of Tourism at the Beginning of the 21st Century

Consider further of tourism and the challenges it will face at the beginning of the twenty-first century. The prognosis is very optimistic as suggested in publicized report. The report talks about quick development and states that during the next twenty years tourism will be one of the fastest growing industries in the world's economy. However, tourism is far from the end of its development, as for now it consists of a small percentage of the world's citizens. The main hazards in development are problems with the political situation in the world, especially conflicts within the Balkans, the instability of the Arab world, and the disorganization between authorities and conflict in the former territory of the Soviet Empire. Slightly less hazardous factors deal with economics such as recession and the increase of gas prices. Nevertheless the outlook on tourist development remains optimistic.

The quantitative development of tourism is accompanied by multi-aspects structure of tourism The downfall of communism and democratization of societies in former socialist countries are events which have an impact on modern tourism, and other parts of the world have witnessed similar processes within their societies. The development of international tourism will take on new dynamic and important changes in spatial structures. Generally speaking an increase in share of the tourist structure shows no connection with an increase in share of the profit structure. There is no guarantee of an even distribution in the benefits of tourism. A good example is Africa, which last years shares in total scale of tourist arrivals increased while the total scale of shares in receipts from tourism rapidly decreased. The forecasts about the tourism development are made by using econometric models. So, very important to remember is that a basic variable is time. Therefore, forecasting quick development of tourism, on the bases of fast developing countries like in nineties is risky. Many of these countries achieved so-called market maturity. The best opportunities for development of tourism are in areas (e.g. China) where it's development is depended on stabilized political situation, what is very far in the future. We cannot forget about that organizations e.g. World Trade Organization that make forecasts which are not impartial. They have got a good interest in forecasting of increasing tendencies.

Some interesting changes in the quality of the tourist market are connected with the supply and demand. These aspects of needs, motivations, and demands lead to new directions in tourist firms. A quick tempo of bringing modern technologies into tourism may herald a real revolution in the organization of the tourist system. These examples show that tourism, like all repeats of civilization, odder-go changes and the question remains; what tasks will tourism face in the beginning of the new century?

There are many factors which will shape the future of the tourist market and it should be noted that some are out of the control of the market. In an attempt to answer some of these questions there must be an analysis of the trends involved with tourism. The end of the twentieth century was a time of great transformation in all fields of life. There were many fast paced changes throughout social conditions, the economy, and technology, which brought about many transitions within tourism. The constant tendencies to observe and gain knowledge about the markets basic condition are needed to succeed with each activity and the trends within tourism can change quickly.

The ability to forecast and stimulate these developmental processes is the key to making the correct decisions for the future. The fluctuation and competition within the tourist market not only requires constant observation and the ability to anticipate change, but also being able to react to the new trend before it becomes the norm. This shows the importance of knowledge in the action of these megatrends, which can be classified into six basic groups; demographics, politics, social and cultural, economics, technology, and ecology. In each of these groups there are positive factors, which will either stimulate or deter the development of tourism, each with variability in strength and effect. These megatrends, especially demographics, social, cultural, ecology, and technology hold such a strong influence on the maturation of tourism that such events as a political crisis or economic recession (in some regions) would be unable to hinder such progress.

Demographic factors, especially

- age of societies;
- tendencies to set up home late;
- a smaller number of households;
- a dominant model of family 2+1;
- increasing number of lonely people;
- increasing number of childless couples;
- increasing number of working women.

Political factors, especially:

- changes in Central-West Europe;
- integration of the European Union;
- liberalization of international migrations;
- convenience passports, foreign currency;
- unstable political situation in many regions of the world;
- international terrorism;
- increased importance of safe travel

Social and cultural factors, especially:

- shortened time of working, more free time and longer vacations;
- increase of time for additional work;
- earlier retirements;
- increasing number of "two-income" households; which were thought of as a healthy life;
- a family crisis;
- conflicts between identity and modernization, especially in developing countries
- a radical demands and increase of importance of ethnic movement etc.

Economical factors, especially:

- continuation of moderate economical increase in the world scale;
- a bigger disproportion between rich and or countries;
- a bigger financial crisis in a number of countries (especially, among "economical tigers" in South Asia and Pacific);
- a stable price of petroleum;
- liberalization and development of an international trade;
- capital concentration in world's economy;
- globalization of economical activity;

Technological factors, especially:

- automation and computerization;
- developing of telecommunication;
- developing of computing systems;
- developing of transport and infrastructure (airports, motorways);

Ecological factors, especially:

- smaller environmental resources;
- a greater ecological awareness in society;
- government's concern to environment;
- conflicts caused by developing of a big agglomerations in developing;
- use of modern technologies in everyday life (household articles, sport, tourist equipment);
- developing of soft technologies; developed countries;
- development of the ecological movement;
- international collaboration in field of natural and cultural environment protection.

The Main Trends in Tourist Demands

There are many interesting publications about change within the field of tourist demands and many studies, which analyze the direction of these changes in development, have been publicized recently. The majorities are unanimous regarding the expansion and direction on the transformations of demands, so much so that there is even an accepted concept known as "Hard and Soft Tourism". It is based on the observational changes within the sphere of former and actual clients in travel agencies and set the standard characteristics of two opposite kinds of tourism: the traditional tourist and the modern tourist. Package tours; Individual travelling; A lot of time, short-term residences; A lot of time, long-term residences Model of one big travel during holidays; Model of two shorter travels during a year. Everything organised earlier from "a" to "z" (sights, a route, program etc.); Program decisions made individually and spontaneously; Comfort and passivity; An activity and effort; Expectation of number of travels and attractions; Expectation of new experiences and higher quality; Sense of superiority, demonstration effect; Respect and relationship with hostess; Lack of knowledge about attractions, culture and tradition in visiting areas; Knowledge about countries we want to visit; Imported life style and behaviour; Lifestyle following to an example of local Population Purchases; Gifts Noise; Silence; Freely available souvenirs (e.g. a mass production of Eiffel Tower figurines; Individual souvenirs (e.g. photo and picture took individually, private video film); Lack of interest in language of visiting country; Studying local language (at least a few words); Fast transport and frequent moves; Less importance of moving speed; Curiosity; Tact; Expectation of comfort; Comfort is not essential; A distance between client and tourist staff; A good relationship with tourist staff; there is a vision of which tourism will dominate the future, characterized by a more active tourist and less interest in passive tourism. The prediction is that traditional tourism, refereed to as 3 × S (sun sea and sand) will be squeezed out by tourism based on a new formula involving 3 × E (entertainment, excitement, and education). During recent years there has become intensified interest in travelling to historical cities, the so-called "green tourist" with additional concern for a tendency in business tourism. Nevertheless it could be halted through the development of telecommunications and shorter but more frequent trips consisting of sightseeing and holiday could become more popular. The useful system of "bridges" between a national holiday leading to the extension of weekends has brought about a prognosis for a renaissance in national tourism. V.T.C. Middleton claimed that for tourists, who quite often may be 'experienced,' a trend in national tourism may become more attractive now then ever, including the sixties. The smaller interest in international tourism is in the neighbouring countries or places where many Europeans have had vacation. In 1990 European travel represented about seven percent of all international travel, although this number was up to about ten percent in 1996, and Europeans are the only ones concerned with these numbers. A poll conducted recently by the Travel Trade Gazette concerning international tourism showed these tendencies in change also pointed to the tourist industry representatives. One director of a travel agency was quoted saying 'a person who was in Spain ten years ago at present is probably in Penang'. The quick increase in numbers of individual trips along with package tours is the prediction of the future. Today Individuality has a strong influence on cars, clothes and other daily needs as well, and the gaining interest of individual travel is one of the most important tendencies in today's tourist demands.

The Main Trends in Tourist Supply

The advancements and inclinations characterized previously have caused fundamental changes in present and future actions of travel agencies. During the last thirty years the developed markets have been dominated primarily by the supply, however, in the future we can expect to see increased importance in the demand factors as well. Agencies, which are not well informed about the market, could feel the effects and begin losing clients. Today a tourist offer has a different meaning then it did several years ago, when the identical packaged product was selling to a maximum number of clients. This is when the main task of an agency was to secure transportation and hotels for the tourists in an identified town near similar beaches and the local supply had to answer the whimsical requirements of the tourist. Today's tourists expect something different and the prognosis for the twenty-first century is different then it has been in past centuries. The totality of tourist activities will be one of the most important features in the early dawn of the twenty-first century, and covering borders in economical activity and the concentration of capital are visible in all spheres of the international economy. These inclinations at the tourist market level are quite visible where huge companies are creating the new direction in trend bringing the end of the small travel agencies drawing to a close. The tourist market has been captured by the huge American and Western European companies with Asian, Japanese, and Chinese companies expected to join them in the near future. Obviously there are some smaller travel agencies which will be needed to look after some special services, but for the most part this will be the change of the movement in the international tourist structure. The expected changes in Russia and China could bring the largest investments into these two countries. It seems that the tourists supply will have a more violent nature than the demand and the odds are that the supply, at the same time, will be the main point of stimulation and transformation.

India has grown considerably in recent years due to the various attractions of Orissa, ranging from wildlife reserves and beaches to temples and monuments.

Eco-tourism in Orissa

One of Orissa's major attractions is its 500 km long coastline and beaches and natural scenery such as Chilka Lake, Asia's largest brackish water lake. Thařea is an important bird sanctuary for millions of birds, and is also noted for its population of Irrawaddy Dolphin (*Orcaella brevirostris*), the only known population of Irrawaddy dolphins in India. It is one of only two lagoons in the world that are home to this species. Dolphin tourism provides an important alternative source of income for many local residents. There are four tourist associations in

Satapada employing three hundred and sixty 9-HP long-tail motor boats taking tourists to a 25 km^2 (9.7 sq mile) area of the lake for dolphin watching. About 500 fishing families are involved in this business. The Orissa Tourism Department and the Dolphin Motorboat Association, an NGO at Satpada, report about 40,000 tourists visit Chilika every year for dolphin Watching. October-January and May-June are the peak season for tourists at Chilika, with a maximum 600-700 per day during December-January. The Dolphin Motorboat Association has 75 8-passenger motorboats for dolphin watching. Tourists pay Rs. 250 for 60–90 minutes per trip. According to the Association, most tourists see dolphins. Only 5 percent return disappointed. Besides the Association, the Orissa Tourism Department organises "dolphin-watch" for tourists. Even during monsoon, about100 tourists/day visit the lake. Major beaches in Orissa include Gopalpur, Puri, Chandipur and Chandrabhaga and the waterfalls of Barehipani and Joranda, Badaghagra, Sanaghagra and Khandadhar are common attractions. The hot springs at Atri, Deulajhari, Taptapani and Tarabalo also attract tourists.The state has rich flora and fauna inhabited the lush green forest and is home to the Royal Bengal Tiger. Eco-tourism is important in Orissa and notable wildlife sanctuaries include Bhitar Kanika, Chandaka, Chilika, Simlipal, Tikarpada, Gahirmatha and Nandan Kanan.[3] Locations which attract tourists because of their natural scenery include Darjeeng, Dairingbadi, Barunei, Dhamra, Chandbali, Tensa, Narayani and Saptasajya. Eco-tourism provides a degree of alternate employment to the local community and generates environmental awareness, among local residents as well as visitors, about the conservation and sensible use of the lake's natural resources. Notable locations within the lake are: Ramba Bay at the southern end of the lake with the group of islands including: *The Becon Island*, with an architectural conical pillar (to put a light on the top) built by Mr. Snodgrass, the then collector of Ganjam of the East India Company, on a mass of rock in the Rambha Bay near Ghantasila hill. It is surrounded by the Eastern Ghat. *The Breakfast Island*, pear shaped, known as "Sankuda Island", with remnants of a dilapidated bungalow constructed by the King of Kalikote, has rare plants and is full of greenery with appealing flora. *Honeymoon Island*, 5 km (3.1 mile) from Rambha Jetty, known as Barkuda Island, with clear waters has abundant red and green macro algae in the bed is also known for the limbless lizard, an endemic species found here. Somolo and Dumkudi islands, located in the Central and Southern sectors of the lake, in the backdrop of scenic Khalikote hill range, are inundated remnants of the Eastern Ghats with rich flora and fauna and also known for sighting of Irrawaddy Dolphins. The birds island, located in the southern sector of the lake has huge exposed hanging rocks, are painted white due to folic acid of the droppings of the birds and is known for rich algal communities and few mangrove species and also migratory birds in winter. Parikud is a group of composite islands in the Garh Krishnaprasad Block for nature lovers and provides an avian spectacle during winter season Kalijai Temple located on an island is considered to be the abode of the Goddess Kalijai Satapada village, at the new mouth of the lake, provides a beautiful view of the lake and also views of the Dolphins. Hundreds of boats here provide tours of the lake for tourists. Barunkuda, a small island situated near Magarmukh, mouth of the lake, has a temple of Lord Varuna. Nabagraha is an ancient deity located along the outer channel. Chourbar Shiva Temple is located near Alupatna village, along the outer channel. Manikpatna, located on the outer channel has historical evidence of a port which was used for trade with Far East and also has the Bhabakundeswar temple of Lord Shiva, an old Mosque whose entrance door is made of the jaws of the whale. Sand-Bar and Mouth of the lake is a striking and un-explored stretch of 30 km (18.6 mile) of empty beach across the sand bar which separates the Lake from the Sea.

Orissa land is studded with numerous temples that elevate its beauty and glory. Some of the famous temples for which Orissa tourism has got a prominent place in world tourism map include but not limited to Sun temple at Konark, Jaganath temple at Puri and Lingaraja temple at Bhubaneswar. The most interesting thing that anyone can find in all these temples usually comprise sanctum, a dancing hall, one or more different front porches normally with pyramidal roof, and a hall of offerings. Crowned with nature's gifts like mighty waterfalls, coastline of around 500 km with virtuous beaches, rich wild life, meandering rivers, forest-covered blue hills of Eastern Ghats, Orissa is among the best tourist places in India that is full of wonderful temples, historic commemorative plaque as well as pieces of recent engineering achievement. The ground while declaring its grandeur, also presents the visitors modern conveniences. Its verdant green countryside and rich plains, tiny hamlets fringed with palm, coconut trees and mango groves represents rustic loveliness while the urban pockets, the four cities in particular, with the magnificence of modern technology provide the amenities necessary for a relaxed staying. This wonderful land of natural beauty boasts of bright festivals around the year. Orissa is also the land of unique handicrafts and other excellent artifacts.

The Golden Triangle is the centre of tourist's attraction being a place for paying homage to the cultural, religious marvels that proliferate here. Some of the most enchanting places that draw tourist's attention include sculptural Sun Temple, Puri Jagannath Temple, Rajarani Temple, Lingaraj Temple, Chandrabhaga and Puri Beaches. Also some other sculptures that can't be neglected are Buddhist stupa in Dhauli, Mahavira Jain Temple in Khandagiri; Hot Sulphur Spring with medicinal properties at Atri; Satapara with dancing dolphins throughout the year; Biological Park and Zoo in Nandankanan;Yogini Shrine at Hirapur; the illustrious embroidery work at Pipli, and Patachitras of Raghurajpur.

Tourists can take advantage of visiting Buddhist complex at the hillsides of Ratnagiri, Udayagiri, and Lalitgiri; Chilika Bird Sanctuary; Berhampur; Huma's Lord Bimaleswar temple; Lord Baladeva temple at Kendrapara; Paradeep port and the crocodile sanctuary at Bhitarkanika. Some other fascinating tourist places that must be traveled include Sambalpur to witness famous textiles, tribal heritage and wonderful forestlands; Ushakothi wildlife sanctuary; Gupteswar; Hirakud Dam and the Vidala-Nrusimha Temple at Nrusinghanath. Indira Gandhi Park, Rourkela's famous Steel Plant, and the highest Hanuman Statue of India; Khandadhar waterfall etc.

Conclusion

The evolution and transformations in tourism during the last one hundred years must be considered one of the most interesting processes in the recent history of humanity. In Orissa lots of places are there, popular and unpopular. No doubt tourism sector contributes a substantial in economic development, but lots of things to be done. Tourists from across the country and globe always visit to the major places like, Puri, Konark, Bhubaneswar, Gopalpur beach. For which government earn huge revenues and local people too are benefited. Recently lots of Buddhists heritage places have been excavated. Lots of Buddhists people have started visiting Orissa from Japan, China, Sri Lanka, Thailand etc. Not only that, recently a debate as "Orissa is the Birth Place of Buddha" attracted foreign countries to visit Orissa. For the proper management the followings factors to be taken Care: 1. Imfructural development, 2. Proper Communications, 3. Use and Development of tourists places, 4. Construction and maintenance of public toilets, 5.Finally, security of tourists.

REFERENCES

Alejziak W., Turystyka w obliczu wyzwan XXI wieku, Albis, Kraków 1999.

Antunac I., Prognozy rozwoju turystyki na swiecie, a zwlaszcza w Europie, w: Problemy Turystyki Nr 1, Instytut Turystyki, Warszwa 1988.

Archer B.H., Demand forecasting and estimation, w: Travel, Tourism and Hospitality (Ed.) J.Ritchie & C. Goeldner, Wiley, New York 1989.

Cooper Ch., Fletcher J., Gilbert D., Wanhill S., Tourism—Principles & Practice, Pitma Publishing, Surrey 1993.

Global Tourism Forecasts to the Year 2000 and Beyond — Executive Sumary, WTO, 1995.

Grabinski T., Wydymus S., Zelias A., Metody prognozowania rozwoju spolecznogospodarczego. Wyd. II poprawione i uzupelnione, AE Kraków, Kraków 1993.

Huntington S.P., Zderzenie cywilizacji, PWN, Warszawa, 1998.

Kahn H., The Next 200 Years—A Scenario for America and the World, Morrow, New York,1976.

Kozak M., Remmington M., Developments in Information Technology: Implications for theTourism Industry and Tourism Marketing, W: Anatolia: *An International Journal of Tourismand Hospitality Research*, Vol. 8, 1997.

McIntosh R., W., Goeldner Ch., R., Tourism—Principles, Practries and Philosophies, Grild Publishing Company, 1984, p.189.

Middleton V.T.C., Marketing w turystyce, PAPT, Warszawa 1996.

Naisbitt J., Megatrends": Ten Mew Directions Transforming Our Lives, Futura Publikations, New York 1982.

Obermait K., Future Trends in Tourism, Stockholm, June 1998.

Opaschowski H.W., Frteizeit 2001. Ein Blick in die Zukunft unserer Freizeitwelt, BAT, Freizeitforschungs institute, Hamburg 1992.

The TTG World Travel Report: 1995–2000, Market Tracking International Ltd, London 1997,

Toffler A., Szok przyszliosci, PWN, Warszawa 1974.

Toffler A., Trzecia fala, PIW, Warszawa 1997.

Tourism: 2020 Vision. A New Forecast, Executive Summary, WTO, Madrid 1998.

Travel and Tourism's Economic Perspective — A Special Report from the World Travel & Tourism Council, WT&TC, 1995.

Ritzer G., Mcdonaldyzacja spoleczenstwa [Przelozyl S. Magala], Warszawskie Wydawnictwo Literackie MUZA SA, Warszawa 1997.

Winiarski R., Czas wolny i rekreacja w perspektywie roku 2000. Prognoza i bariery rozwoju, w: Kultura Fizyczna Nr 9-10, 1997, s. 13-15.

Van Doorn J.W.M. Trafnosc prognozowania—dyskusja trwa, w: Problemy Turystyki Nr 4, Instytut Turystyki, Warszawa 1985, pp.103-106.

Vukonic B., Turizam ususret buducnosti,Ekonomski Fakultet, Zagreb 1994.

3

Management Practices in Hospital Administration—A Study of the Prominent Participants in Hospital and Hospitality Industry in Bangalore and Hyderabad

Bindi Varghese

This paper envisages the need for innovation in management practices in hospital administration, which is indeed the need of the hour. The paper emphasizes on the need for quality assurance and standardization norms for the hospital administration. The paper will mull over how management is practiced currently in number hospitals situated in Bangalore and Hyderabad. Thus addressing the lack of research into leadership-in-practice noted by a number of authors (Stogdill, 1974; Bryman, 1992; Gronn & Ribbins, 1996; Yukl, 2005) and hence the paper makes a contribution towards understanding management practices in India effectively. The research addresses Medical Tourism as a meeting point which is comparatively new in the vast ocean of travel & tourism industry. To describe Medical Tourism—it is a provision of 'cost effective' private medical care in collaboration with the tourism industry for patients needing surgical and other forms of specialized treatment. This process is being facilitated by

> the corporate sector involved in medical care as well as the tourism industry—both private and public. There is also a constant effort taken up by the corporate hospitals to support medical tourism with its fullest potential. Unlike other countries, India is a safe place and people are known for their hospitality. It's the most touted healthcare destinations for Medical or Health tourism has become a common form of vacationing, and covers a broad spectrum of medical services. It mixes leisure, fun and relaxation together with wellness and healthcare. India today has copious opportunities to compete with other developed nations and building a quality health care system of its own. The research project is descriptive and aims to give a snapshot of current views on management practices with regard to the corporate hospitals.

Healthcare service industry is one of the flourishing sectors of the Indian economy which is cashing in on the opportunities that liberalization of markets around the globe opened. Increase in awareness to keep oneself healthy coupled with rise in standard of living have led to increase in demand for quality healthcare services. According to the General Agreement of Trade in Services (GATS) definition, "trade in health services occurs via four modes of supply; these are: cross-border delivery of trade, consumption of health services abroad, commercial presence and movement of health personnel." (Adlung Rudolf and Carzaniga Antonia, "Health Services under the General Agreement on Trade in Services", WHO Bulletin, 2001, Issue 4, Vol. 79). The most recent trend in privatization of health care services is medical tourism, which is gaining prominence in developing countries. Globalization has promoted a consumerist culture, which has had its effect in the health sector too, with the emergence of a private sector that thrives by servicing a small percentage of the population that has the ability to "buy" medical care at the rates at which the "high end" of the private medical sector provides such care. This has changed the character of the medical care sector, with the entry of the corporate sector. Corporate run institutions are seized with the necessity to maximize profits and expand their coverage. These objectives face a constraint in the form of the relatively small size of the population in developing countries that can afford services offered by such institutions. In this background, corporate interests in the Medical Care sector are looking for opportunities that go beyond the limited domestic "market" for high cost medical care. This is the genesis of the "medical tourism" industry. Medical Tourism is comparatively new in the vast ocean of travel and tourism industry. When described Medical Tourism in simple terms, it is a provision of 'cost effective' private medical care in collaboration with the tourism industry for patients needing surgical and other forms of specialized treatment. This process is being facilitated by the corporate sector involved in medical care as well as the tourism industry—both private and public.

Although, India is a recent entrant into the medical tourism arena, it is poised to emerge as a major global player. India offers world-class healthcare that costs substantially less than those in developed countries, using the same technology delivered by competent specialists attaining similar success rates. Indian hospitals do not face problem with the technical skills as they are acquired through education and training but the difficulty lies in leveraging the soft skills of the employees. Soft skills are one of the underlying principles that trademark a hospital for professionalism and excellent customer service. The need also foresee the role of various stake holders in promoting healthcare business to uplift the Indian economy. Medical tourism news 29 July (2010) reveals that the Government mulls funding hospitals and the overseas promotion. The Ministry of Tourism (MOT) plans to extend its Market Development Assistance (MDA) scheme to cover Joint Commission International (JCI) and National Accreditation Board of Hospitals (NABH) certified hospitals. The MDA scheme offsets overseas marketing costs for travel companies earning foreign exchange. With the MDA scheme, eligible hospitals will be able to apply for financial assistance to cover publicity through printed material, travel and stay expenses for sales-cum-study tours and participation fees for trade fairs and exhibitions. MOT director Dr Prabhakar Dubey states, "The MDA scheme for medical tourism is under active consideration and will be applicable only to accredited hospitals. This should be finalized soon. This will apply to about 60 hospitals". The ministry is prompting all players to form a government-industry partnership to strengthen the Indian healthcare brand overseas. Efforts will be made to launch uniform pricing bands and to combine medical packages with travel products. The potential for this is huge. In India, 11 hospitals have JCI status and at least 18 are known to be at various stages of seeking or achieving it. On the other hand, the official NABH website lists 23 hospitals and 60 at various stages in the process of achieving accreditation, but it is not up to date. Latest figures show 25 private and 108 state hospitals have achieved NABH status, and over 100 are in the pipeline. While most JCI hospitals and large healthcare groups are in the medical tourism business, many with or seeking NABH status are not and do not plan to be.

Scope of the Study

There is ample scope for exploring the potentials of medical tourism and ascertaining the Quality or standardization norms for global healthcare competency. This could be attained by focusing on the factors like, Up-gradation of basic amenities and hospital infrastructure, co-ordination between the healthcare and tourism sectors, creating a resource pool of highly skilled and cordial manpower, standardization of services and accreditation of hospitals, increasing visibility of India on the world map, the impact on domestic healthcare services. There is a need for emerging healthcare segments in India to develop the regional specialized areas (South India) as a global healthcare destination. The broader scope covers emphasis on enhancing a wider perspective for Medical Tourism as an emerging industry. Hence there is impending requirement for comparison on different destinations in South India which ensures competitiveness towards development for working out a global healthcare destination.

For getting an exceptional growth in the healthcare system, India needs to lay a wider role in developing integrated healthcare units. This could be practiced by either government owned ventures or by partnership with globally competitive private participants. This creates India to mull over for Value creation in a networked healthcare environment and also building professional competency through healthcare managers. Medical Tourism falls under the category of consumption of health services abroad. It has evolved through the coming together of two services hitherto unrelated, i.e., healthcare and tourism. Due to the escalation of this industry in India, massive tasks lie ahead to synergize the resources of the two sectors. However there are issues and challenges that need to be addressed to overcome the roadblocks to facilitate the growth of this industry in India. The issues that call for attention are:

- Progression of basic amenities and hospital infrastructure —Basic amenities in India are not up to international standards, especially air connectivity, road links, conveyance services and Internet connectivity. This gives a poor image of the country to health travelers, and also raises doubts about the quality of healthcare facilities. The state of basic amenities in a country has a considerable impact on the choice of destination for health travellers. Basic amenities need to be upgraded and made hassle free. Travel visa is another critical issue which the Indian government plans to address by introducing special medical visas for foreign tourists coming to India for specialised treatment. This visa will allow the patient to bring along two attendants and will also enable him to access the finest medical care in the most recognized hospitals in the country, that specialize in the treatment he is seeking. Recognizing this, the government of India through various measures is encouraging private sector investment in the sector. It has conferred 'infrastructure' status for the healthcare industry, and allowed foreign collaboration. In addition, concessions in tax to raise cheaper long-term funds, reduction in import and custom duties on medical equipment, increase in depreciation limit and income tax exemption for the first five years if the hospital has a capacity of hundred beds or more, have been granted. The concern here is whether corporates will use these incentives as intended by the state, and whether they will repay society in equal measure.

- Co-ordination between the healthcare and tourism sectors —Co-coordinating the resources and services of two unrelated sectors-healthcare and tourism is challenging. Strategic coordination essential between these two sectors can be done through facilitation by the government. The Indian Healthcare Federation, Medical Tourism Council of Maharashtra, FICCI, government of India and respective state governments are coordinating to promote this industry. The services of both the healthcare and the tourism sector are required simultaneously once the patient finalizes the hospital from where he/she wishes to avail of the healthcare services. Arrangement for passports, visas, airline tickets and conveyance has to be made. The availability of doctor, date of surgery, days to be spent in the hospital and recuperation services have to be confirmed. All this requires co-operation from both the hospital and the tour operator. Thus there is a need to train the people of these two sectors to meet the requirements of this special segment of tourists. Conferences, interaction between the two sectors, knowledge up-gradation workshops, coaching for personality development and investment in information technology are the ways to strengthen this synergy.
- Generate a resource pool of highly skilled and cordial manpower—Indian doctors are well-known abroad for their qualifications and skills. This is a big advantage for hospitals in India in attracting more medical tourists.

There are 5,00,000 doctors and 7,37,000 nurses serving in the Indian healthcare sector and 18,000 persons get qualified as doctors each year from 170 medical colleges, according to a CII-McKinsey report. This skilled human resource pool can help to meet the increasing demand for healthcare services in India. In addition to hiring and retaining skilled manpower, service expectations of medical tourists have made it imperative for hospitals to create an ambience of wellbeing and cordiality so that their clients feel comfortable and well-attended while on treatment. Corporate hospitals are investing in furnishing their facilities and in training and development of personnel through seminars and short-term courses to gear them up to meet the requirement.

- Standardization of services and accreditation of hospitals —Standardization in pricing of various surgeries and healthcare services is required as vast price differences exist across hospitals. The Indian Healthcare Federation (IHF) has brought in the concept of 'price banding' to bring some consistency in the prices of different therapies and procedures, along with the move to accredit hospitals. Currently the 'price banding' concept is in the consensus stage; once all the IHF members approve it, it will be legalized through the government. Accreditation will be used to negotiate with overseas health insurance companies to extend their cover to include treatment in India. Both standardization in pricing and accreditation will help Indian hospitals in attracting more medical tourists. There is also a requirement for a standard accreditation system. A quality accreditation institution called The National Accreditation Board for Hospital and Healthcare Service Providers (NABH) is likely to be constituted under the aegis of the Quality Council of India. The NABH will have three committees—Accreditation committee, Technical committee and the Appeals committee. The proposed system will assess hospitals based on organizational and clinical governance, operational management, focus on patients, clinical services and human resources, while primary healthcare centres will be assessed on their management and clinical services by designated agencies under the overall control of NABH. The challenge lies in getting the consensus and legalization of this system done. If it gets delayed in the consensus and legalization stages there will be delay in reaping benefits it can bring for the medical tourism sector as well. Huge investment is required to build and maintain this system. There is thus apprehension about mismanagement of funds and resources as this task will be carried out on a large scale around the country. There may be scope for fake accredited hospitals to flourish along with the well-established ones.

- Increasing visibility of India on the world map—India's healthcare services cost far less compared to even Thailand, Singapore and many other healthcare destinations. But it is the poor visibility on the world healthcare tourism map and poor image of the country in terms of poverty and basic amenities that deter people from coming to India. Thailand and Singapore are promoting their healthcare services aggressively which has turned their countries into healthcare hubs. Lately, the government of India, the state governments, the Confederation of Indian Industry and the Indian Healthcare Federation have begun promoting India through road shows in some countries, participating in international trade shows and exhibitions and placing advertisements in various media abroad. Tour operators too are taking advantage of this opportunity. Kuoni has tied-up with the Apollo group, and Cox and Kings with Dr. Batras, Vedic India and Omkar Trust. More such tie-ups are on the anvil. Tourism packages specifically designed for the healthcare tourists are being aggressively promoted by these tour operators. Some hospitals now have their own Marketing and Public Relations department. Websites too have been set up for easy availability of information and for immediate contact.

- The impact on domestic healthcare services—India is one of the cheapest healthcare tourism hubs in the world especially for advanced life saving surgeries. The inflow of medical tourists is on the rise in India, and private hospitals are ever ready to serve this special segment. However, concerns are being raised about the far reaching impact of medical tourism on the public healthcare system that serves a larger section of the Indian society. Although healthcare services provided by private hospitals in India to foreign patients are cheap for them, these are still exorbitant for many Indians. The private hospitals are registered under the Public Trust Act which makes them liable to provide healthcare services free upto 20 percent of their resources in return for subsidies received from the government. But, it is a question that remains unanswered as to whether they are actually providing free healthcare services to the public. Another concern is about increasing concentration of doctors in urban hospitals. Currently more than 50 percent of the doctors is concentrated in the urban hospitals, especially in the metros. Private hospitals cater to nearly 65 percent of the healthcare services market. The number of medical tourists is increasing, which means demand for private healthcare services will increase. Private hospitals will need more medical professionals to meet the increasing demand, and the lucrative offers and the work environment they offer will attract many. The public healthcare sector which is disadvantaged vis-à-vis the private hospitals on these counts will be put under further strain. If more subsidies are given to private hospitals and changes in regulation made to suit them, their concentration in the sector will increase. The public healthcare system will remain neglected.

Indian hospitals are now being acclaimed the world over for the standards of healthcare delivery. The country boasts of superior technology with skilled super specialists along with sound infrastructure & professional outlook. Major hospitals in Chennai, Mumbai, Hyderabad & New Delhi have recorded a 125 patient flow from the neighboring & South-East Asian countries. This is because people have realized that they can now have access to international quality medi-care at 10 percent of international costs in India. Thus, there is apprehension about the benefits of medical tourism to the Indian public. There is an enormous potential for Indian healthcare system to reach out with its services beyond frontiers. The purpose of the study also necessitates the role of hospitality sector in promoting medical tourism in coordination with the hospital sector. Hence the thrust could be leveraged by promulgating an effective tourism economics. This enables a wider sphere for a better proximity to global success. The potential is explored in the study through analysis of the market for medical tourism in south India and identification of its link to economic growth. Medical tourism is not a universally feasible growth strategy. Instead, it is successful only in countries with economic and political advantages that enable them to navigate around international and domestic obstacles to trade in medical services. A successful medical tourism industry, when coupled with cooperation between the private and public sectors, may lead to public health improvements in developing countries.

In many developing countries it is being actively promoted by the government's official policy. India's National Health Policy, says: "to capitalize on the comparative cost advantage enjoyed by domestic health facilities in the secondary and tertiary sector, the policy will encourage the supply of services to patients of foreign origin on payment. The rendering of such services on payment in foreign exchange will be treated as 'deemed exports' and will be made eligible for all fiscal incentives extended to export earnings".

Latest study of CII, medical tourism in India could become a $1 billion business by 2012. The Indian government predicts that India's $17-billion-a-year health care industry could grow by 13 percent in each of the next six years, boosted by medical tourism. In India, the Apollo group alone has so far treated 95,000 international patients, many of whom are of Indian origin. Apollo has been a forerunner in medical tourism in India and attracts patients from Southeast Asia, Africa, and the Middle East. The group has tied up with hospitals in Mauritius, Tanzania, Bangladesh and Yemen besides running a hospital in Sri Lanka. Reports also show that foreigners account for 10-12 percent of all patients in top Mumbai hospitals despite absence of uniform quality standards. However some claim that the industry would flourish even without Western medical tourists. Afro-Asian people spend as much as $20 billion a year on health care outside their countries—Nigerians alone spend an estimated a $1 billion a year. Most of this money is spent in Europe and America, but it is hoped that this would be directed to developing countries with advanced facilities. Former Union Minister Ambika Soni recently announced that a total investment of $6.5 billion is in the pipeline for medical tourism industry in the country and the amount will also be used for setting up affordable hospitals and budget hotels for patients' relatives in the country. This announcement highlights the increasing number of Indian private hospitals that are finding themselves mentioned in travel itineraries and are sought out by more and more foreigners.

Analyzing the past trends of medical travelers from the late 1980s and early 1990s, most medical travelers coming to India were from the Arab countries, Africa and south-east Asia. But today, medical travelers to India can be divided into three distinct geographical categories that travel for distinctly different reasons. The first category is made up of the Americans and Europeans. The prime factors driving the Americans to travel abroad was their lifestyle surgeries and recurring costs. The natures of treatments were because of age like; facelifts, dental treatment, botox treatments, tummy tucks etc and since, cosmetic surgery is not covered by medical insurance. Many Americans prefer to travel abroad. The British were being forced to seek medical treatment in other countries by the sheer waiting lists caused by the National Health Service (NHS). The second big group of medical travelers comes from the Middle East. These are citizens of oil rich nations flying India to seek medical facilities that are either unavailable or in short supply in their own countries. A research in Saudi Arabia estimated that every year more than 500,000 people from the Middle East travel seeking medical treatment for everything from open-heart surgery to infertility treatments. By some estimates, India itself attracted 70000 plus medical travelers from the Middle East in 2009. Finally, the last group of medical travelers forms an assorted lot. They are from the least developed countries and countries with generally poor infrastructure, who seek treatment for facilities at some neighboring country with better infrastructure. In 2009, it was estimated that at least 50000 people from Bangladesh, Burma and Nepal came for medical treatment to India.

India is a big player in the medical tourism industry. In fact, it has been ranked the most popular medical tourism destination by many. India is now moving into a new area of "medical outsourcing," where subcontractors provide services to the overburdened medical care systems in western countries. The health care sector in India has witnessed an enormous growth in infrastructure in the private and voluntary sector. Apart from the contribution of government and hospitals in improving the health care service in India, what truly give that edge to India over other medical tourism destinations are the innumerable rejuvenation options it offers and the easiness of stay in India. There is no compromise on the quality of medical services provided in this country and thus India can confidently compete with that of even the most developed nations. Hospitals of India are well equipped with the latest technology and houses highly qualified and experienced staff that can provide timely and quality medical treatment to patients. As a move in promoting medical tourism, many hospitals are deemed as "corporate hospitals" that specially cater to the needs of medical tourists in India. Apart from offering world class treatments, they offer various services that make medical tourists' stay in India hassle free. Many hospitals in India have international accreditations that certify the quality of health care service. In a shot-in-the-arm for healthcare tourism, the tourism ministry is planning to extend its market development assistance (MDA) scheme to cover Joint Commission International (JCI) and National Accreditation Board (NABH) certified hospitals. The MDA scheme offsets overseas marketing costs for travel companies earning foreign exchange. By opening up the MDA, hospital groups will be made eligible for financial assistance, including publicity through printed material, travel and stay expenses for sales-cum-study tours and participation fees for trade fairs and exhibitions, subject to an upper ceiling. There are about 60 accredited hospitals in India, of which the big groups have independently facilitated tie-ups with US-based insurance companies such as Bluecross Blueshield and Anthem Wellpoint but smaller players have relied on agents due to high costs.

The ministry is prompting all players to form a government-industry partnership on the lines of Nasscom to strengthen the Indian healthcare brand overseas. Efforts will be made to launch uniform pricing bands and to combine medical packages with travel products. The potential for forex earnings through this route is huge. On an average, a medical traveller spends about $7,000 as opposed to a holiday traveler who spends $3000. Indian Government has acknowledged the growth of medical tourism in India and is now offering Medical Visas. South India has become one of the preferred medical tourism and health holiday destination with some of the best hospitals providing services at the cheapest rates found in the city. Cost effectiveness is the main USP for the developing counties like India along with its clinical expertise. India has world's best centers, besides having internationally qualified and experienced specialists. Price advantage is a major selling point. The slogan, thus is, "first world treatment at third world prices". The cost differential across the board is huge. India offers a vast array of services combined with the cultural warmth that is difficult to match by other countries.

Unlike the prospects of medical tourism, the vulnerable

business environment has its own downsides. The challenges faced are:

- Restraint on follow-up care, the patient usually is in hospital for only a few days, and then goes on the vacation portion of the trip or returns home. Complications, side-effects and post-operative care are then the responsibility of the medical care system in the patients' home country.
- Government and basic medical insurance, and sometimes extended medical insurance, often does not pay for the medical procedure, sometimes the patient has to pay of his own.
- Most of the countries that offer medical tourism have weak malpractice laws, so the patient has little recourse to local courts or medical boards if something goes wrong.
- There are growing accusations that profitable; private-sector medical tourism is drawing medical resources and personnel away from the local population, although some medical organizations that market to outside tourists are taking steps to improve local service.

Experts have identified a number of challenges before Indian medial tourism on its global competency. Problems with medical tourism are to be dealt with care as it can reinforce the nation's economic condition.

- Without strong support or initiative taken by government no country can promote any niche segment as medical tourism. India spends 1.2 percent of its GDP on health, but takes care of foreign patients—the country ranks second in medical tourism. In 2007, Indian hospitals treated 4.5 lakh patients from other countries against topper Thailand's 12 lakh.
- Poor coordination between the various players in the industry—hospitals, air line operators and hotels can tamper the potentials of medical tourism. A joint venture can prove high ratio of efficiency and can boost private public partnership.

- It's obligatory to reorient the customer perception from being an unhygienic country to be equipped with high quality assuring system which will accelerate penetration of quality healthcare services in India.
- Lack of proper regulatory system for hospitals. The hospitality sector was first to introduce grading system which was indicator of quality of hotels and the different parameters of service delivery, along with this with growing consumer awareness and consumer protection initiatives by government and realized the need of importance of service delivery system in healthcare quality accreditation system and compliance to the same came into practice.
- India has strong competition from countries like Thailand, Malaysia, and Singapore, but Indian clinical and paramedical talent is globally appreciated and with JCI accreditation of some hospitals, the international standard is proven. Third party intervention through health insurance has also given it a boost. Moreover these far east Asian countries which revolutionized medical tourism, is more into cosmetic surgery; where as India focuses on cardiac, neurological or orthopedic problems.
- Many recognized Indian healthcare units still lack international accreditation. If the governing body takes interest in inviting the accrediting bodies to assess the quality system it can boost medical tourism.
- It could be a bane with overseas medical care not covered by many insurance players.
- Limited role of government involvement in healthcare infrastructure is a barrier to diversify the total stream of development in medical tourism. There is an opportunity in medical tourism because Indian healthcare institutions is in a position to offer quality medical services at one-tenth the cost compared to that in many countries in the west.

The biggest challenge is to position India as a favourable

healthcare destination by setting high health standards and work in association with the government and the medical council to see to it that all hospitals keep up to those standards. At present the Indian healthcare federation is working along with different industry chambers to promote medical tourism in the country. The road map ahead has to be focused. The strategy to get global visibility can be through gathering more information from potential outlets. Secondly, Indian healthcare industry should work more closely with the industry chambers and various government departments to spread the awareness and remove hurdles. Finally, we have to work towards getting accreditation for various hospitals to build up perception of quality among foreign tourists.

Healthcare sector on the other hand has direct correlation with the external influences drawn from business environment. However, healthcare has not been totally immune to the global financial crisis. The economic situation has hit demand *"because elective surgery is being delayed"*, says Paul Keckley, executive director of the Deloitte Centre for Health Solutions.

Confederation of Indian Industry (CII) organized the 3rd Medical Technology Conference 2010: *"Innovations in Medical Technology-Enabling India to 'Leapfrog' to the next level Healthcare"* at New Delhi. The existing healthcare infrastructure and skills in India alone cannot solve India's huge unmet needs in Healthcare. It needs to be supported by Technology which has the potential to increase accessibility, significantly reduce the burden of disease and the load of Healthcare delivery services through early diagnosis, better clinical outcomes, less invasive procedures and shorter recovery times.

India foresees innovative approaches in medical tourism which is being patient centric and balancing the internal medical travel in India. India may not only see advanced technology within medical equipment, but also an opening up of the possibility of large indigenous manufacturing to serve Indian masses. This possibility is also taking shape as various development centers of multinational companies have started development and customization of their high end products such as digital x-ray as per Indian requirements, re-affirming the need for certain "Made in India, Made for India" products.

There are wider issues to be addressed considering new array of subjects like: Innovate for access, cost and convenience, collaboration from all stakeholders in the innovation ecosystem, impediments and solutions to growth of this industry, need for an unambiguous and supportive regulatory environment & enabling India to become a manufacturing base for medical technology industry. This innovative approach will enable latest medical technologies reoriented not limited to the upper crust of society alone. However it is important to look into the challenges faced by medical technology companies in India—awareness, regulations, lack of proper health infrastructure, affordability hindering access, insurance and return on investment, which if nurtured and addressed appropriately, will accelerate penetration of quality healthcare services in India. This will enhance connotation of a Quality System. There was a time when quality was a much heard term in product industry. But over a period of time the consumers became more demanding even in the service sector and with the achievement of next levels of service delivery practices, the term "Quality" started to gain significance in service industries.

Trends in Medical Tourism in India

Healthcare sector has enormous business potential but public expenditure on healthcare remains a priority issue to be addressed. India needs to increase its public expenditure on healthcare and improve the legislative framework for medical tourism. Technopak estimates that around $20 billion will be invested in healthcare facilities in Tier II and III cities during the next five years.

Medical Tourism World Launches Versatile Portal on Medical Tourism in India

Medical Treatments & Tourism India (MTTI) is one of the first ISO 9001: 2000 Certified Company in this field in India. It is a well thought, supported & well promoted endeavor of an established International Trading Organisation. The portal is a "One Stop-Treatment Shop" offering World Class and affordable Medical Treatments & Services to people from around the globe in India. It offers World class Medical Care & Treatment Solutions connecting people from around the globe to a vast network of major associated Hospitals, Clinics & Doctors. Co has a transparent, clear and well explained Step by Step Procedures & Medical Packages and provides customized Medical Packages as per the specific need & situation. Company's USP is Personalised care & support right from Query, to Registration, to Receiving the Patient, till completion of the Medical Treatment & Procedure and Departure, backed by a professionally managed team.

Cosmetic surgery packages at Goa and Kerala in India at low cost for international medical tourists

Medical tourists and international aspirants can now get cosmetic surgery packages at Goa and Kerala in India at low cost. Cosmetic surgery packages at Goa and Kerala in India not only offers you beauty enhancement procedures but also provides you health recovery physically and mentally by providing you extensive holiday tours and holiday vacations.

Indian medical tourism has brought the economical but international quality healthcare facilities available at the cosmetic surgery clinics of Delhi, Mumbai, Goa and Chennai into lime light creating curiosity among abroad natives from US, Canada, Europe and Africa who are very adventurous and exploring in nature. Cosmetic surgery packages in India are now also being financed by some top rated finance institutions of Canada and US with less or zero payment options. The clinical care and cosmetic surgery technology being provided in India at cities of Mumbai, Chennai, Goa, Hyderabad and Delhi are comparable to that being provided in countries of Europe and America only the difference is concerned to cost. The cost of cosmetic surgery in India is 1/10th of the amount charged at other places. Plus medical visa, travel and hospitality arrangements by Indian medical tourism services and affiliated cosmetic surgery hospitals in India are very convenient to persons coming from abroad. Holiday tours at Indian wild life sanctuaries and holiday vacations at Indian tourism destinations are added attractions that are being offered under exclusive cosmetic surgery packages in India.

Indian aura plans to set up three spas in Gujarat

Indian aura, a Non-Resident Indian (NRI) venture is planning to come up with three spas in Gujarat state for capturing major share of Rs 3,300 crores medical tourism industry in the state. I.J. Patel chairman, said these spas will come up by 2011 in Vadodara, Ahmedabad and one more city which is yet to be selected. These spas will provide the meditarranean, Indian, oriental system of medicine, naturopaty, allopathy and aurveda treatment.

Indian aura is taking lead in the state with a plan of three spas which requires an investment of Rs 11 crores. The aim is to promote Gujarat as Asia's number one health destination". The Gujarat government had promoted the concept of medical tourism industry during 'Gujarat Vibrant' meet in 2003; however it did not succeed completely, due to many lapses.

IFC to invest Rs 55 crore in Rockland hospitals

World Bank group member International Finance Corporation will invest Rs 55 crore (14 million dollars) in Delhi-based Rockland Hospitals to support its expansion plans. Rockland Hospitals plans to expand its facility in the national capital and set up a 250-bed hospital in Manesar, Haryana. The project will help broaden access to high-quality health care and good administrative and patient care to common people. The project demonstrates IFC's commitment to social sector development. It also aligns with the strategy to invest in health care, one of India's largest service industries where the private sector's involvement is most critical. IFC, a member of the World Bank Group fosters sustainable economic growth in developing countries by financing private sector investments.

Govt plans medical tech park in Chennai—The government is setting up a medical technology park in Chennai soon to help cut costs of healthcare equipment and research for new vaccines. The park would include medical device manufacturing units, healthcare infrastructure and vaccine technology facilities. The medical park will help manufacture cost-effective medical equipment for the country. The vaccine park will research on developing new vaccines. The work for setting up the vaccine park has already started, the ministry of health and family welfare will shortly invite private players to set up facilities in the park. The state government has already given 300 acres for the vaccine technology park at a concessional price. The park is expected to be in place within four years. State-owned Hindustan Latex will set up its facility in the vaccine centre. According to industry estimates, 90 percent of the medical equipment used in India are imported. The medical technology park is likely to help tackle this situation as manufacturing products in India for domestic use would reduce the cost of equipment by 40 percent. The medical equipment market in India is estimated to be around a billion dollars. The government plans to keep the park open to both national and international companies.

Maldives explores medical tourism, health education tie-up with city hospital in Chennai

The Republic of Maldives is exploring the possibility of a tie-up with K.G. Hospital for medical tourism and health education. The hospital has said in a press release that Maldives Minister for Education Mustafa Lutfi and his deputy Ahmed Ali Manik visited it recently as part of their tour of India to explore collaboration in medical tourism, healthcare education and information technology (IT). The Government of Maldives had also invited Dr. Bakthavathsalam and the hospital's team to that country to identify appropriate areas where the hospital's expertise could be used effectively. Dr. Bakthavathsalam said a high-level team of the hospital would visit the Maldives to enter into a memorandum of understanding with its Government in the area of healthcare.

Narayana Hrudayalaya, the Bangalore-based Heart Hospital, Embarked upon Building a "health city"

Narayana Hrudayalaya, the Bangalore-based heart hospital, has embarked upon building a "health city" with a capacity of 2,000 beds in another one and half years. Today a 250 bed institute of neurosciences, equipped with state-of-the-art facilities, would be set up with an investment of Rs 250 crores, in the first phase. The hospital has already acquired 20 acres, adjacent to the cardiac super specialty hospital, to develop the health city. By this ambitious venture, it proposed to turn Bangalore city into the healthcare hub of the world. The health city project would cater to orthopedics and eye care treatment, besides an additional 500 bed hospital for neurology and neurosurgical care. Statistics have shown that there are 25 lakh patients in need of heart operations, but every year only 60,000 operations are performed by hospitals across the country.

Quality healthcare should be affordable and accessible to all because even developed countries like the UK and the US are struggling to meet their people's healthcare needs. Governments should be a health-insurance provider rather than only a healthcare provider. Access to quality healthcare is a fundamental right and not a privilege, and in achieving this objective, Narayana Health City has been a model to the world." Kiran Mazumdar Shaw, whose cancer hospital is also housed in the health city, said: "The world is challenged with the burden of diseases. Forty million people in the US don't have access to healthcare; in India, only 20 percent do, and 80 percent of non-insured people in India have to pay from their pockets. Even US President Barack Obama is trying hard to bring healthcare reforms. And models like Narayana Health City in India can address these healthcare problems". Similar health cities with 5,000-bed capacity will be set up in Hyderabad, Jaipur, Kolkata and Ahmedabad. In Karnataka, apart from Bangalore, a 2,000-bed facility on 14 acres of land has been sanctioned with the vision to treat 10,000 out-patients and 5,000 in-patients every day. Through tele-medicine 53,000 cardiac patients have been reached and they are still reaching out to patients in 53 countries in Africa. 20 percent of patients in health city are from abroad, from around 65 countries. With the increase in surgeries, cost of treatment will reduce and every year, our objective is to reduce treatment costs by at least by 5 percent.

According to an official from the Karnataka Tourism Department, healthcare in Bangalore came into the limelight when Noor Fatima from Pakistan came to Narayana Hrudayalaya in July 2003, and was operated on by Dr Devi Shetty. After that, there was no looking back for the city. Her surgery was a landmark because not only did it help in thawing the hostility between the two neighboring countries, but also drastically reversed the table in the medical scenario of the city for the better. Hospitals and corporate establishments in the city have realised the potential of this niche market and have accordingly channelised their needs and facilities. Travel agents and hotels are structuring their packages and holiday schemes in accordance with the inflow of foreign patients coming into the city.

Karnataka's Foray into the Healthcare Sector

The department of tourism, government of Karnataka, has ambitious plans for the state. According to D.B. Inamdar, then minister for tourism, "The idea is to make Karnataka a top health tourism destination, not only in India but internationally. We want to lure foreigners to Karnataka to avail of our sophisticated facilities and subsequently induce them to enjoy our multiple tourism offerings. This endeavour will have a positive impact on the entire economy of the state." In fact, the government is setting up a Bangalore International Health City Corporation which will cater to patients for a wide variety of health care products and treatments. The recent operations of children from Pakistan, who have sought medical treatment in Bangalore, have not only helped to boost the state economy but more importantly, helped in fostering goodwill, peace and harmony between India and Pakistan. Without doubt, Indian doctors are among the best in the world and given the right atmosphere and environment, they can enhance the image of Incredible India as a health and tourism destination. The state also boasts of having the unique property, Golden Palms Spa & Resort, which is the one and only resort in the country where a guest can have a complete range of pathological tests, dental treatment, electro-cardiograms, stress tests, X-rays, and even sonography tests. To crown it all, there is even a mini-operation theatre for cosmetic surgery performed by world renowned surgeons in the field.

The Karnataka Government is taking a slew of initiatives in promoting medical tourism in the state. Most experts from the industry have acknowledged the fact that the State Government is supportive and enthusiastic in promoting medical tourism in the city in particular and the State as a whole. The Karnataka government right now is working in a meticulous manner. They first conduct research to study key players in the field, which include not just the top hospitals but travel agents and consulates in the city. Their performance over the year is reviewed and simultaneously suggestions are taken. Consulates and travel agents have their networks abroad. So, it is easier for us to have international conferences and contacts. The Government also holds health tourism expos. A recent one was held at Bahrain. Such meets are a platform for the Government to meet international experts from the medical fraternity and brief them about the competence of Indian healthcare industry.

Travel agents and hotels are cashing in on the situation and are coming up with schemes and packages to attract foreign patients to the city. They are gradually realising that immense benefits can be reaped. The Leela Palaces and Resorts, Bangalore, which purely caters to the corporate class, have now decided to spread its wings according to the change in times and trends. The five-star hotel group has decided to tie up with Manipal Hospital. The five-star hotel has also joined hands with Globe Health Tours.

The survey conducted on "Medical Tourism in Chennai and Bangalore", helped in making a few observations. They are:

- The survey revealed that awareness of hospitals and medical tourism in Chennai and Bangalore was mainly obtained from the Internet as well as by Word of Mouth. Magazines/Newspapers played only a small role.
- All the respondents were aware of Medical Tourism in Chennai and Bangalore and said that India came to their mind first when they spoke of Medical Tourism, followed by Thailand.
- A large number of people said the facilities provided were very good and could be compared to international standards.
- The survey revealed that majority people could not go around visiting the tourist sites while they came for their treatment.
- Majority of the respondents had not faced any trouble at the destination; however problems faced by few people were communication problems and lack of adequate post-medical treatment.
- Most of the respondents were aware of the various kinds of treatments available in India.
- Majority of patients were seen coming in for cardiac surgeries, followed by dental and then other treatments such as oncology etc
- The survey revealed that the reason people opted for Chennai and Bangalore was because of the affordable rates and the ease in communication.
- The survey showed that most of the respondents were satisfied with their overall stay.

Suggestions

The survey conducted on "Medical Tourism in Chennai and Bangalore", helped in making a few observations. And thus a few of my suggestions for the further development of this form of tourism:

- The survey revealed that Chennai and Bangalore should improve its infrastructure facilities.
- A small number of people were not satisfied with the treatment provided to them. Thus hospitals should ensure that everyone is benefited from the services provided to them, by ensuring that feedback is obtained from the patient and the needs of dissatisfied patients addressed immediately.
- Corporate hospitals should ensure that foreign patients are given a translator from the time they enter the hospital till they leave the hospital.
- Chennai and Bangalore also have various alternative forms of medicine which needs to be promoted to a greater extent.
- Hospitals should ensure that patients are given adequate post-medical treatment.

Conclusion

The research brought to light the potential south Indian cities has to grow as the healthcare destination; however what is required today is standardization of existing healthcare institutions. The Karnataka and Tamilnadu government is working in a meticulous manner. Travel agents and hotels are cashing in on the situation and are coming up with schemes and packages to attract foreign patients to the city. They are gradually realising that immense benefits can be reaped. However we cannot afford to compromise on quality which is important today. Destinations covered are some of the top medical tourism destinations of India, with professional experts, technological sophistication and health care services that easily match the best in the world. Its reputation as the global technology hub and cosmopolitan city has made it a prominent health care destination for foreigners from developed as well as developing countries.

REFERENCES

"Now Medical Visas for Foreign Tourists", (2005), http://inhome.rediff.com, July.

"Medical Tourism: Opportunities and Challenges for India", www.expresshealthcare mgmt.com, March 16-31, 2005.

"Hospitals to bring in 'Price Banding' for Overseas Clients", *Economic Times*, February 26, 2005.

Syed Falknaaz, "Apex Body for Accreditating Hospitals and Healthcare Providers on the Anvil", www.expresshealthcaremgmt.com, February 16-28, 2005.

Dutt Rimin, "Medical Tourism has Legs; Government Help Needed" (2004), www. indusbusinessjournal.com, May.

Gupta Sen Amit, "Medical Tourism and Public Health", *People's Democracy*, May 09, 2004, Vol. XXVIII, No. 19.

"Healthcare Sectoral Report" (2004), http://ibef.org.

Duggal Ravi and Verma Anupam, "Should Public Hospitals Participate in Medical Tourism?"

www.expresshealthcaremgmt.com, December 15-31, 2003.

Adlung Rudolf and Carzaniga Antonia, "Health Services under the General Agreement on Trade in Services", *WHO Bulletin*, 2001, Issue 4, Vol. 79.

"India is Far Cheaper than Thailand", www.ibef.org May 23, 2004.

Zarkovic Bookman, Milica. & Bookman, Karla R. *"Medical Tourism In Developing Countries"*, Palgrave Macmillan, 2007.

Hancock, David. *"The Complete Medical Tourist: Your Guide to Inexpensive and Safe Cosmetic, Medical and Dental Surgery Overseas"*, Blake; Illustrated Edition, March 2006.

Parekh R.L., *"Medical Tourism"*—Alfa Publication, 2009.

"Medical Tourism: Opportunities and Challenges for India", www.expresshealthcare mgmt.com, March 16-31, 2005.

"Hospitals to bring in 'Price Banding' for Overseas Clients", *Economic Times*, February 26, 2005.

Adlung Rudolf and Carzaniga Antonia, "Health Services under the General Agreement on Trade in Services", *WHO Bulletin*, 2001, Issue 4, Vol. 79.

Syed Falknaaz, "Apex Body for Accreditating Hospitals and Healthcare Providers on the Anvil", www.expresshealthcaremgmt.com, February 16-28 2005.

Dutt Rimin, "Medical Tourism has Legs; Government Help Needed", (2004), www.indusbusinessjournal.com, May.

Gupta Sen Amit, "Medical Tourism and Public Health", *People's Democracy*, May 09, 2004, Vol. XXVIII, No. 19.

Medical Tourist—A Bi–annual Magazine by Medical Tourism Association, U.S.

Medical Tourism Magazine—Published by the UK Health Insurance Companies

http://timesofindia.indiatimes.com/india/India-emerges-2nd-in-medical-tourismrace/articleshow/4321310.cms

http://worldmedtourism.blogspot.com/

http://www.expresshealthcaremgmt.com/20020731/bangalore1.shtml

http://www.globalpost.com/dispatch/india/090724/medical-outsourcing-india

4

Tourism in India : Emerging Strategies

Krishan Gopal

In India tourism has been dismissively treated a leisure activity of the rich, a somewhat unnecessary distraction for a poor. Take for instance our understanding of who we recognize as a tourist —the client whom we expect to spend money.

Fortunately of late, official thinking about the potential of tourism has been undergoing a transformation. In part, this is a reflection of a growing number of travelers able and willing to spend money to enjoy a wide variety of goods, services and experiences. Equally, it is being recognized that the income and employment generating potential of tourism per unit of investment is higher than manufacturing or agriculture and more, it cuts across class, social and geographical divides. Given the backward and forward linkages of the sector, resources invested in the promotion of tourism can stimulate demand for an immense range of goods, services and skills, both traditional and modern, and the consequent incomes generated can be widely dispersed and shared.

Despite the proliferation of research and publications on the sector, we still seem obsessed with the white, western tourist, that too from the English speaking Anglo-Saxon world. Consequently, not only do we miss out on the diversity of the western traveler, we are even less sensitive to the concerns of visitors from other parts of the globe, be it from the affluent and growing economies of East and South-East Asia, countries of the Middle East or those from East and South Africa, even China, all of whom today account for a substantial and growing share of global tourist traffic.

We have not been able to map and tap the various segments of the tourist market. People travel to India not only to experience the exotica of the cultural and spiritual East—the golden triangle of Delhi-Agra-Jaipur, the forts, temples and palaces—but increasingly also for business, education, rural and social studies, medical and other reasons, not to forget more specialized and niche experiences like wild life tourism and mountaineering. Without continuous research and monitoring of different kinds of travelers and their varied preferences, it is difficult to arrange for and provide a worthwhile experience.

Even more surprising than the above is the relative blindness to the domestic traveler. It is only now sinking in that many more Indians are travelling, and not merely for social engagements or pilgrimage. Both as a result of increasing disposable incomes as also provisions like the leave travel concession, Indians are now travelling for pleasure and new experiences. It is even less realized that in the last few years, more Indians travelled abroad than our inflow of foreign visitors, resulting in a net outflow of foreign exchange. Hardly surprising since our policies continue to discourage local travel—viz. the airfares from Delhi to Thiruvananthapuram exceed those to Bangkok or Singapore. Equally, we give greater attention to airports than railway stations and bus terminals, or to luxury hotels than budget accommodation, clearly indicating our preference for a specific category of tourists.

Some of these distorted attention are reflected in the practice of clubbing the tourism ministry sometimes with civil aviation, at other times with culture, but rarely granting it the independent status it deserves. Further, we have failed to develop many forward and backward linkages affecting visitor experience

—from visa difficulties and inefficient airports, overpriced hotel rooms, the absence of safe and convenient travel infrastructure and, above all, ill-maintained sites and locations that do little to attract the travelers. Little do we realize that unwholesome and unwelcoming experiences only drive away the potential repeat visitor.

Another major problem is our inability to distinguish between, and thus prepare for, the differential requirements of mass/charter and boutique tourism. The obsession with increasing figures of arrival make thus miss out on the higher revenue per capita potential\of niche tourism. Not only does mass/charter tourism place greater burden on an already stretched local infrastructure, much of the money spent by the charter tourist is cornered by foreign airlines and tourism agencies leaving less for domestic players. It can, as Goa domestically has shown, escalate tensions and lead to cultural clashes. Instead, we need to learn from the experience of boutique tourism in Kerala, some of our wildlife sites and so on, which have succeeded in creating models wherein the local populations gain from visitor arrivals in a sustainable manner and thus develop a stake in preserving and improving the local resources.

All of the above demands that we give tourism the attention it deserves—not only grant it the status of an independent and important ministry but also place the subject on the concurrent list enabling greater coordination between centre and states, rationalize the multiple taxes imposed on various goods and services and, above all, move away from short-run considerations of maximizing immediate returns to foregrounding long term considerations of sustainability. We need, for instance, many more imaginative models of public-private partnership—from financing and maintenance of tourism related infrastructure; expansion of sites and experiences for travelers, both foreign and domestic; marketing and sales of associated goods and services, and so on. Then there is a more 'radical' proposal of treating tourism as a by-product of enhancing the quality of local resources and infrastructure for citizens rather than tailor policy and packages for the external visitor. Therefore, it will improve the environment for all visitors.

Tourism: As an Economic Sector

Tourism as an economic sector has to interface with a large number of other economic, social and administrative sectors in part because tourism itself has to address various dimensions.

Tourism is today's largest industry, with the travel and tourism economy the world over contributing 10.4 percent of global GDP. It is also recognized as the highest generator of jobs accounting for 8.1 per cent of the total global employment or one in every 12.2 jobs, adding 45 million jobs in the travel and tourism economy by 2014. In terms of employment, the travel and tourism economy accounts for 25 million jobs in India. This translates to a 6 per cent share of all employment. With such large numbers at stake, tourism, like any other major industry must also take into account the following essential components—R&D, manufacturing, distribution, sales and marketing. Such fundamentals need to be seriously deliberated as policy determiners in India.

Given India's priorities of population, agricultural production, industrial output, market organization, education and health, the tourism sector traditionally was more or less equated with a holiday, at best a necessary peripheral for the elite. It is now clearer that tourism must be regarded as a core consideration in the life of major sections of the population, even when it means travel on a pilgrimage or for a social obligation like marriage. Only now are we developing a vocabulary and perspective which captures the true expanse and time potential of tourism.

The next major component of this economic sector is 'manufacturing'. Manufacturing in the tourism sector involves a very diverse range. Just in terms of accommodation the range can extend from niche boutique hotels to multi-rise hotels, purely experiential hotels and budget hotels all of which would be required in large numbers. It has been estimated that there is a shortfall of at least 150,000 hotel rooms in the country. If an average of three million rupees per hotel, room is taken as a base figure, the investment required in this sector works out to be a staggering Rs. 45,000 crore. One can imagine the huge employment opportunities generated when the country undertakes the development of roads, water supply, electricity supply, sanitation, construction and supplies to the new rooms needed all over the country. This is in addition to the products and employment generated in the transportation sector to ensure the movement of tourists and materials needed to fulfill the requirements of this sector.

Another key word in the tourism sector is distribution. Traditionally, tourism was related to historical sites, the usual attractions like hill stations, sanctuaries, beaches or travel stops on the highways. However, starting from Kerala where destinations were created in the backwaters, on plantations or in residential homes, we have today reached a stage where the "creation of an experience' knows no limitations. There is the possibility of using lake palaces, of forts being turned into museums, spas being created in the hills (like Ananda), tented hotels or even high-end resorts coming up near the small towns (like Alwar in Rajasthan). Not to forget that rural tourism can be made to flourish in the remotest of villages offering the best of experiences from the true cultural strengths of a village community.

Thus distribution in tourism experiences will assume a macro meaning and a macro opportunity for creation of economic wealth and development and equitable distribution of incomes ensuring alleviation of poverty. While research will form the backbone of the distribution system, the sheer opportunity for increasing flows from the present level of 3.37 million tourists to a target of 15 or 25 or 50 million will boost the fortunes of many an entrepreneur.

Entrepreneurship has to be the cornerstone of the 'sales strategies' which will have to draw on the sales network and acumen of the personnel responsible for generating turnover volumes in the tourism industry. Markets will have to be identified and focused upon.

Cultural Tourism

Cultural Tourism in India relies on a combination of emerging trends in tourism as a whole, and the ever growing sophistication of cultural heritage conservation activities, particularly for the major monuments and historic cities.

Tourism in Asia is growing exponentially and is expected to continue over the coming years. Increasing wealth among the middle classes of Asia is generating a great deal of international travel within Asia as well as an increasing level of domestic tourism in many countries. The Borobudur World Heritage Site in Indonesia welcomes nearly 2.5 million visitors per annum, of which only about 150,000 are international arrivals.

The Government of India should focus tourism development policy on benefits from tourism for the myriad regional and local communities that make up the nation. The current emphasis of promoting the country as an international destination merely to increase the number of tourists who might visit, a very common approach worldwide, is no longer appropriate.

Packaged tourism is increasingly recognizing the potential of world heritage and other major cultural heritage sites. This carries the danger of high concentrations of visitors in very restricted locations. Packaged tourism is tending to move people from attraction to attraction more quickly than was the traditional pace of tourism. In many major sites, visits are often reduced to one or two days before moving on to the next attraction. These places increased strain on transportation, hotels, local infrastructure and the local environment.

The short duration stays make it difficult for visitors to interact with local people and local cultures. Packaged tours tend to concentrate the economic benefits from tourism activity into the hands of a small number of operators, restricting the flow of economic benefits to local economic benefits to local economies.

The cultural identity of individual communities, and its manifestation as tangible and intangible cultural heritage, is increasingly being seen as a major factor that can enable them to withstand and respond to the power of globalised market forces. Cultural identity enhances the capacity of human beings, whether individually or in groups, to recognize and manage their environment. Culture positively enables individuals to establish, maintain and extend their social relations (social capital) just as much as their ability to manage their economic and physical environment.

Capitalizing on their cultural distinctiveness presents individual communities throughout the world with a significant opportunity to reduce poverty and provide a sustainable future by drawing down some of the direct economic benefits from tourism expenditure. A key part of this process is the presentation and interpretation of their cultural heritage.

Current tourism promotion for India is based around the 'Incredible India theme. This promotes a number of key aspects of India's tourism attractions:

- The spectacular historic monuments including the Taj Mahal, historic forts and towns and a number of major world heritage sites.
- Lifestyle tourism based around spas and yoga, often including luxury hotels and resorts.
- The colours of India, from the wonderful textiles of Rajasthan to the exotic face masks of Kerala.

This promotional campaign seeks to condense tourism in India into a single image of exotic colour and lifestyle. There is little emphasis on the broader history, cultural heritage, living culture and enormous diversity of India. This is a weakness in that it seems to be targeted at a limited audience and offers only a limited range of experiences.

Medical Tourism

Asia has become a prominent destination for global medical

tourists. Within it, India has a relative advantage, as is evident from the institutions involved and the services offered.

Current Status of Medical Tourism

Quality care, relatively cheaper services compared to the west, package deals and cheap services from the tourism and hospitality sectors and the options offered by holistic medicine are MT's biggest attractions in India. The price differentials of various procedures for Singapore and India with the west reveal the economic advantage offered to interested patients by Asia. This is the most important factor in promoting MT even though along with the best medical treatment, a patient also has a chance to discover India through assured travel facilities for tourism and pilgrimage.

India's comparatively better tertiary health care-services draw clients from neighbouring countries like Bangladesh, Nepal, Pakistan and Sri Lanka that lack such facilities. Earlier too, patients from these neighboring countries were coming to tertiary teaching hospitals like the All India Institute of Medical Sciences (AIIMS) and were treated according to their economic status. Patients from Pakistan, especially children with heart afflictions, have been regularly coming to Hyderabad and Bangalore corporate hospitals. Today, even government's teaching hospitals are being encouraged to promote MT by strengthening their private facilities. Given the extremely low levels of public investment, this could only be at the cost of facilities for the poor—local or regional. Private hospitals are advertising their services on the web and the Ministry of Tourism has put up its own list of mostly private and one or two public hospitals as destinations for medical tourists in the major cities of India. These hospitals are destination for patients from neighboring countries as well as from the Gulf countries, and a few non-resident Indians (NRIs) from the US (Dogra 2003).

These hi-tech hospitals attract patients from the Middle-East as well as the West by offering them "First World Quality at Third World Rates". Patients flow from neighboring and South-

East Asian countries has increased nearly 12 percent at hospitals in Chennai, Mumbai, Hyderabad and New Delhi. Apollo has been a forerunner in health tourism for patients from south-east Asia, Africa, and the middle-east. It has set up a chain of hospitals in Delhi and Ahmedabad with the intention of attracting NRIs from the world over. A combination spa and hospital in Goa, with a focus on non elective surgeries, has boosted the medical tourism in that state.

In the wake of this newfound potential for MT, most of the private tertiary hospitals are investing heavily to give a facelift to their facilities, to make them visible to not just the local elite but also to overseas clients.

Corporate hospitals in metropolitan and smaller cities like Pune, Goa and Ahmedabad have brought in five-star facilities and hi-tech medicine. Both the state administration and the corporate sector see the benefits of synergy for profits and have hence evolved separate as well as combined promotional strategies.

The state is proposing MT in its own institutions. It invests directly in infrastructure and tourism to push its policy support to the corporate sector in earning foreign exchange by treating MT as a trade. This encourages all the players directly or indirectly involved in MT to invest and expand their businesses corporate hospitals; the aviation industry, private tour services, travel operators, the hotel and hospitality industries.

The tourism debate in this country is not about tourism alone, it is far deeper than is made out to be. It is not about night bazaars and monuments hosting soirees. Nor is it about pretty pictures and advertisements in international and national media vehicles, and certainly not about global summits. It is essentially about the attitude we as a nation have, first to brand building and, within that, to specific targeting. It is here that we are often found wanting. It is a sobering thought that India today attracts fewer tourists than Singapore, a city-state. Equally worrying is the lack of comprehensive infrastructure to support flexible price point tourism. While we need to be justifiably proud of chains like The Oberoi, The Taj and ITC Hotels, the spread needs to be more even which it is not.

The linkages in terms of connectivity are equally miserable as are our access points, be they rail terminals or airports.

The reasons for this malaise are many but the manner in which they have so far been addressed remains insular. Tourism as an industry cannot be built by a single ministry, nor for that matter by one government. It must emanate from the recognition of the potential that the tourism industry provides for employment on the one hand and national showcasing on the other. We have instead viewed tourism from a silo-perspective with the result that we have not progressed as much as we should have.

5

Strategic Use of Information Technologies in the Tourism Industry

Lakhvir Suneja

Information Technologies (ITs) as a Business Tool

Developments in ITs revolutionize both economies and enterprises. ITs are defined as the "collective term given to the most recent developments in the mode (electronic) and the mechanisms computers and communication technologies) used for the acquisition, processing analysis, storage, retrieval, dissemination and application of information. At the macroeconomic level, ITs become instrumental in the development and prosperity of regions, as they determine their competitiveness in the global marketplace. At the micro-economic level, ITs prevail all functions of strategic and operational management and impel the competitiveness of enterprises.

The enhancements in ITs' processing power in the last decade revolutionize their capabilities as they constantly increase computing speed; decrease equipment size; reduce hardware and software costs; and improve the reliability, compatibility and inter-connectivity of numerous terminals and applications. A great degree of innovation is incorporated in hardware, software and network developments, whilst intellect becomes a critical asset in ITs' management. Paradoxically, the more powerful and complicated ITs become, the more user-friendly and inexpensive they are, enabling more people and organisations to take advantage. Hence, Hopper proposes that "in the not-so-distant future, computers will be as familiar part of the business environment as telephones are today. They will also be as simple to use as telephones or at least nearly so". The emergent information society and the knowledge-based economic powers will therefore redefine the ability of regions and enterprises to prosper in the new millennium. Inevitably the tourism industry is also affected by the technological revolution. Both tourism destinations and enterprises increasingly need to adopt innovative methods and to enhance their competitiveness. On the demand side, the new, sophisticated, knowledgeable and demanding consumer increasingly becomes familiar with the emergent ITs and requires flexible, specialized, accessible, interactive products and communication with principals. Hence, new best management practices emerge, taking advantage of the ITs revolution and re-engineering the entire business processes of the industry. This paper aims to analyze some of the most critical IT developments and to demonstrate how they influence the tourism industry. It blends the theoretical background of its with the strategic functions of the industry and proposes a multi-dimensional framework for the incorporation of ITs in tourism. Information Technologies as a major contributor to competitiveness and competitive advantage. The fusion of ITs provides unprecedented tools, which facilitate the creation of new industries, restructure existing industries and radically change the way firms and regions compete. ITs reshape the nature of competition in most economic activities, whilst they link consumers and suppliers, adding value to organizations products. Hence, ITs change the competitive game for almost all organizations, regardless the industry they operate in, their location or size. In particular, technology affects competitive advantage as it determines the relative cost position or differentiation of organizations. A firm can achieve several strategic benefits by using ITs, namely establishing entry barriers; affecting switching costs; differentiating products/services; limiting access to distribution channels; ensuring competitive pricing; decreasing supply costs and easing supply; increasing cost efficiency; using information as a product itself; and building closer relationships with suppliers and customers. Using ITs, as bargaining power is gradually relocated from institutional buyers and wholesalers to suppliers, due to the more effective and interactive communication they can achieve with their target markets. Small size in combination with innovation and effective networking by using ITs also enables them to develop "virtual size" and empowers their competitiveness. Smaller firms can therefore develop and deliver the right product, to the right customer, at the right price and place, without over-depending on intermediaries. This would enable small firms to enhance their position and increase their profit margin.

Hence, ITs offer new management and business opportunities and can be applied strategically in at least four different ways: gain a competitive advantage; improve productivity and performance; facilitate new ways of managing and organizing; and develop new businesses. Ultimately, firms investing in ITs attempt to gain a competitive advantage by lowering their cost or by improving customers' perception about the quality of their products and services, and hence differentiating their offering. Prerequisites for Achieving Competitive Advantages Through Information Technologies. Despite the potential benefits, ITs do not guarantee profitability and they may even worsen the competitive position of firms and the attractiveness of an industry. There is also a debate on whether ITs-originated competitive advantage can be sustained, as investments in technology are often matched by competitors. Strassmann suggests that there is no significant correlation between spending on ITs and profitability. There is also criticism that ITs often fail to add value in an organization's operation, whilst the costs associated (capital, training, staff) sometimes exceed the benefits generated. This is often attributed to the lack of long term ITs vision, which deters enterprises from capitalizing on opportunities and gaining benefits. ITs are not a panacea and in fact incorporate several risks as well as considerable costs. Organizations should therefore realize that ITs contribute to both sides of the general business equation, since they add to both revenue and cost streams. However, ignoring and under-utilizing ITs could be disastrous as it would create strategic vulnerability and competitive dis-advantage. Thus, no action is not an option. ITs can be fruitful, only if certain prerequisites are satisfied, namely: long term planning and strategy; innovative business processes re-engineering; top management commitment; and training throughout the hierarchy. Using ITs as a stand-alone initiative is inappropriate. Their usage has to be coupled with the re-engineering of all business processes as well as with a redesign of organizational structures and control systems. Perhaps the greatest challenge is to identify and train managers who will be effective and innovative users of ITs and would lead technology-based decision making towards quantifiable gains and advantages. Intellect, therefore, becomes one of the major assets of organizations, while continuous education and training are the only methods to develop and maintain this asset. Provided that rational and innovative planning and management is exercised constantly and consistently, ITs can support the success of organizations.

Tourism and Information Technologies

Tourism is inevitably influenced by the business process re-engineering experienced due to the technological revolution. As information is the life-blood of the travel industry, effective use of ITs is pivotal. Hence, "a whole system of ITs is being rapidly diffused throughout the tourism industry and no player will escape its impacts". Unlike durable goods, intangible tourism services cannot be physically displayed or inspected at the point of sale before purchasing. They are bought before the time of their use and away from the place of consumption. Hence they depend exclusively upon representations and descriptions, provided by the travel trade, (e.g. information in brochures), for their ability to attract consumers. Timely and accurate information, relevant to consumers' needs, is often the key to satisfaction of tourist demand. Therefore, ITs provide the information backbone that facilitates tourism. The revolution of ITs has profound implications for the management of the tourism industry, mainly by enabling efficient co-operation within the industry and by offering tools for globalization. In few other economic activities are the generation, gathering, processing, application and communication of information as important for day-to-day operations. The rapid development of both supply and demand makes ITs an imperative partner and thus they increasingly play a more critical role in tourism marketing, distribution, promotion and co-ordination. The re-engineering of these processes generates a paradigm-shift altering the structure of the entire industry. Thus, ITs have a dramatic impact on the travel industry, because they force the sector to rethink the way in which it organizes its business, its values or norms of behavior and the way in which it educates its workforce.

Information Technologies and Tourism Demand

WTO argues that "the key to success lies in the quick identification of consumer needs and in reaching potential clients with comprehensive, personalized and up-to-date information". The rapid growth of both the volume and the quality requirements of contemporary travelers, require powerful ITs for the administration of the expanding traffic. Tourists become sophisticated and more demanding, requesting high quality products and value for their money. Thus, destinations and principals need new methods to serve the new types of demand. The usage of ITs in the industry is driven by both the development of the size and complexity of tourism demand, as well as by the rapid expansion and sophistication of new tourism products, which address mini-market segments. Increasingly, new, experienced, sophisticated, demanding travelers seek information about more exotic destinations and authentic experiences, as well as require to interact with suppliers in order to satisfy their specific needs and wishes. The contemporary/ connected consumer "is far less willing to wait or put up with delays, to the point where patience is a disappearing virtue."

In order to satisfy tourism demand and survive in the long term there is no choice but to incorporate technology and enhance the interactivity with the marketplace. Increasingly, ITs enable travelers to access reliable and accurate information as well as to undertake reservations in a fraction of time, cost and inconvenience required by conventional methods. ITs improve the service quality and contribute to higher guest/traveler satisfaction. Customer satisfaction depends highly on the accuracy and comprehensiveness of specific information on destinations' accessibility, facilities, attractions and activities. This is because the gap between consumers' expectations and perceived experiences is smaller and thus, unpleasant surprises from the destination or principals are minimized. In addition, several other ITs facilitated factors enhance consumer satisfaction, namely, consumers have more information and enjoy a greater choice; a reduction of the bureaucracy and paper-work effectively frees time for customer service; customizing the product and establishing "one-to-one" marketing by using intelligence collected by loyalty schemes (e.g. dietary require-ments, product preferences); providing new services, (e.g. as in-flight or in-room entertainment and information channels); facilitating operational tasks (e.g. in-room TV checkout); personalized services (e.g. telephone operator acknowledges guest by his name); and finally better integration of departments and functions of organizations towards better service.

Computer Reservation Systems (CRSs) and increasingly Internet providers satisfy the needs of consumer for convenient access to transparent and easy to compare information. They cover the entire variety of choices of travel, lodging and leisure services, destinations, holiday packages, as well as display the actual prices and availability of such services. These services also provide immediate confirmation and speedy documentation of reservations, allowing a greater degree of flexibility and enabling prospective travelers to book at the "last minute". Experienced travelers are therefore empowered by information and booking systems and increase their personal efficiency by creating tailor-made products independently. ITs also assist principals to understand consumer needs through marketing research and loyalty/partnership schemes. Improved access to information covering all aspects of tourist activities provides the framework for offering personalized services at price levels comparable to those of standard packages.

The revolutionary developments in ITs, which have been experienced through the proliferation of the Internet and the World Wide Web since 1995, illustrate that consumers increasingly rely on the Internet for travel information. They utilize commercial and non-commercial Internet sites for planning, searching, purchasing and amending their travel. Non-tourism organizations tend to seize the emergent opportunity by utilizing the ITs tools. This is already the case with major ITs providers, (e.g., Microsoft developed Expedia, an electronic travel agency) to satisfy tourism demand.

The Re-Engineering of Tourism Production and Distribution

The impacts of ITs are evident in the tourism production, marketing, distribution and operational functions of both the private and public sectors. ITs can also boost staff morale, managerial effectiveness, productivity and ultimately profitability of tourism organizations, provided that managerial attitude is adapted to the new business environment and takes advantage of the emergent opportunities. In particular, ITs have pivotal implications for the distribution channel, as they introduce unprecedented and innovative methods. Distribution is one of the few elements of the marketing mix, which can still enable tourism enterprises to improve their competitiveness and performance. Distributing the right marketing mix, to the right segments, through the right intermediaries, will be instrumental for the long-term success of principals. ITs not only facilitate distribution, but they also enable differentiation and/or cost advantage, as well as empower interactive communication between principals and target markets. This is accomplished by reengineering the entire processes of producing and delivering products, in order to optimize efficiency and productivity, and to maximize the value-added provided to consumers.

The evolution of ITs demonstrated that destinations and principals will be unable to compete effectively, unless they were able to promote themselves in the emergent electronic distribution channels. ITs transformed distribution to an electronic marketplace, where access to information and ubiquity is achieved, while interactivity between principals and consumers is empowered. Three main waves of technological developments established ITs in tourism enterprises, namely Computer Reservations Systems (CRSs) in the 1970s; Global Distribution Systems (GDSs) in the 1980s and the Internet in the 1990s. Although these technologies emerged with gaps of about 10 years from each other, they currently operate both separately and jointly, controlling different functions and target markets.

Computer Reservation Systems (CRSs)

Computerized networks and electronic distribution in tourism emerged in the early 1970s, through internal CRSs. They became central to the distribution mix and strategy of airlines. CRSs are widely regarded as the critical initiators of the electronic age, as they formulated a new travel marketing and distribution system. A CRS is essentially a database which manages the inventory of a tourism enterprise, whilst it distributes it electronically to remote sales offices and external partners. Intermediaries and consumers can access the inventory and they can make and confirm reservations. The rapid growth of both demand and supply, as well as the deregulation of the American air transportation demonstrated that the tourism inventory could only be managed by powerful computerized systems. Airlines pioneered this technology, although hotel chains and tour operators followed by developing CRSs enable principals to control, promote and sell their products globally, while facilitating their yield management. In addition, they integrate the entire range of business functions, and thus can contribute to principals' profitability and long term prosperity. CRSs often charge competitive commission rates in comparison with other distribution options, whilst enabling flexible pricing and capacity alterations in order to adjust supply to demand fluctuations. CRSs also reduce communication costs, while providing intelligence information on demand patterns or the position of partners and competitors. Hence, CRSs contribute enormously to both the operational and strategic management of the industry.

Global Distribution Systems (GDSs)

Since the mid-1980s, airline CRSs have emerged into Global Distribution Systems (GDSs), by gradually expanding their geographical coverage, as well as by integrating both horizontally (with other airline systems) and vertically (by incorporating the entire range of tourism products and services, such as accommodation, car rentals, train and ferry ticketing, entertainment and other provisions). To avoid unnecessary over-lapping principals integrated their CRSs with GDSs, by developing interfaces. Several "switch" companies, such as THISCO and WIZCOM, emerged to facilitate interconnectivity. This enabled the display and purchasing of the majority of tourism products on-line. As GDSs connect most tourism organizations with intermediaries around the world, they lead the standardization processes and control a considerable market share.

GDSs emerged as the "circulation system" or the "backbone" of the industry by establishing a global communication standard and a new tourism electronic distribution channel. Evidently GDSs became businesses in their own right, as they changed their nature from tools for vendor airlines and accommodation corporations, to "electronic travel supermarkets" and strategic business units for their corporations. However, fierce competition forced a number of mergers and acquisitions in the GDS industry. It is predicted that only two or three of the major ten GDSs will survive and therefore, further concentration and integration is anticipated. Currently four systems, namely Galileo, Amadeus, Sabre and Worldspan, dominate the global market. Since GDSs are connected with most major principals, they offer similar services. In June 1996, for example, Amadeus displayed availability for 432 airlines, 29,000 hotels and 55 car rental companies through 162,329 terminals in 106,394 travel agencies around the world. However, each GDS has a stronger market share at the region where its parent airlines operate, as traditional links with travel agencies have been utilized for the penetration of GDSs.

GDSs increasingly offer both leisure and business products, by providing information and allowing reservations for theatre tickets, holiday packages and tourism destinations. Eventually core GDSs are expected to be based on a network of smaller, regional and specialized computerized systems for their leisure products. The development of Destination Management Systems will enable small and medium sized tourism enterprises to be represented. Diverting into the leisure market responds to demand trends, while enabling GDSs to diversify their portfolio in order to take advantage of their technological infrastructure and network as well as economies of scale. This will assist them to deliver diversified services to broader markets and therefore suffer less from their business market saturation. GDSs' efficiency and reliability enable principals to distribute and manage their reservations globally, by bridging consumer needs with the tourism supply. Hence, great synergies are achieved, where globalization drivers stimulate GDS developments and vice versa. Go48 identifies four major sets of conditions, namely, cost, market, government and competitive drivers and demonstrates why the globalization of the tourism industry is closely interrelated with its ability to use computerized systems. Ultimately GDSs should aim to increase the satisfaction of their stakeholders, (i.e. consumers, principals, travel agencies and shareholders), offer superior products.

6

Tourism for Peace and Stability: A Case Study of Kashmir Valley (India)

Mondira Dutta

Introduction

Tourism is often considered as a suitable engine for economic development, especially for relatively backward regions. It is perhaps the only activity which successfully utilises those regional resources which otherwise remain unused. Many regional attributes for example, rugged topography, relative isolation and cultural conservatism which act as disincentives to other activities can be all turned into assets by the tourist industry. Tourism has been sought after worldwide, as the most efficient tool for ushering in economic development into a region.[1] In fact it is an important instrument in triggering off a series of interrelated induced effects. Tourism which has fewer disadvantages of industrial pollution or the introduction of intrusive element into the landscape is a more acceptable means for ushering in economic development than most alternatives. It contains a pleasing element of self-advertisement and encourages contacts outside the region that benefit development generally. Undoubtedly, tourism is an important tertiary activity helping many a country to improve their balance of payments, generating income and expanding employment opportunities.

These opportunities may be direct, indirect or induced. It also generates entrepreneurial activity and brings about a better distribution of population. The outward migration from the rural area to the conurbation decreases and inward migration to the rural areas increases. Most of the underdeveloped regions, best suited to national and international tourism are peripheral, situated in the rural hinterland, mountainous tracts or along the sea coast where natural beauty are in abundance. These areas are in need of new employment opportunities. Such opportunities can be initiated out of tourist activities. This dispersion of development to the under developed parts is perhaps the greatest benefit brought about by tourism. The increasing social contacts between the tourists and the local people lead to a cultural interaction and their quick diffusion in the areas of relative isolation. Tourism, perhaps, is the only economic activity whose raw materials or 'tourist attractions' can be substantially upgraded at low cost and these are essentially inexhaustible. Despite the several advantages of tourism, it is a pity that the theory of regional economic policy has neglected tourism as a strategic element of regional development. In fact, it can be argued that in promoting the regional economic growth, tourism encourages a diffusion of economic benefits, through a wide area, whereas manufacturing industry encourages concentration. The tourist industry is an excellent example of the export base theory in regional development. A basic industry which reduces imports and/or contributes to exports.

Throughout the history of tourism literature, a common factor that frequently emerges ascribes tourism, as a potential for promoting international understanding and world peace.[2] It is believed to be a world movement that fosters peace and promotes understanding between people of various countries thereby, reducing the tensions between unfriendly nations. However, the recent years have witnessed a phenomenal rise in the spurt of terrorist activities, creating a substantial impact on the tourist industry all over the world. The tourist industry is extremely sensitive and highly susceptible to political upheavals, instability, and risks to personal safety. Although the number of deaths from acts of terrorism is far more insignificant in comparison to the number arising from car accidents or heart attacks; nevertheless, the impact of terrorism on the tourist industry in general has been quite drastic and hard felt all over the world. The main problem is that there is a need for the tourism industry and those policy makers who have invested in tourism to acknowledge the unique vulnerability of the industry both to actual terroristic activity and general perceived insecurity. This fact was very well attested when the high jacking of Air India flight and the Kargil war in the not too distant past resulted in mass scale cancellation of tickets not only to Nepal and Kashmir but even to Delhi and other parts of the country making the impact deep and strong. The unrest situation within the state, the constant reporting of violence by the media and the existing strategy, which lacks proper planning and inter-sectoral coordination, only adds to destabilizing any tourism development plan which may be in progress. Such an impact is hard felt effecting people from all walks of life. Significant contributions of propaganda does come from the mass media but another massive contribution is from the political leaders who allot a high priority to anti-terrorism programmes often disproportionate to the terrorism's effects, thereby magnifying the importance of the events manifold. Diffusing a situation with the help of military forces at times may actually make the situation worse. Such situations usually portray a desperate picture. Thus an over-reaction could increase the impact and importance of terrorist events. A few terrorists can actually make a decisive and crippling impact on travel patterns and the economies of particular destinations in the world. Whether it is a networking of terrorism, a political conflict, violence, criminal activities or war, the tourism industry is quick to react, often leaving the economy completely shattered. It is therefore natural, that most tourists will after all not be prepared to spend their hard earned money in order to go to a destination where the safety of their limbs and life may be in jeopardy. The tourists will simply not think twice to immediately change for an alternative safer destination.

A review of selected tourism literature and statistics in relation to terrorism does show an alarming picture and depicts a pessimist viewpoint as far as the future of tourism is concerned. In fact violence of any kind leaves a long lasting impact on the tourist industry of that region. In the late 1980s, Fiji faced a similar situation because of military coups and political instability. Egypt was estimated to have lost more than US$ 1 billion in tourism revenues in 1992-93, as a result of terrorist attacks. In 1994 an increase in the crime rates in Florida had sent its total inflow of foreign tourists to an all-time low. Its share declined from 23 percent to 20 percent within the first seven months of 1994. A similar trend was also witnessed in countries like Brazil, Papua, New Guinea, South Africa and others. The terrorist attack of November 1997 had claimed as much as 58 lives.[3] The hijacking incidents and attacks on the Rome and Vienna Airports had also caused serious reductions in the number of American tourists visiting Europe and the Middle East (60 percent decline). Even wars between nations have also left long-term scars damaging and sometimes totally destroying the tourism-based economy. Moreover, the spread of destruction is not only restricted to the boundary of administrative confines of the countries' involved. Such effects have been devastating to other tourism destinations. The impact of the Gulf War and the prolonged war in the former Yugoslavia suffered serious declines in the trends of tourist arrivals in the entire region.

The tourist industry is often accompanied by negative impacts if its growth is not properly channelled. Instead of transforming a region, it can cause immense social, environmental as well economic consequences which are of serious concerns. It has been found that tourism development has often been accompanied by the twin economic evils of displacing local communities from traditional dwelling and working areas as well as depriving them of jobs and employment opportunities.[4] The tourist industry usually encounters three stages of tourism growth, if not monitored and coordinated by proper planning and involvement of the community.[5] The first stage refers to 'Euphoria', where the host welcomes the tourists and ready money flows in. The second stage is referred to as 'antagonism' where the local population is sometimes subjected to inflationary tendencies and decreasing access to commodities and goods, which get diverted to meet the tourist needs.[6] The employment provided to them are usually under-paid, servile and often exploitative. The forthcoming of such a stage can be delayed with proper planning. Without proper comprehensive tourism development plans the degradation and underplay of local culture and tradition is under constant threat, in favour of an imported consumer culture. The encouragement of 'five star tourism' controlled by outside forces deprives the local people of prospective job opportunities and training of technical skills and know-how. Certain tourist spots within the region gets undue promotion, ignoring the 'carrying capacity', which seriously affects the ability of the area and its people to absorb the increasing number of tourists, both in economic and social terms. With the onset of time, all these factors contribute to the creation of the most unwanted third stage referred to as 'Hostility'. The host turns hostile towards its guest where tourists may be a target by the local community. Proper planning can ensure that such a stage never arrives.

In India, tourism was recognised as an industry only in 1986, but it has been one of the fastest growing sectors, turning over an earning of US$2300 million in 1998.[7] The country received more than 2.36 million foreign tourists, which forms about 3.5 percent of the total tourist inflow to India, with the remaining majority being domestic tourists. The percentage share of foreign tourists in the world hardly forms a meagre 0.38 percent. In terms of receipts, India receives hardly 0.62 percent of world tourist receipts.

India, like many other countries has been no exception in terrorist attacks. Terrorism in India is a phenomenon for the last three decades. The entire north India was rocked under the grip of terrorism by the Punjab terrorist in the 1980s. The terrorist activities culminated in large-scale destruction leading to disruption of buses and trains, a series of bomb blasts, hijacking and massive killings of a particular community. The 1980s were a witness to several cancellations of trains, discontinuing the plying of night buses through Punjab ultimately leading to a mass exodus of Hindu population from the state. Terrorism reached its peak in 1984, when the then Prime Minister of India, Mrs. Indira Gandhi was assassinated by her own Sikh guards within the premises of her residence. Within a span of seven years, history was repeating itself. In 1991, suicide bombers killed Mr. Rajiv Gandhi the ex-Prime Minister. Such instances no doubt, go to prove the level of terrorism existing at a particular time in the society, but these cannot be accepted as terrorism targeting the tourists. Nevertheless, the impact on the tourist industry was a serious one. The figures of the tourist arrivals to India during that period shows a decline in the growth rate of tourist inflows that drooped to a minus 8.5 in 1984-85 from 1.3 in 1983-84. The industry limped back to normalcy but only after a considerable time had run out.

Backdrop of the Study Area

The state of Jammu and Kashmir in the Himalayas has always been famous for its natural beauty holding three distinct regions within it, namely, Kashmir, Jammu and Laddakh regions. The valley of Kashmir is known as paradise on earth, with its scenic charm, the plains of Jammu with its famous shrines like the Vaishno Devi and the mountainous landscape of Laddakh with its fascinating history has always attracted travellers from far and wide. The state does not contain a single industry, which could provide a vibrant economic base for the state, as it has a highly fragile ecological set up. Inadequate capital investment in creating tourism infrastructure and limited private sector participation are other significant factors responsible in creating hurdles for a 'take off' of the tourism development process.

The spindle shaped valley with its semi-closed eco-system, is famous for its enormous endowment of tourist potentials. However the recent spurt of terrorism has eroded the tourist industry drastically. This however does not mean that the tourist industry be shut down or operated only with the help of gun trotting soldiers. It is important to recognize the various types of tourists that visit destinations and cater to their demands accordingly. The tourists who are regular visitors to the valley for business purpose, official delegates and the pilgrims are some of the most potential tourists. The famous pilgrimage to Amarnath cave in the Kashmir Himalayas continues despite terrorists' threats. Records show that even when the valley did not receive a single tourist, Amarnath cave had an inflow of 5,000 pilgrims.[9] In 1998, more than 1.5 lakhs of pilgrims visited Amarnath despite the militants' ban on the 'yatra'. Similarly the Vaishno Devi temple in the Jammu region attracts several lakhs of devotees throughout the year. The unique landscape of Laddakh has constantly been a famous haunt for the foreign tourists; most of these being 'repeat' tourists. Thus the situational differences prevailing at a tourist destination necessitates to widen the scope and cater to the demand accordingly for a variety of tourists visiting the region.

There is a tremendous scope to manage local tourist sites within Jammu division with proper infrastructure facilities like accommodation, recreation, marketing, ticketing facilities and adventure tourism etc. Currently millions of Pilgrims visit Vaishno Devi shrine and usually spent a couple of nights in Jammu division. These tourists need to be encouraged to spend a few more days for visiting other scenic spots, scattered all over the Pirpanjal ranges. This will boost the economy of the region and will help in creating employment avenues for the local population. This will be possible only through proper management of the tourism sector in collaboration with the private sector. The plateau of Laddakh also has enormous potential for developing the international tourism because of its rich cultural heritage and the majestic landscape along with scenic grandeur.

Despite its semi-closed eco-system, the valley has been a popular destination for travellers from far and wide. The origin of Kashmir itself is wrapped up in mysterious legends, which defy the scientifically discovered facts of Geologists. Kashmir attracted its visitors as early as the 15th and 16th century. The first Europeans to visit Kashmir were the Portuguese and Italian who accompanied Emperor Akbar in 1597. Most of the Englishmen visited during that period. Several works on Kashmir written by scholars during that period exists. Kashmir thus became a favourite destination of the Mughal rulers and their personnel. Even during the colonial period there was a steady growth of European visitors to the valley. Unfortunately, Kashmir today is not looked upon as merely a beautiful valley enclosed by awe inspiring and peace bestowing mountains. The picture of Kashmir thrown up by newspapers is not of snowy mountain peaks anymore but as a terrorist torn state.

It was much after independence that the tourist industry got its proper shape and content as an independent sector in Kashmir. In the pre-terrorism period during the 1970s and early 1980s, the valley attracted a considerable number of visitors (about 50,000 to 1,100,000). Most of these belonged to the middle-income group and their average duration of stay varied from 5 to 8 days (Dutta, M 1990). However even these tourists formed hardly 5 percent of the total foreign tourists visiting India according to 1980-87 statistics. Nevertheless, according to a study conducted during that period, it was estimated that Jammu & Kashmir earned almost 1/3rd of its total income[10] from the tourism sector alone (TECS, 1982). It is more than a decade now since terrorism started in the valley creating distortions of all kinds, like hijacking, destruction of transportation systems, uprooting bridges through bomb blasts and rocket launching, disrupting the normal life of a common man. These have had a tremendous impact on the tourist inflows, which is steadily dwindling away to alternative destinations.

The virus of "Terrorism" hit the valley towards the second half of 1989, whereby thousands of terrorists owing unflinching loyalty to multiform fundamental religious organizations poured into the tranquil hills and mountains of Kashmir. The peace and tranquil atmosphere in the valley got quickly converted into a terror-torn state 'where even the angels feared to tread'. The tourists are an easy prey, unsuspecting, usually unarmed and disoriented targets who are trying to acclimatize with the alien environment. Terrorists usually get attracted to tourists and the tourism infrastructure because these provide easy and soft targets, which enable them to meet their goals. A typical example of this is the tourist industry of Jammu and Kashmir. It is on record that there had not been a single domestic tourist who visited the valley in the year 1990 bringing the tourist industry to almost a standstill.[11] During the time of normalcy in late 1980s, the valley attracted more than 4 to 5 lakhs of tourists per year.

Early Period of Terrorism in the Valley

Taking recourse through religious fundamentalism the state has been torn apart in order to open up to all kinds of terrorist violence. In addition, the growth of several terrorist groups having divergent objectives has left the movement with no clear-cut goals. Some of them aim for the revival of classic Islamic rules of societal behaviour. These are aimed in order to combat the ills of so called distorted modern ways of life, which they consider as a deviation from Islam. The beauty parlours for women, the cinema halls, the video parlours and wine shops were all ordered to close down by particular militant groups in the 1990s. Several others insisted that the women wear a veil or the 'burkha'. A second group of militants spoke of autonomy, freedom and independence. Yet, there is a third who professes their loyalty to Pakistan. The goals of these various terrorist groups contradict each other, sometimes leading to inter-group rivalry, which simply makes living of a common man impossible! Initially terrorism in Kashmir did enjoy the support of the local population, who sympathised with their cause and were manoeuvred and willing to sacrifice anything in the name of

'Jehad' or the holy war. This was the time when terrorism had been at its peak (1990-91). The killings began by targeting the military and paramilitary personnel, the Govt. of India officials, media personnel, and people considered to be informers or agents of the Indian Government. This was extended later to rope in people from the ruling political party, the minority community of Kashmiri Pandits and the non-Kashmiris including the labourers from other parts of the country. This was the period when large-scale migration mainly of Kashmiri Hindu population from the valley took place. The killings continued unabated to include prominent personalities and finally the tourists, who were an easy prey. Several of the tourists have been kidnapped and murdered in more than one occasion. Some of them remained missing.

Table 1: Foreign Mercenaries Killed in Jammu & Kashmir (1991-1998)

From	1991	1992	1993	1994	1995	1996	1997	1998	Total
Pakistan/ Pak Occupied Kashmir	2	12	27	39	28	44	55	43	250
Afghan	1	6	62	53	39	48	38	20	267
Sudanese	-	-	2	1	1	2	2	-	8
Others	-	1	6	32	51	100	163	102	455
Total	3	19	97	125	119	194	258	165	980

Source: *Journal of Himalayan and Central Asian Studies.* Vol 2, No 2, April-June 1998.

Table 1 shows almost 1000 foreign mercenaries had been killed during 1991 to 1998. Data reveals that most of the foreign mercenaries belonged to Pakistan/Pak occupied Kashmir, Afghanistan, Sudan and others. The maximum number of foreign mercenaries that were killed during this period was in 1997 totalling to the tune of 258.

Figure 1 clearly shows the no of incidents were maximum in the early 1990s especially in the years 1994/1995. The attacks

Figure 1: Militant Activities in Jammu and Kashmir (Data as on 31.12.1999)

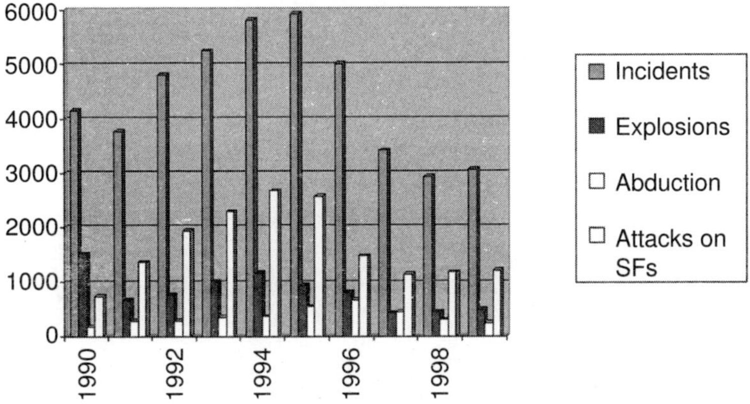

Source: http://mha.nic.in/mil.htm#iov

on security forces were also the maximum then. The magnitude of women and children that were killed in the valley were the highest in the years 1996 and 2002 (Refer Table 2).

Table 2: Jammu & Kashmir
Magnitude of Women and Children Killed by Terrorists

Year	Women	Children	Total Civilians
1991	63	3	382
1996	89	24	1341
2001	116	43	996
2002	139	63	1008
2003	110	32	795
2004	92	32	707

Source: Rajya Sabha Starred Question No. 24, dated 2.03.2005.

Figure 2 depicts the number of lives lost annually. The year 1996 showed the maximum number followed by the year 1995. During this period, several important political leaders, professionals, government officials, and also foreign tourists were kidnapped—most of who were either killed or believed to be dead. These were the years of the Taliban period. There does seem to have some relation with the Taliban period and the increased terrorist activities in the state.

Figure 2: Loss of Life
(Data as on 31.12.1999)

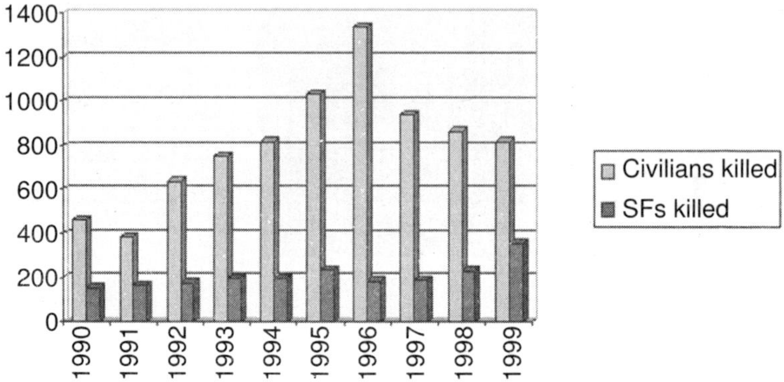

Source: http://mha.nic.in/mil.htm#iov

According to the ministry of Home Affairs, during 1990 to 1999 (April), an estimated 936 Hindus and 46 Sikhs were killed in various incidents of attacks on minorities. Selective targeting of minorities by the militants lead to large-scale migration of these families from Kashmir valley making them refugees in their own country. These people are now settled in various parts of the country. Out of about 50,248 families, 28,561 are in the Jammu region (15 camps), 19,338 are in Delhi (14 camps) and 2,347 are scattered all over the country.

Table 3, given below shows the largest number of civilians that were killed during 1990 to 2006 was 1031 in the year 1995. The same year also recorded a maximum number of violent incidents.

Tourist Flow

The tourist season of Kashmir valley has never managed to reach the peak as before even after considerable time had passed enabling the tourists' memory to fade out the unpleasant

Table 3: Persons Killed in Jammu and Kashmir (1990 to 2006)

	1990	1995	2000	2003	2004	2005	2006*
No of Incidents	4158	5938	3074	3401	2565	1990	1442
Civilians Killed	461	1031	847	795	707	557	340
Security Forces/ Personnel Killed	155	237	397	314	281	189	131
Terrorists Killed	550	1332	1520	1494	976	917	516
Foreign Terrorists Killed	14	85	436	470	289	N.A	N.A

Note: Upto 31.10.2006

Source: Rajya Sabha Unstarred Question No. 1554, dated 7.12.2005; Rajya Sabha Unstarred Question No. 216, dated 26.07.2006; & Rajya Sabha Unstarred Question No. 811, dated 29.11.2006.

incidents. It only goes to show how a distorted perception of risk among the tourists may drastically affect surpassing factors of time and space. Mass scale cancellation of tourist reservation shows the drastic change in destination from Laddakh to alternative tourist destination after the Kargil war.

According to the department of tourism, Government of Jammu & Kashmir, 1990 has had the lowest record of tourist inflow during the last one-decade. The total tourists for the year 1999 which registers a substantial improvement still lags behind at 17130 foreign tourists creating a huge gap as compared to the 1989 figures. The scenario of domestic tourists is no different. The 1999 figure shows a staggering 200162 number of home tourists, hardly 40 percent as compared to the figures of 1989, which shows a total number of 490215 home tourists. The drastic fall in the tourist numbers was no doubt substantial but the impact was much more and was felt far beyond the regional boundaries as the tourist traffic almost came to a standstill in 1990 with zero home tourists. The official figure shows an absolute zero in terms of domestic tourists visiting the valley, while the foreign tourists hardly trickled to a measly number of

4627 as compared to 67762 of 1989. Even these were hesitant to enter the valley. In fact a study of the table (Refer table 4) clearly states the sharp fall in the tourist inflow has been particularly during the years 1984, 1990 and 1994-95 known to be the most eventful years.

Tourism in Kashmir valley is bound to revive provided there is a perception of decreased violence in the state. People's

Table 4: Tourist Flow to Kashmir Valley (1981-2006)

Year	Home Tourist	Foreign Tourists	Total Tourists
1981	598555	43745	642300
1982	560987	42851	603833
1983	398428	41101	439529
1984	192684	36458	229142
1985	465599	38015	503614
1986	536598	53118	589716
1987	664081	57573	721654
1988	662097	59938	722035
1989	490215	67762	557977
1990	Zero	4627	4627
1991	1400	4887	6287
1992	1175	9148	10323
1993	1135	12918	14053
1994	2080	15369	17449
1995	322	8198	8520
1996	375	9592	9967
1997	7027	9111	16138
1998	99636	10247	109883
1999	200162	17130	217292
2000	104337	7575	111912
2001	66732	5859	72591
2002	23370	2511	25881
2003	182205	8959	191164
2004	358095	18234	376329
2005	585708	19608	605382
2006	412879	20009	432888

Source: Annual Report 2003-2004, Ministry of Home Affairs, Govt of India.

memory is short lived and efforts need to be initiated in portraying a peaceful Kashmir. However what would have been a record in Kashmir's history of tourism may now be another 15 years in the coming, provided total peace prevails in the valley for a long duration. The state's highest ever tourist inflow was 7,22,035 in 1988 before militancy peaked, following a steady and direct drop in tourism. Following a rise in the tourist inflow to the valley there was again a sharp fall in June 2010. Cancellations began and in a short span of time, around 80 per cent of all bookings for the period from June to mid-September were cancelled.[12]

Table 5: Tourist Inflow to Valley in Different Phases

Phases	Years	Foreign Tourists	Domestic Tourists
Pre-Terrorism Period	1981	43745	598555
	1984	36458	192684
	1989	67762	490215
Peak-Terrorism Period	1990	4627	Zero
	1995	8198	322
Pre-Kargil War	1999	17130	200162
Post-Kargil War	2000	7575	104337

The entire scenario of the tourist traffic to the valley can be studied in various phases (Table 5). Prior to terrorism the tourist traffic to the valley, had been fairly consistent and regular. Excepting for the year 1984—the year in which Prime minister of India was assassinated, the tourist traffic ranged from 4 to 7 lakhs. The peak terrorism period in 1990 brought the figures crashing down showing an absolute stand still. The number of foreign tourists that year was less than 5000, while not a single home tourist ventured into the valley! The tourist industry was still trying to recover when five foreign tourists were kidnapped from within the valley in 1995. Only one or two of them have now been proclaimed as dead according to official authorities. The rest are still missing. Whenever the terrorist activities occurred the tourist industry was sharp to react instantly. The rise and fall in the number of tourists shows the extent of sensitiveness existing within the industry displaying sharp, sudden and abrupt changes to any terrorism activities. As evident from the table, it takes almost four to five years for the tourist industry to start showing the slightest signs of recovery after a setback. The year 1999 seemed promising with 217292 total tourists and the tourist industry looked ready to take off once again. One has however, got to wait and see what the effects of the Kargil war and the hijacking will be like, which are yet to unfold its claws on the already weak and under nourished tourist industry in the valley. In order to diffuse any negative impact on the tourism sector in the immediate future, authorities and all concerned need to get active. The role of the media could play a significant part in contributing to such a scenario.

A mere comparison of terrorism in the valley vis-à-vis other parts of the world where the picture is even more gruesome will not cut much ice in portraying a rosy scenario back home. Even though the total number of tourists that had been specially targeted and killed in the entire period of terrorism in the valley was hardly a handful, but the force of the factor of risk perception operated actively in obstructing a heavy tourist traffic to the valley. In order to reverse such a perception of the picture a new scenario of no risk or a low risk level needs to be prominently displayed across the world canvas through governmental plans, policies and programmes which shows success in combating terrorism in the valley. Though the total number of tourists killed in the valley due to terrorism over the last decade may not seem so gigantic, but the huge number of civilians and army personnel that were killed certainly goes well above the five-digit figure. This leaves an impact sufficient enough to send the potential tourists scurrying away to alternative destinations. Besides the misconception of risk, the spread of message travelling beyond the regional and national administrative confines make things worse. The Kargil war, would have forced the tourist inflow into the valley to a minimum level had it been the tourist season during that period. This is despite the fact that the two regions are situated way off from each other and differ drastically in terms of spatial characteristics. The immediate impact however will die off considerably given the lapse of time. Such factors however can get easily activated in full swing within a short span of time taking the necessary toll even if a single tourist is killed.

There is a serious need of creating a database for tourism-linked activities. Intensive research studies on the basis of reliable data needs to be encouraged. Such studies need to be continuous and on a regular basis. This will help in building the spatio-temporal linkages, which will assist in the understanding and tackling of the problem within the situational framework at a grass root level. A data bank needs to be created in order to help the tourism-based industry to develop and grow. The present data available with the tourist department has far too many shortcomings and requires more details to be furnished in order to make meaningful study. The tourist characteristic is badly in need of an age and sex structure classification.

In terms of domestic tourists' inflow, J&K still has a long way to go. Unfortunately, Jammu & Kashmir do not figure among the top ten states in terms of domestic tourist inflow according to 2004 data (Refer table 6).

Table 6: Share of Top Ten States (Home Tourist Inflow) in India (2004)

States	Share (%)
Uttar Pradesh	24.4
Andhra Pradesh	24.4
Tamil Nadu	11.5
Karnataka	7.4
Rajasthan	4.4
Maharasthra	3.6
West Bengal	3.4
Uttranchal	3.2
Madhya Pradesh	2.3
Bihar	2.2
Other	13.2
India	**100.0**

Source: Ministry of Tourism, Govt. of India.

Though it receives a substantial number of domestic tourists every year nevertheless it does not figure among the top ten states of India.

Tourism amidst Terrorism

Over the decades Kashmir valley has started getting famous for violence and terrorism rather than its earlier image of the peaceful 'Vitasta'. It is necessary to identify and flush out certain pockets in the valley, which can be declared as safe zones. These could be the areas within the valley where the tourists would be at a lower risk and the governmental machinery will be able to handle the situation with ease. Police officers in disguise need to keep constant vigil and checks on the movement of suspicious people. They need to keep guard and at times accompany every transport system. Gulmarg, the famous meadow is popular for winter skiing and golf. The Dachigam wildlife sanctuary in Srinagar (which has restricted entry) is another such place. The innumerous fishing zones, the several nodes of religious importance and many others could be segregated from areas, which are under constant threat. The vulnerable areas may be restricted from tourist entry temporarily. It is necessary to identify such areas of the Kashmir Valley where tourists are at high risk and vulnerable. They need to be pre-informed not to travel or to travel only with an escort in these areas. Helicopters could be introduced for short distance travel within the valley.

The role of the media is extremely important in reaching home the right kind of messages. While giving publicity to a terrorist act, it is essential to give equal importance to the other side of the picture. People, who have had a pleasant stay during that period, need to be interviewed about their experiences, and these may be amply publicized. The state machinery of publicity needs to spring into action in addition to the media. This leads to a balance being struck between the positive and negative impacts so that the view is not of a distorted one. They are like both sides of the same coin, which cannot see each other. A correct viewpoint will be possible only after portraying both the aspects in detail. Therefore the media can play a dominant role in creating either the right picture or a distorted one. In order to counter a distorted image, vigorous and professionally guided promotions need to be developed. These should be such that, it can provide wide exposure sufficient to capture the international media's attention, thus demanding not only creative thinking but also innovative action. Good contacts need to be maintained with the international media for ensuring a balanced report. Detailed briefing to international tour operators, travel agents and the press is absolutely essential.

Besides the above, a certain period of the year could be declared as a festival period. Such practices do exist in Ladakh as well as for Jammu regions. But not in the Valley of Kashmir except for the sport activities of winter skiing in Gulmarg and the Amarnath pilgrimage. Special folkloric shows, trade shows and friendship weeks could be held in many tourist-generating countries of Europe and America. Declaring a particularly significant year as the 'Year of Kashmir Tourism' could be held through convening and organizing a major world tourism conference for peace. Holding of monthly speeches by dignitaries, politicians, movie stars, university professors and famous businessmen on the security and safety in Kashmir Valley could help. Probably, the 27th of September—the world tourism day, could be celebrated as an annual celebration date in the Valley through special shows, food festivals, free sightseeing tours, shopping open for 24 hours, etc. The involvement of the mass is a must and therefore awareness needs to be created especially among the people engaged in tourism activities like handicrafts, hotelliering, shikara and houseboat owners, transport services, porters and others. Right from the planning stage till the implementation, the local populations' participation will go a long way in giving the industry the necessary thrust and the right push.

A proper scientific market based plan at a regional level needs to be developed in collaboration with the national level. From a financial viewpoint, it is always considered to be safe to have a tourist destination budget as 1 to 3 percent of the tourist receipts. It is yet to be seen how far this has been implemented in the case of Kashmir Valley or even the state as a whole. Not forgetting that the image of the tourist industry in the valley is a tattered one at the moment. The total budget for the publicity sector needs to be distributed in such a manner so that 20 percent of the total budget will be set aside for advertising campaigns through general and specialised press in chosen markets. The televised ads in these chosen markets should include another 60 percent. The conventional promotional efforts and trade shows should account for about 8 percent each and the road shows could claim the balancing amount. Implementation of policies will remain incomplete without a proper feedback. There is a need to monitor and evaluate the implementation of such policies. A permanent committee composed of representatives from the ministry of tourism and other government agencies need to be entrusted with this job. This committee could meet on a regular basis and be responsible to review and amend the promotion plan if necessary.

Tourism by itself hardly has any influence on the management of terrorism. However, peoples' memory is usually short-lived. With conscious ongoing efforts for ushering in normalcy into a terrorist torn region, the harsh reality of terroristic activities do tend to fade away over time, regenerating the tourist activities. Effective planning and management, responsible environmental policies, well guided integration within the national economic and social development, the raising of popular awareness about the benefits of tourism and cautious integration of guests and hosts, uprooting the corruption within the society will all actively contribute to achieve sustainable economic and social benefits to the destination through tourism and emphasize its importance to the country and the economy.

Despite the negative impact of terrorism resulting in a decline of tourist traffic, there seems to be a ray of hope coming from the influx of pilgrims. The famous pilgrimage to Amarnath cave in the Kashmir Himalayas has continued despite terrorist threats.

In 1990, even when the valley did not receive a single home tourist, Amarnath cave had an inflow of 5,000 pilgrims consisting mainly of Hindu pilgrims. In 1998, almost one and a half lakh pilgrims had visited Amarnath despite the militants' ban on the 'yatra'. A substantial section of these pilgrims do visit the valley. Besides the Amarnath pilgrims, there has been a consistent tourist inflow throughout the terrorism period to Ladakh. Such tourists would be easily manoeuvred to visit the valley provided the picture is not a gory one.

Tourism and travel is positively co-related with peace and stability. When the tourist market is up for an area, it is sure to be peaceful. It is in the interest of the tourism sector, that international agencies and private sector be made to involve in the revamping process. Their role in providing the co-ordinating thread can be of crucial importance.

Recommendations

- Media, advertising agencies and the Tourism Department, J&K Government, needs to develop a synergy of efforts in developing an image of peaceful Kashmir. The image building of the state needs a thorough revamping. So an effective publicity and media campaign should be launched to make people aware of the brighter side of the picture. The website and portals could be utilized greatly. Celebrities also can play a major role in this respect.
- Identification of tourist attractions for different target groups such as pilgrims, pleasure tourism, adventurous tourists and so on.
- Establishing community participation in dealing with the domestic tourists/foreign tourists, local communities, women and other stakeholders at all levels of planning for designating specific areas of tourism development and identifying the thrust areas. Empower local people to become decision-makers.
- Regular evaluation of the impact of tourism linking

tourism with other resource conservation measures (e.g. parks and protected areas). Impact studies need to be extended to cover the socio-cultural impact of tourism/ pilgrims, prevent negative impacts, and reinforce positive outcomes.

REFERENCES

1. Dutta Mondira, 1990: Towards a Spatial Model of the Tourist Industry in Kashmir Valley; Unpublished PhD thesis, Srinagar, J&K, India.
2. D'Amore, Louis, 1988: Tourism—The World's Peace Industry in *Journal of Travel Research*, Vol. 27(1), pp. 35-40.
3. Brown Hillary, 1999: Tourism for Development. ABC NEWS.com 12th Jan.
4. Zutshi B. and Mondira Dutta, 1988: Tourism for Whose Benefit? Annals of National Association of Geographers, India, (NAGI), Vol. VIII, No. 2, December, Pune, p. 35.
5. Doxey, G.V., 1975: 'A Causation Theory of Visitor Resident Irritants: Methodology and Research Influences' in *Proceedings of the Travel Research* Association, 6th Annual Conference, San Diego, California.
6. Zutshi B. and Mondira Dutta, 1988 : Ibid.
7. Ministry of Tourism, 1998: Highlights, Tourist Statistics, Government of India.
8. Dutta Mondira, 2006: Chapter on Tourism in 'Bihar Human Development Report', (IHD) Institute of Human Development, New Delhi, June, 2006 (Project was sponsored by the Planning Commission)
9. Dutta Mondira, 1999: Terrorism and Tourism: A Case Study of Kashmir Valley, Spatio–Economic Development Record, July-August 2000, New Delhi
10. Tata Economic Consultancy Services (TECS), (1982): Tourist Survey in J&K, Bombay.
11. Dutta Mondira, 2010: 'Impact of Terrorism on the Tourist Economy in Kashmir Valley' in Global Terrorism and Security, Vol. II, Part V, Edited by Narayan Singh Rao, Mittal Publication, New Delhi.
12. Nandini R. Iyer, *Hindusthan Times*, 17 July 2010.

7

World Heritage Sites and Promotion of Tourism in Tamil Nadu

M. Thilakavathy

According to the famous American traveller and writer Mark Twain, "India is one country under the sun that is endowed with an imperishable interest for alien prince and alien peasant, for the lettered and the ignorant, the wise and the fool, the rich and the poor, the bonded and the free one-land that all men desire to see, and having seen once, by even a glimpse, would not give that glimpse for the shows of all the rest of the globe combined".

Heritage pronounces the age old culture, traditions and customs of a country. Heritage tourism in India has registered an immense growth in the last few years, ever since additional initiatives were taken by the government of India to boost India's image as a destination for heritage tourism. India is famous for its rich heritage and ancient culture. India's glorious past and cultural diversity make a potent blend which attracts millions of tourists to its heritage tourist attractions.

As one turns the pages of history, the rich heritage of India comes alive with all its fragrance and colour which are still breathing in the heritage forts, palaces, temples and monuments. The splendid architecture, minutely carved motifs, embellished facades of the heritage monuments narrates the immense skill of the craftsmen of the yore which have been fascinating the world for many centuries. UNESCO has come up with the mission to protect these treasures which are the finest gifts to world from India.

Tourism in India has been on rise and is expected to emerge as the most important revenue earner for India by 2012. Heritage tourism has emerged as one of the niche segments of tourism in India and worldwide. It is often offered in combination with other elements like religion, wildlife, ecotourism, and even adventure.

Cultural heritage tourism is a niche element of the overall tourism spectrum. It is meant to gain an appreciation of the past or something we have got in legacy. It is one of the oldest forms of travel, and involves heritages of all kinds—colonial heritage, urban renewal, religious tourism, genealogy, industrial heritage, and ethnicity.

Objectives of the paper

- To analyse the World Heritage Sites and its impact on tourism
- To outline the efforts of preservation of the sites
- To evaluate the work of the Tamil Nadu Tourism Department in improving the Heritage Tourism

Heritage Tourism Spectacle of Tamil Nadu

Tamil Nadu is one of the 28 states of India which lies on the eastern coast of the south Indian peninsula bordered by Puducherry (Pondicherry), Kerala, Karnataka and Andhra Pradesh.[1] It is the eleventh largest state in India by size and the sixth most populous state. Tamil Nadu is the homeland of the Tamils and has existed since prehistoric times. The culture and artwork of this region are considered to be some of the oldest in the world...

Tamil Nadu has many amazing monuments, which attracts tourists from all over the world. The southern state of Tamil Nadu is referred to as the cradle of Dravidian culture, an ancient culture distinguished by unique languages and customs. The cultural icons are everywhere—huge temples with their towering gopurams are not seen anywhere else in the country.

Tamil Nadu is one of those areas of the country which remained comparatively safe from the repeated foreign invasions that ransacked the northern parts of the country repeatedly. This helped the state to retain most of its rich heritage and religious monuments; It is one of the foremost states in the country in terms of overall development.

Tamil Nadu holds a unique position in the sphere of cultural as it is a distinguished region where the cultural symbols of the country is preserved in its original form. The state's cultural heritage consists of fascinating monuments, architectural splendours, religious shrines, performing arts and the customs and traditions of the people. UNESCO has conferred World Heritage status to some monuments and heritage manifestations in Tamil Nadu. This study elucidates on the World Heritage Sites in Tamilnadu and its tourism potential.

World Heritage Sites in Perspective

In India 28 sites are recognized by the United Nations Educational, Scientific and Cultural Organization (UNESCO) as World Heritage Sites. The Suggestion of World Heritage site was initiated by United States with merging cultural conservation and natural conservation. The programme was founded with the *Convention Concerning the Protection of World Cultural and Natural Heritage*, which was adopted by the General Conference of UNESCO on November 16, 1972.[2]

UNESCO refers each World Heritage Site with an identification number. While each World Heritage Site remains part of the legal territory of the state wherein the site is located, UNESCO considers it in the interest of the international community to preserve each site.

With the aim to restore and properly maintain the heritage structures, properties of natural importance etc., UNESCO has designated a number of sites across the world as Heritage sites.

An ancient land, India has a 5,000 years old history and has been ruled by various dynasties and rulers. Over the centuries the rulers had erected a number of interesting structures across the country. Today those rulers are no more, but the old structures provide a glimpse of the bygone era. For proper maintenance and promoting the sites, UNESCO has designated a number of sites as World Heritage Site.

The following World Heritage Sites in Tamil Nadu, Accredited by UNESCO are taken for this study:

- Mahabalipuram,
- The Brihadeeswara temple at Thanjavur,
- The great Siva temple at Gangaikondacholapuram,
- Airavateeswarar temple at Darasuram, and
- Nilgiri Mountain Railway.

Mahabalipuram

Mahabalipuram also known as Mamallapuram, was a famous sea port found by a Pallavan King in the 7th Century. Today it is a fascinating archaeological site and a pleasant sea-resort. Mahabalipuram is just 60 kms. South-west of Madras and has great ancient monuments made out of solid granite rocks by master stone-cutters.[3]

Mahabalipuram is pre-eminently testimony to the Pallavas civilization of south-India.The sanctuary, known especially for its rathas (temples in the form of chariots), mandapas (cave sanctuaries), and giant open-air reliefs, is one of the major centres of the cult of Siva. Most of the monuments, like the rock-cut rathas, sculptured scenes on open rocks like Arjuna's penance, the caves of Govardhanadhari and Ahishasuramardini, and the Jala-Sayana Perumal temple (the sleeping Mahavishnu or Chakrin at the rear part of the Shore temple complex) are attributed to the period of Narasimhavarman I Mamalla.

The entire group of monuments at Mahabalipuram is a exquite example of early temple architecture. They are classified under four main heads:

- Monoliths i.e. free standing temples cut out of solid rock locally called Rathas or Chariots.
- Cave temples excavated on the sides of the rock called Mandapas.
- Sculptured scenes carved on the edges of the hills known as Base-reliefs.
- Shore-temple, a structural monument i.e. built up masonry temple.[4]

The first three are hewn out of the rocks and the last one is built with stones.

The monuments are subdivided into five categories

Ratha temples in the form of processional chariots, monolithic constructions cut into the residual blocks of diorite which emerge from the sand. The five *ratha* of the south, which are the most famous, date to the reign of Naharasimhavarman Mamalla (630-68), the great Pallavas king.

Mandapa, or rock sanctuaries modelled as rooms covered with bas-reliefs (the *mandapa* of Varaha, representing the acts of this avatar of Vishnu; the *mandapa* of the Five Pandavas and, especially, the *mandapa* of Krishna and the *mandapa* of Mahishasuramardini).

Rock reliefs in the open air illustrate a popular episode in the iconography of Siva, that of the Descent of the Ganges. The wise King Baghirata having begged him to do so, Siva ordered the Ganges to descend to Earth and to nourish the world. The sculptors used the natural fissure dividing the cliff to suggest this cosmic event to which a swarming crowd of gods, goddesses, mythical beings (Kinnara, Gandherya, Apsara, Gana, Naga and Nagini), wild and domestic animals bear witness.

Temples built from cut stone, like the Temple of Rivage, which was constructed under King Rajasimha Narasimavarmn II (695-722), with its high-stepped pyramidal tower and thousands of sculptures dedicated to the glory of Siva.

Monolithic *rathas*, from single- to triple-storeyed, display a variety of architectural forms, while the Dharmaraja, Arjuna and

Draupadi rathas are square in plan, the Bhima and Ganesa rathas rectangular, and the Sahadeva *ratha* apsidal. Structural architecture was introduced on a grand scale by Pallava Rajasimha (700-28), culminating in the erection of the Shore Temple.[5]

Another piece of architectural beauty is the Shore temple, standing against the background of the ocean. It belongs to a period when the constructional style of the Pallavas was at its peak in its decorative beauty and intrinsic quality. This building has become eroded by the corrosive action of seawater and air and the sculptures have become indistinct.[6]

Now Mahabalipuram has become a popular tourist centre and a place of pilgrimage to the students of art and architecture. It attracts thousands of tourists from all over India as well as from countries anroad. All types of temple architecture in the south can be seen at Mahabalipuram. They provide an eloquent commentary on the glory and greatness of the Pallava rulers. It bears testimony to the ancient art and culture of South India.

Great Living Chola Temples

Considering the outstanding universal value of Brahadeeswara Temple, it was inscribed as a World Heritage Site in the year 1987. This meticulously planned metaphorical and physical structure envisaged and implemented by Raja Raja I at Thanjavur were followed by subsequent rulers including his son Rajendra at Gangaikonda Cholapuram as a continuing dynamic tradition. Subsequently in the same tradition, Airavatesvara temple was constructed at Darasuram. Each of this temple is a living temple having a well defined system of worship and rituals based on vedic traditions. In recognition of the fact that these three temples formed a unique group demonstrating a progressive development of high Chola architecture and art at its best, the UNESCO has inscribed all the three temples as World Heritage Sites under the caption "The Great Living Chola Temples" in the year 2004. These Great Temples had been built during the Chola rule in South India.These temples demonstrate the tremendous power, wealth, imperial domain, and religious commitment of the Chola Dynasity in the cities of Thanjavur and Gangaikonda Cholapuram.

Brahadeeswara Temple (Tanjavur)

This city of Tanjavur also called Tanjore, was the capital of the Chola Empire during the 10th and 14th centuries. It is today a small town, but still the 'Art Capital of South India'. Besides being the centre of art and culture it has many temples; the most famous being Brihadeshwara Temple, which dominates the entire landscape. Built by the Chola King Raj Raja (985-1014), this temple with 63 meter high tower marks the crowning glory of the Chola architecture. Dedicated to Lord Shiva this masterpiece of Dravidian art has its Viman crowned with a dome of a monolithic rock of granite weighing over 80 tons. This was hauled up inch by inch along an eastern ramp, especially built for this purpose, and which extended 6 kms. in length.

In the sanctum sanctorum under the superb tower, is enshrined a huge Shiva Lingam. The temple stands encircled by a huge courtyard with cloisters. Before the sanctum lays the Nandi Bull, the second largest of its kind, made up of a single block of black granite. The 13 storey tower is covered with fine sculptures including those depicting the 108 poses of Natyam enumerated in Bharat's classic Natyashastra. As evidenced by the inscriptions that found in the compound wall of this temple, the temple had always been serving as a platform for the dancers who excelled in the traditional dance form of Bharatha Natyam. The inner walls are decorated with excellent paintings and frescoes which remind the visitor of the Ajanta cave paintings.

The temple is also an architectural exemplar showcasing the pure form of the Dravida type of temple architecture and representative of the Chola Empire ideology and the Tamil civilisation in Southern India. The temple "testifies to the brilliant achievements of the Chola in architecture, sculpture, painting and bronze casting".[7]

Features

The temple is made up of 130,000 tons of granite. The 60-metre tall vimana is still the tallest extant in South India And the most important feature of the building is that, at no time of the day the shadow of the gopuram will not fall on the ground. This temple was declared as the World Heritage Site in 1987.

Millennium celebrations

Built in the year 1010 AD by Raja Raja Chola in Thanjavur, Brahadishwara Temple also popularly known as the 'Big Temple' has turned 1000 years and to mark the 1000th year of existence of the grand structure, the state government conducted many cultural events. It was on the 275th day of his 25th regal year (1010 AD) that Raja Raja Chola handed over a gold-platedkalasam for the final consecration to crown the vimana of the temple.

Bharathanatyam Yajna

To mark this occasion, the State Government has organised a Bharathanatyam Yajna, classical dance show under noted dancer Padma Subramaniam. To mark the 1000th year anniversary of annisary of the building, 1000 dancers from New Delhi, Mumbai, Pune, Tamil Nadu, Andra Pradesh, Karnataka, Kerala, Singapore, Malaysia and the US danced for the recorded 11 verses of *divine Music Thiruvichaippa* (ninth of Thirumurai) composed by Karuvur Thevar (the guru of Raja Raja Chola) called Tiruvisaippa.[8]

Commemorative Stamp and Coin

On 26 September 2010 (Big Temple's fifth day of millennium Celebrations), as an dignification to Big Temple's contribution to the country's Cultural, Architectural, Epigraphical history, a Special 5 Postage Stamp of the 216-feet tall giant Raja Gopuram was released by Indian Postal department. A special commemorative 5 coin with the model of temple embossed on it was released by the Reserve Bank of India.[9]

Travel Information

Tanjavur is well connected with Madras, Trichy, and Kumbakonam with trains and buses. Trichy (58 kms) is also the nearest airport.

Gangaikonda Cholapuram

Gangaikonda Cholapuram in Tamil Nadu was the headquarters of the Cholas till the 13th century. This place is well known for the Temple which was built in 11th century, to celebrate Chola King's acquisition up to the Gangetic plain. The Temple is one of the very age-old temples of Tamil Nadu, built in the Chola style. The temple is extravagantly sculpted with beautiful stone sculptures including a dancing Ganesha, a lion headed well and a stunning freeze portraying Rajendra Chola being crowned by Lord Siva and his wife Parvathi. The meticulous accounts of the Cholas are inscribed on the copper plates and temple walls. The exotic structure took approximately nine years to complete. The temple was erected to extol the accomplishments of king Rajendra I.[10]

History

For about 250 years, Chola clan ruled over a large part of South India. In those times, the Chola dynasty was at its apex and conquered many a parts of the northern territory. On one of the expeditions, Rajendra Chola brought Ganga water in a golden pot and consecrated the reservoir 'Ponneri or Cholaganga'. Consequently, Rajendra was titled as 'Gangaikondan' (the one who brought the Ganges). The king wanted to erect a 'larger than life' temple correspondent to the Brihadeeswara Temple. During 1020–29 AD, Gangaikondacholapuram. Saw its construction.

Architecture

The superb architecture of the temple boasts of a 9 storey vimanam that extends to the height of 185 feet. Facing the east direction, Gangai Konda Cholapuram embraces incredible sculptures and carvings. Not less than 54.86m in height, the temple structure follows the style of Brihadisvara Temple. The whole temple is thrived with rich and intricate carvings that are exclusive to Chola style of artistry. Known to comprise a little northern style, the structure embraces intricate carvings in the Vimanams.

The architecture is a portrayal of complex carvings on the hard granite stones,. Mind-blowing sculptures adorn the walls and ceilings of Gangaikondacholapuram. The creativity of sculptors is reflected in the figures of dancing Nataraja and peaceful Saraswati. The temple is declared as a UNESCO World Heritage Site.

Travel Information

Gangaikonda Cholapuram is a 45 minutes drive from Chidambaram. Chidambaram is well connected with Madras, Trichy, and Kumbakonam with trains and buses.

Airavateswarar Temple at Darasuram

Darasuram is a small town adjacent to Kumbakonam on the route from Kumbakonam to Thanjavur. It is in the Thanjavur district of Tamil Nadu. Airavateswarar temple at Darasuram is elegant, exquisite, and grand in scale and splendor.

The Chola king Rajaraja Chola II built this temple in 12th century. The town is initially called as Rajarajapurm and in course of time corrupted into Darasuram. As per temple legend, the vehicle of Indira, the white elephant called Airavata, worshipped at this temple. Hence, Lord Siva is known in the name of Airavateeswarar. Yama also is said to have worshipped Lord Siva here and got cure from a rishi's curse whereby his body was constantly feeling a burning sensation. The consort of the lord is Devya Nayaki. The main sanctum is in the form of a chariot drawn by elephants. The temple is declared as a UNESCO World Heritage Site. The temple is a treasure trove of painting, inscriptions, stone carvings, and musical pillars.[11]

Travel Information

Darasuram is at a distance of 3 km from Kumbakonam. Buses frequently ply from Kumbakonam to Darasuram. The temple town of Kumbakonam is well connected by roads and railways. Kumbakonam is at a distance of 275 km from Chennai To travel by air, the nearest airport is at Trichy. To travel by train, the nearest train heads are located at Thanjavur and Kumbakonam.

Nilgiri Mountain Railway

The Nilgiri Mountain Railway was built by the British in 1908, and was initially operated by the Madras Railway Company. The railway still relies heavily on its fleet of locomotives. The Southern Railway, with headquarters in Chennai, Tamil Nadu which operates the NMR, incurs an annual shortfall of Rs 4 crores, (~US$1 million).

In July 2005, UNESCO added the Nilgiri Mountain Railway as an extension to the World Heritage Site of Darjeeling Himalayan Railway, the site then became known as 'Mountain Railways of India' after it satisfied the necessary criteria, thus forcing abandonment of the modernisation plans.

For the past several years diesel locomotives have taken over from steam on the section between Coonoor and Udhagamandalam. Local people and tourists have led a demand for steam locos to once again haul this section.

NMR issues old style tickets, keeping in line with the World Heritage Site status. Even though the NMR stations have networked computerised ticketing systems for onward journeys, it still issues Edmondson style manual tickets for the Ooty-Mettupalayam journey to preserve the 'World Heritage Site' status of the railway. However, ticket booking is similar to other conventional trains and can also be done via the Indian Railways' website.

The Toute

The 'Nilagiri Passenger' train covers a distance of 26 mile (41.8 km), travels through 208 curves, 16 tunnels, and 250 bridges. The uphill journey takes around 290 minutes (4.8 hours), and the downhill journey takes 215 minutes (3.6 hours) It has the steepest track in Asia with a maximum gradient of 8.33 percent.

Development of Tourism in India

Today tourism is the largest service industry in India, with a contribution of 6.23 percent to the national GDP and providing 8.78 percent of the total employment. India witnesses' more than 5 million annual foreign tourist arrivals and 562 million domestic tourism visits. The tourism industry in India generated about US$100 billion in 2008 and that is expected to increase to US$275.5 billion by 2018 at a 9.4 percent annual growth rate. The Ministry of Tourism is the nodal agency for the development and promotion of tourism in India and maintains the *'Incredible India'* campaign.

According to World Travel and Tourism Council, India will be a tourism hotspot from 2009-18, having the highest 10-year growth potential. As per the Travel and Tourism Competitiveness Report 2009 by the World Economic Forum, India is ranked 11th in the Asia-Pacific region and 62nd overall, moving up three places on the list of the world's attractive destinations. It is ranked the 14th best tourist destination for its natural resources and 24th for its cultural resources, with many *World Heritage Sites*, both natural and cultural, rich fauna, and strong creative industries in the country. India also bagged 37th rank for its air transport network. The India travel and tourism industry ranked 5th in the long-term (10-year) growth and is expected to be the second largest employer in the world by 2019.India made it to the list of "rising stars" or the countries that are likely to become major tourist destinations in the next five years, led by the United Arab Emirates, China, and Vietnam.

Development of Tourism in Tamil Nadu

"The guest arrived he tends, the coming guest expects to see:

To these is a heavenly home that dwell a welcome guest is he."

Tourism promotes hospitality as enunciated by poet Thiruvalluvar in Tirukural. Tourism plays a vital role in promoting goodwill among the people and socio-economic development of the country. Tamilnadu tourism is an industry to a very large section of society. Tourism promotes handicrafts and fine arts of a nation; it helps in preserving the national integration and universal brotherhood.

Promotion of tourism received attention in the post independent Tamilnadu. From the year 1971, tourism in Tamilnadu was made official and a full-fledged department of tourism was created. In the same year, Tamilnadu Tourism Development Corporation was created to look after the commercial features. Tourism has been declared as an industry. The government of Tamilnadu extends Capital and General subsidy to the private parties, those who are participating in the tourism industry. Tamil Nadu's tourism industry, centred on Hindu temples, wild life sanctuaries, hill stations and waterfalls is the second largest in India, with an annual growth rate of 16 percent.

In Tamil Nadu, Heritage Tourism plays a vital role for the development of Tourism sector.

Tourists irrespective of their varied interests, have one thing in common i.e. they would like to go around heritage monuments which are in plenty in Tamil Nadu, viz.,

(i) 4 world heritage monuments identified by the UNESCO.
(ii) 48 centres declared as heritage towns by the Government of Tamil Nadu.
(iii) Innumerable heritage monuments declared by the Archaeological Survey of India and the Archaeology Department, Government of Tamil Nadu.

Tourist Arrivals to Tamil Nadu

Aggressive promotion and marketing campaigns through print and electronic media at the domestic, national and international levels and up gradation of basic amenities at tourist/spots have resulted in the increase of tourist arrivals to Tamil Nadu as furnished below:

(in lakhs)

Year	Domestic	Foreign	Total
2005	323.39	11.79	335.18
2006	392.14	13.35	405.49
2007	506.47	17.53	524.00
2008	626.18	20.40	646.58
2009	781.37	23.69	804.06

The above table clearly shows that there is a steady growth in the arrival of the tourists in Tamil Nadu.

According to a PTI report, domestic and International tourist arrivals in Tamil Nadu have witnessed a 25 percent increase in 2009 with the number increasing the eight crore mark. "In 2009 the number of arrivals both, domestic and foreign travellers was 8,04,06,657 compared previous year's 6,46,58,671, thus registering the growth of 24.36 percent."[12]

Conclusion and Suggestions

Tamil Nadu is a splendid destination with rich cultural heritage and ecological resources. This study assumes importance in the context of tourism promotional activities cantered on World Heritage Sites in Tamil Nadu. The promotional campaign improved by Tamil Nadu Tourism under the banner "Enchanting Tamil Nadu" has fetched great benefits both cultural and economic for the state.

We have to maintain the World Heritage tag obviously it can boost tourist destination image and create awareness among the tourists. Even the private sector can be roped in like some European countries (Spain for instance) to offer pro-active support to the destinations. Knowledgeable and well trained guides could be posted in the World Heritage sites to provide information and assist tourists. The package tours to World Heritage Sites can be a value addition to promote tourism.

Tamil Nadu is rich in its cultural heritage and history. Its invaluable treasures managed well with proper resource support can attract the tourists in large numbers and help in promoting heritage tourism and thus led to an overall development in Tamilnadu. 'Enchanting Tamilnadu' is a much sought after destination owing to the spectacular mix of ancient and modern tourism products.

Tamil Nadu has the potential to becoming a global metropolis in view of the blend of the new and the old, excellent connectivity, educated man power and wide base of technical institutions.. With the Government providing adequate support and effective guidance to formulate new plans for promoting tourism, Tamilnadu Tourism is poised to take a big leap in future.

REFERENCES

1. *Manorama Year Book* 2010, p. 658.
2. http:.//whc.unesco.org/en/list/
3. Sivaramamurti C., *Mahabalipuram* (New Delhi, 1972), p. 3.
4. Padmanabhan, S, *Temples of South India*, (Nagarkovil, 1977), p. 65.
5. Percy Brown, *Indian Architecture* (London, 1940), p. 299.
6. *Op. cit.*, Sivaramamurti, C., p. 24.
7. Balasubrahmanyam, S.R., *Early Chola temples* (Orient Longman Publicantions, 1971), p. 234.
8. *The Hindu* (1 August 2010), "A grand dance spectacle at the Thanjavur Big Temple".
9. *Deccan Herald* (26 September 2010). "Stamp, coin release mark 1,000 years of Big Temple" and Express Buzz, *The Indian Express* (26 September 2010). Rs. 1000 note of popular in Tanjavur.
10. Somasundaram, J.M., *The Great Temple at Tanjore* (The Tajore Devasatanams, 1st Published, 1958), p. 46.
11. Sastri, K.A.N., *The Cholas* (University of Madras, 1959), p. 389.
12. Balasubrahmanyam S.R., "*Early Chola Temples: Parantaka I to Rajaraja I, 907-985 A.D*", Orient Longman Publicantions, 1971.
13. Harish Batt, B.S. Badan, *Sustainable Tourism*, Cresent Publishing Corportation, 2006.
14. Padmanabhan, S., *Temples of South India*, Nagarkovil, 1977.
15. Percy Brown, *Indian Architecture*, London, 1940.
16. Pran Nath Seth, *Fundamental of Tourism*, Sterling Publishers Private Ltd, 2008.
17. Pran Nath Seth, *An Introduction to Travel and Tourism*, Sterling Publishers Private Ltd, 2008.
18. Sastri, K.A.N., *The Cholas*, University of Madras, 1959.

19. Sivaramamurti C., *Mahabalipuram*, Director General Archaeological Survey of India, New Delhi, 1972.
20. Somasundaram, J.M., *The great Temple at Tanjore*, The Tajore Devasatanams, 1st Published, 1958.
21. Vijaya Kumar, R., *Indian Tourism Industry in 21st Century Challenges and Responses*, Sonali Publication, 2009.
22. *South Asian Journal of Tourism and Heritage* (2011) Vol. 4, No. 1.
23. *Tourism India India's Tourism Magazine*, December, 2003.
24. http:.//www. Wikipedia.org/
25. http:.//whc.unesco.org/en/list/
26. www.tourismindiainluine.com

8

Tourism in Barddhaman Town, West Bengal: Constraints and Prospects

N.C. Jana

Introduction

Tourism was originally conceived as foreign exchange earner to support balance of payments and to promote international understanding. Today, it is considered as a major instrument of socio-economic development. For the developing countries it offers an alternative source and reliable route to employment generation, advancement of deprived section of society, especially the youth and women, and in fact, a sure way of removing poverty. India is a vast subcontinent with a billion strong population, diversity of languages, culture, cuisine and heritage, where tourism has assumed a special role in national integration and conservation of its natural and man-made assets of fauna, flora, arts, crafts, architecture, customs and traditions. Tourism, which in the rest of the world has emerged as the largest and the fastest growing industry, "failed to receive due importance on India's development agenda" as the Planning Commission put it in its mid-term appraisal of the Ninth Plan. The result is that India has been left far behind in its quest for tourism compared both to the developed western world as well as our Asian neighbours.

According to the WTO, international tourism will have positive contribution to reduce the increasing gap between developed and developing countries and securing fast growth in socio-economic progress of the later. The practical role of tourism in national economy, international trade and balance of payments makes it one of the world's important industries. Tourism is regarded as a large and labor-intensive industry and also an important earner to the national exchequer.

From the economic point of view tourism is a general industry having relationship with a lot of social activities. Tourism creates jobs, recovers traditional fine art and contributes a large percentage to the national GDP. From the sociological viewpoint it may be pointed out that tourist services are very beneficial to human society. Its positive effects are to provide employment to workers, improve the people's educational attainment, promote standard of living, restore and preserve traditional values and national identity, alleviating hunger and reducing poverty.

Mr. David Eizenberg, Resident Representative of UNDP, emphasized on the importance of the linkage between tourism and poverty reduction, for two reasons: (i) tourism is a labour intensive sector and offers small-scale business opportunities, and (ii) it has potential to generate employment in rural areas.

Barddhaman is the largest and possibly the richest district in West Bengal. Culturally, it possesses a very rich heritage and finds mentioned from ancient times. The architecture of Barddhaman town is a brilliant combination of the folk and the classic-Terracotta with Gothic and Persian. Sheer Afghan's beautiful wife, Meher-un-nisa (later known as Empress Nor Jahan) was abducted by the Mughal Emperor Jahangir from this town and the tombs of Sheer Afghan and his opponent Kutubuddin lie, side by side, as sad but eloquent testimonies of imperial caprice. Hindu temples, mosques, churches, along with tombs of Sufi saints adorn this town. *Mahavir Bardhaman* came to this area in order to preach Jainism in Bengal. Guru Nanak also came to this town. The town itself has been identified with

Parthalis or Portalis which, according to Greek Geographers, was the Royal City of the Gangardae or Gangarides.

The history of Barddhaman is associated with the rise and fall of the Barddhaman Raja. Original founder of the house was Sangam Rai, a Khattri Kapur of Kotli in Lahore. Then Abu Rai was appointed Choudhury and Kotwal of Rekabi Bazar in the town in 1657. Raja Krishna Chandra Roy was the founder of Raj family and Maharajadhiraj Uday Chand Mahatab Bahadur was the last King of Bardhaman Raj Family, till 1954, when Estate Acquisition Act came into force.

The history and civilisation of Barddhaman is associated with the rule of other so many kings like Kantideb, Ichhai Ghosh, Bijay Sen etc. and also cult of village Gods, Temples, Mosques, Tombs, Churches, diversified social and economie life of the people of this area.

Barddhaman is a place of historical importance, because it has been evolved through the longstanding rules of Nawabs and Rajas. So, the reflection of architectural beauty in places and temples established by the past rulers can be observed. It is also an ideal place of cultural assimilation as the past rulers were alien to Barddhaman. A significant number of people came from western India with Nawabs and Rajas who are presently the permanent residents of the place (Konar, 2003). Barddhaman has a vast potentiality of tourism development that needs appropriate planning and management measures.

Importance of the Study

The present study is limited to Barddhaman town. Barddhaman, the district headqurter, is well connected by the Eastem Railway and G.T. Road. Situated on the bank of River Damodar, the town is traversed by its tributary viz. Banka. It is less than 100 kms from Kolkata. Despite enjoying the locational advantage betwen Kolkata and Durgapur-Asansol industrial complex, tourism at Barddhaman town has not been developed to the desired level. Therefore, it is necessary to identify the causes responsible for the underdevelopment of tourism in the study area and accordingly appropriate measures should be taken to establish the area as a remarkable centre of tourist attraction.

Places of Tourist Attraction

Barddhaman town is enriched with a number of tourist places comprising of temples, icons of deities, tombs, mosques, monuments, majars, ponds, parks etc. These places can be classified into historical, religious, aesthetic, science and architecture, which are as follows (Konar, 2003):

1. Historical Places

Mahatab Manjil: The 300 years old history of royal family of Barddhaman started with their establishment of residence at Baikunthapur, a village near Gangpur. Then they moved to Kanchannagar, a place between the Rivers Damodar & Banka. The royal palace 'Mahatab Manjil' was built by the then Maharaja of Barddhaman Mahatab Chand in the year 1851 AD. It was situated in the recent Barabazar locality on the north of the River Banka, about 4 km away frorn Kanchannagar. There were orchestra house, ball room, Queen's house, art gallery, revenue compound and many others in this royal palace. Nowadays the rani mahal (queen's house) is converted to M.U.C. Women's College and the main building is occupied by the University of Burdwan & Department of Settlement. Despite lack of maintenance, still it is considered as a piece of historical importance and remains a must visit place in Barddhaman.

Golapbag, Darul Bahar and Hawa Manjil: Golapbag, Darul Bahar and Hawa Manjil stand as a token of love for beauty of Maharajadhiraj Mahatab Chand. This beautiful garden was planned and designed by Ramdas, who was previously the gardener-in-charge of Raja Rammohan Roy. The magnificent Places at Golapbag, Darul Bahar and Hawa Manjil are still the main attractions for visitors. Nowadays this beautiful place is converted into the campus of the University of Burdwan. Some new buildings have been added to establish different departments of Arts, Science and Commerce as well as library and auditorium. A Hawa Manjil on the '*Lahar*' was built for the purpose of recreation and relaxation under the full moon is also note worthy.

Tombs of Sher Afgan and Kutubuddin: This is one of the most important archaeological remains in the town and its origin is traced back to the reign of Emperor Akbar about four hundred years ago.

Barddhaman was the country residence of Sher Afgan (Jaigirdar of Barddhaman), the first husband of the famous Meherunnisa, (aftenwards Empress Nur-Jahan meaning Light of the World), who was treacherously attacked and slain just outside the town by Kutubuddin, the foster brother of Emperor Jahangir. Kutubuddin was appointed as the Subedar of BengaI by the Emperor as a reward to procure Meherunnisa for his Royal Master Jahangir, who subsequently married her. The graves of both Sher Afgan and Kutubuddin are still to be seen in the mahalla of Pir Baharam.

In the honour of Sher Afgan and Kutubuddin, marble tombs were built by the Barddhaman Raj and are kept in a fair state of preservation under the ancient Monuments Act by the Archaeological Survey of India.

Khaja Anwar and Khaja Abul Kasem Nawab Bari: Tombs over the graves of Khaja Anwar and Khaja Abul Kasem, who laid down their lives and became martyrs in their encounter with Rahim Khan, were built in 1715 during the reign of Emperor Farukhsiyar of Delhi. A mosque alongwith beautiful palace was built in the midst of a squre tank (Hawa Mahal) covering an area of 10 bighas at the then Poddarhat Mouza (now Khaja Anwar Berh) in the town. This Nawab Bari is a wonderful specimen of Mughal Architecture. During mid-January of every year pilgrims from different places come here for holy dip and accordingly a big fair is organised.

Will Bari: Opposite to Sarbamangala Temple Will Bari was an attraction for many people. The building was constructed on a land of about 4 acres. This property was donated by Tarachand Kapur to his youngest brother Maharaja Mahatab Chand in a Will (Deed) and since then it was known as '*Will Bari*'. Every year doll shows on the themes of Ramayana, Mahabharata and Krishnaleela as well as a month long photo festival were organised starting from Saraswati Puja to Shivaratri. Nowadays it has lost its past glory, but the older people are still remember it.

Bardwari Gate: To commemorate the victory of Maharaja Kirtichand over Shova Singh, Zamindar of Chitua Baroda and the King of Bishnupur, 12 vast gates were built on the style of mediaval architecture in the year 1737 AD. Eleven out of twelve gates have been completely ruined, only one is still remaining. Even today it stands as a historical relic. Some historians marked the gate as out-ward gate (Bar Dwar) towards the palace.

Satir Math: This famous place is situated in the southern part of Barddhaman town on the way to Tejganj from Alamganj. A Kali temple is situated inside. Once this holy place was famous for '*Satidaha*' (The practice of burning widows themselves on their husband pyre). There were a large crematory, lofty Kali temple, attached Shiva temple, a pond and some shops containing materials of Satidaha. Orchestras, Pundits were also available there to help the whole procedures. Nowadays Satidaha is declared illegal and it is completely stopped. But still the Kali temple, Shiva temple and many others are standing with the evidences of this tragic custom.

Curzon Gate: Situated at the heart of the town it was built in the year 1904 by Sir Bijoy Chand Mahatab, the Maharajadhiraj of Barddhaman to commemorate the visit of Lord Curzon, the then Governor General of India as the gateway to the town. Originally its name was '*Star of India*' and later '*Curzon Gate*'. Now it is known as '*Bijoy Toran*'. The structure of the gate speaks for itself and attracts many tourists particularly those interested in architecture.

2. Religious Places

Darga of Khakkar Shah: Shah Mohammad came to Barddhaman long before Pir Baharam to preach the principles of Islam. He originally belonged to the Thakori region of Peshwar, who later on became *Pir*. After his death he was buried within the precincts of the Palace of Pairakhana Lane. The '*Majar*' is sacred to both the Hindus and the Muslims. Many pilgrims of both the communities visit this holy place regularly.

Jama Mosque: On the side of Mahatab Manjil at Pairakhana Road Jama Mosque was built in the year 1699 AD by Azim-us-shan, grandson of Mughal Emperor Aurangazeb. It is a three-dome mosque reflecting unique work of Mughal sculpture.

Pir Baharam: Pir Baharam, then named Shah Wordi Bayat of Tabriz in Persia took the name of Pir Baharam Sakka (Vistiwala) as he used to supply water to pilgrims. He came to Barddhaman on his way to visit holy places and took shelter in the hermitage of Yogi Joypal in the Puratan Chawk area of Barddhaman. The Pir died in 1563 AD and a tomb was built by the order of the Emperor Akbar. This memorial located near Mayur Mahal is a worth visiting place.

108 Temples of Lord Shiva: These temples are located at Nawabhat village, about four kms west of Barddhaman town, on the junction of G.T. Road and Suri Road. There are actually 109 Shiva temples. Out of the 108 temples form a rectangular garland and the rest one is found separately. The temples were built in the year 1789 AD by Maharani Bishnu Kumari, wife of Maharaja Tilok Chand Bahadur. Daily worship is performed there. A week-long fair is held every year on the occasion of Shiva Ratri Festival. Now it is maintained by a Board of Trustees of which District Magistrate as the Chairperson. The temples are visited by thousands of devotees throughout the year.

Barddhamaneshwar: At Bhikharibagan in the Alamganj area, Barddhamaneswhar Shiva was unearthed on 10th August 1972 AD from a wasteland. Its weight is about twelve and half tonnes; its circumference, Gouripatta and height are 6 feet, 18 feet and 6 feet respectively. According to the opinions expressed by different Historians it may belong to the 7th or 8th century AD. On the day of Shivaratri, pilgrims gather here and a large fair is also organised for 2-3 days. Except that, devotees come here throughout the year.

Sarba Mangala Temple: Mata Sarbamangala, the Principal Deity of Barddhaman, was recovered by Maharaja Kirtichand in the year 1740 AD from the Bagdis (lime manufacturer by profession) of Bahirsarbamangala Mouza who found it in the adjacent '*Chunuri Pond*'. This eighteen handed icon of Devi Durga carved on 11 × 8 inches touch stone was established by the King in this present Temple of Nabaratna Type. It is more beautiful and attractive to the religious tourists.

Kankaleshwari Temple: Kankaleshwari is worthy of its name, as it is a rare specimen of Stone-Sculpture. It is a six feet high, eight handed icon of goddess *Chamunda*, carved on the black basalt stone depicting muscles, nerves, veins and skeleton of human body. It was found out from the sandy bed of the River Damodar and accordingly established during the late 18th century in this Jor Bangla Nabaratna type temple at the outskirts of Kanchannagar. The icon is very old and it can be related to Pre-Aryan Yakshini icon. On the Kartiki Amabasya (New Moon in the month of Kartik) every year special Pujas are arranged and also a fair is organised which continues for 2-3 days.

Dhaneswari Temple: Shree Shree Dhaneshwari Devi Temple was built by Dhandeyi Devi, the only daughter of Maharajadhiraj Mahatab Chand Bahadur. It is situated in the northern side of Sarbamangala Temple. The idol of Devi Dhaneshwari was placed in this south facing temple. Here different festivals are organised throughout the year.

Bhairabeshwari Temple: Just on the western side of the Sarbamangala Temple, Shree Shree Bhairabeshwari Kali Temple was built by Bhairab Chand Kapur. The idol is made up of '*Neem*' wood. People have great faith and regard on this deity. It is about three hundred years old.

Kamalakanta Kali Bari: In the Kotalhat area of Barddhaman, this Kali Temple was built by Maharajadhiraj Tej Chand Bahadur in the year 1216 BC. He received Kamalakanta as his spiritual guide and brought him from '*Channa*' village to Barddhaman. Kamalakanta was the priest of Devi Bishalakshmi at Channa where he attained spiritual power. He died in the year 1821 AD. Till today people of Barddhaman pay regards to Kamalakanta and his Kali.

3. Aesthetic Spots

Krishnasayar Eco-Park: Krishnasayar was excavated by Maharaja Krishnaram Roy in the year 1691 AD to meet the water crisis. Its area is about 33 acres. As a joint venture of the University of Burdwan, Zilla Parisad and Burdwan Municipality an Eco-park with flower garden, aviary and snake garden was built under the endeavour of Krisnasayar Acchi Parisad. There are arrangements for boating, sight seeing, restaurant. Cultural programmes are organised every year during the celebration of *Barddhaman Utsav* and *Basanta Utsav*. Exhibition on handicrafts, flowers, sculpture, photography and other visual arts as well as musical programmes are organised besides seminars on different topics.

Ramna Deer Park: This reserved forest is located near Golapbag Campus of the University of Burdwan, containing different valuable trees like Sal, Teak etc. Its area is about 14 hectare. A deer park has been established in this forest where cheetas, rabits and some kind of birds are found. In another part of the forest alongside University Road there is the mausoleum of Bijoy Chand Mahatab (1941 AD) within a beautiful garden named '*Bijoyananda Bihar*'. There is a separate guesthouse of the Forest Department.

Ranisayar: Ranisayar was excavated by Maharaja Kirtichand Roy in memory of his mother Brojokishori Jagatram Roy in the year 1609 AD. It is situated at the heart of the town with about 1 sq. km area. Although the sides of the Sayar are covered by lofty buildings the vast area and the landing ghats still attract many people.

Shyamsayar: Situated almost in the central place of Barddhaman, Shyamsayar was excavated by the then Maharaja of Barddhaman, Ghanashyam Roy, son of Babu Roy in the year 1675 AD, with the objective for meeting the water crisis of the town.

Kamalsayar: It was excavated by Raja Tej Chand Bahadur in the name of his wife Kamal Kumari in the year 1698 AD. It is a vast pond and the University Institute of Technology (UIT) is situated on the side of it.

4. Places of Science and Architecture

Barddhaman Science Centre: It is adjacent to the Ramna Deer Park, just opposite to the second gate of the University of Burdwan. It has been established in the year 1994 with the help of the National Council of Science Museums, Govt. of India. Different experiments on popular science are exhibited here with an aim to augment scientific awareness among rural people and children. Science Centre has its own air-conditioned auditorium for holding seminars, workshops etc.

Meghnad Saha Planetorium: Just opposite to Ramna Deer Park (opposite to the first gate of the University of Burdwan), the second Planetorium in West Bengal was built in the premises of the University of Burdwan (5 acres approx.). It has been established as a joint venture of the Govt. of India, Goto Optical Manufacturing Co. of Japan, Govt. of West Bengal and common people of Barddhaman in January, 1994. Different programmes on astronomy are shown like '*Man and Space*', '*Dinosaur World,*' '*In Search after World,*' etc., which attracts the children and the elderly persons as well.

Sanskriti Lokamancha: Just on the opposite of Bijoy Toran, within the collectorate compound, Sanskriti Loka Mancha was constructed in the year 1993 under the joint venture of District Administration, Zilla Parisad and Burdwan Municipality. This air-conditioned auditorium can accommodate 1400 audiences at a time. Movies are shown here on a regular basis. In addition, Bardhaman Chalachchitra Charcha Kendra also screens movies on account of their film festival. Other cultural programmes are also organised here.

Krishak Setu: Barddhaman town is situated on the bank of River Damodar. A bridge popularly known as *Krishak Setu* has been constructed over the River Damodar connecting Barddhaman proper with south Damodar area of Barddhaman and Hooghly, Bankura, Midnapur Districts. A large kite fair is organised during mid January every year at Sadarghat from the traditional past. Besides, the sand beach here is pleasant for picnic.

Locational Advantages

- Regular train services to Barddhaman are available from Howrah and Sealdah Stations. Two different routes, the chord line and the main line connect Barddhaman with Sealdah and Howrah by rail, about two hours journey.
- By road from Kolkata Sahid Minar Terminus by bus, one and a half hours journey, directly to Barddhaman.
- The town has bus links with Durgapur, Haldia, Digha, Siliguri, Malda, Berhampur, Jhargram, Bankura, Purulia, Shantiniketan etc.
- The district in general and town in particular are well connected with all the districts of West Bengal either by road or rail. It is also well connected by rail with other states of India.

Existing Constraints

Throughout the history Barddhaman has been prosperous and the buildings have reflected a rich heritage. However, after independence, like many other towns of West Bengal, it has succumbed to the pressures of rapidly increasing population. The imbalance between infrastructure and human need has led to increasing dilapidation as the resources have simply not matched up. Today, most parts of this historical town are marked by broken roads, poor drainage, unplanned development and shabby buildings. In addition to the above situation, some of the major constraints identified are:

- Barddhaman town is enriched with a number of temples, icons of deities, tombs, mosques, monuments, majars, ponds, parks etc., but there is no such initiative at the government level for a package tour.
- Town Service buses are the only transport available for covering the few of major tourist spots. In addition, tourist may hire only ricksaw on a contractual basis. Barddhaman has not yet equipped with auto and taxi at large for meeting the growing needs of the domestic and foreign tourists.

- A number of private hotels; few govt. accommodations like Barddhaman Bhavan, Damodar Bhavan, Barddhaman Municipality guesthouse and others such as Sikh and Marwari Dharamsalas are available in and around the town. Among them Hotel Siddharth, Hotel Nataraj, Hotel Kalyani, Hotel Manohar Inn, Hotel Konar, Hotel Samrat, Burdwan Boarding etc. are located in the heart of the town. In fact, super star hotels are not available in this town, which are surely to be identified as one of the major contraints in the development of tourism.

Interventions Required

- The Department of Tourism, Government of West Bengal should give due attention to the development of tourism in Barddhaman town by providing sufficient financial grant to the district administration.
- Most of the places of historical importance have either been damaged or gradually are being damaged, which need renovation to have a fresh look.
- Development and improvement of roads, drinking water supply, electricity and power supply, sewage and sanitation systems.
- Opening a branch of foreign bank and establishment of five star hotel are essential for the tourists from abroad.
- Barddhaman Railway Station and Bus Stand should be renovated.
- The Zilla Parisad and Barddhaman Municipality may think over a package tour for the incoming tourists covering all the places of tourist attraction.
- Barddhaman Municipality may open a counter at both railway station and bus stand for extending services to the tourists.
- To develop and promote local tourism products (e.g. food items like Sitabhog and Mihidana), lesser known destinations (Periphery of Barddhaman town), art forms cuisines, monuments and handicrafts.

- To involve Municipality, PRIs and NGOs in the development of tourism infrastructure and tourism awareness.
- To create awareness and tourism consciousness among the people in general and among the taxi drivers, policemen, bus conductors, porters, customs and others with whom tourists interact thereby removing prejudices and misconceptions and to make Barddhaman a tourism friendly society.
- To promote sustainable and eco-friendly tourism based on the carrying capacity of the destinations.
- Organisation of seminars and workshops as well as printed booklets may enhance the importance of tourism in the area concerned.
- Separate website may be introduced for attracting tourists at large scale from different parts of India and abroad. It may be noted that in this context that *barddhamandarshan.com* has recently been introduced for this purpose.

Concluding Remarks

Today tourism is considered as an important industry, which creates new possibility for unemployed youths. Barddhaman is a place of historical importance, which can be developed as an income generating tourist centre by effective planning and management measures. Now this sector is neglected in Barddhaman in the present juncture of employment crisis. Strong efforts and heartfelt will are needed to develop this place as a Tourist Centre of international importance, so that the symbolic name 'Barddhaman' truly reflects the sign of prosperity. In this regard the following points need to be emphasized: (i) cooperation between public and private sectors is essential to foster sound and sustainable tourism development in Barddhaman; (ii) there is a need to bring new quality to education and HR management that would bring benefits to wide segments of society in general local communities in particular; (iii) there is also a need to create a conducive environment for attracting investment in this sector.

Barddhaman town is located in the eastern part of the district, which is a prosperous agricultural belt of West Bengal. In fact, the town is predominated by agri-business and agro-industries. So, the constant flow of inbound and outbound tourists may enhance the growth of agro-based tourism products, which would be an alternative source to boost sound sustainable economy at the local level.

Although few progressive steps have been adopted by both the District and Municipal administration for the overall development of Barddhaman town in general and development of tourism in particular, much has yet to be done. The establishment of Barddhaman Development Authority is a remarkable step in this direction.

REFERENCES

1. Abhijan Gosthhi (2001), *Barddhaman Samagra*, 2001.
2. *Ambukantha*, Special Issue, 1989.
3. *Barddhaman Samachar Patrika*.
4. Burdwan Municipality (2008): *Unnayaner Pathe Barddhaman*, published by Burdwan Municipality.
5. Chowdhury, Y. (1990), *Barddhaman: Itihas O Sanskriti* (Part-I), Pustak Bipani, Calcutta.
6. Chowdhury, Y. (1991), *Barddhaman: Itihas O Sanskriti* (Part-II), Pustak Bipani, Calcutta.
7. Em Puthy, Mecon (2004), *Role of Tourism in Cambodian Socio-Economc Development*, Magazine 09.
8. Govt. of West Bengal (1996), *Barddhaman Zila Sankhya*, Paschim Banga, Dept. of Information & Culture, Govt. of W.B.
9. Konar, Gopikanta (2003), *Glimpses of Barddhaman*, Indu Publications, Burdwan.
10. Mukhopadhyay, Rakhaldas (1914), *Barddhaman Rajbangshanucharit*, Barddhaman.
11. Natural Group: *From History to Modernity: The Pride of Barddhaman*, published by Natural Group, Kolkata
12. Seminar Report on *Role of Tourism in Poverty Alleviation*, December 2, 2004, Baku.
13. Seth Rabindra (2003), *Hopeful Signs in a Vital Sector*, PIB Features, June 2.
14. Ibid.
15. 152nd Report of the Department-Related Parliamentary Standing Committee on Transport, Tourism & Culture (Rajya Sabha Secretariat: March, 2010: New Delhi)
16. Ibid.
17. Lok Sabha Unstarred Question No.276, dt. 20.11.2009, Ministry of Tourism, Government of India, New Delhi
18. *Indian Express*, 1st September, 2010
19. http://www.prsindia.org Retrieved on Februtary 18, 2011.

9

Eco-Tourism in Himachal Pradesh: Need for a Paradigm Shift

Ruchi Ramesh

Tourism is one of the world's largest and fastest growing economic sectors and represents an activity that forms an integral part of modern societies in both the developed and the developing countries. Davos Declaration on Tourism and Climate Change, reached at the conclusion of a three-day UNWTO-backed meeting in the Swiss town, better known for its annual economic forum states that "the tourism sector must rapidly respond to climate change, within the evolving UN framework, if it is to grow in a sustainable manner." This second International Conference (Davos, Switzerland, October 2007) also deliberated upon the role tourism could play in addressing the concerns arising due to climate change to fructify the UN's Millennium Development Goals, and concluded that the tourism sector must lessen its greenhouse gas emissions, derived from transport and accommodation activities, adapt tourism businesses and destinations to alter their practices, utilize technology to bolster energy efficiency and obtain financial resources to assist poor regions and countries. The Conference has been a milestone event laying bare the status of knowledge to understand the complex relationship between climate change and tourism. The publication notes the vulnerability of the sector to climate change and the impacts of tourism on climate itself. The report provides an excellent basis to address the global phenomenon of climate change, as well as to develop practical tools that can be used by tourism policy-makers and managers to foster the sustainable growth of the tourism industry. In the Conference, an Indian delegation wished to put on record the following statement: "India is acutely aware of the considerable challenge we face today from climate change. We, like other developing countries, bear an inordinate share of the burden of climate change even though this is due to high-level emissions of developed countries. In such circumstances, we must significantly shore up our abilities to cope with and adapt to climate change. To be able to do so, we need development, which is also the best form of adaptation." The Conference underscored the importance of tourism in the global challenges of climate change and poverty reduction. It emphasized that there is a need to urgently adopt a range of policies which give impetus to sustainable tourism that reflects a 'quadruple bottom line' of environmental, social, economic and climate responsiveness. In response to these concerns, a term that has surfaced recently is eco- tourism.[1] Since the late 1960s, the impacts of mass tourism have become a subject of discussion in conservation and development circles. David Fennell says that "there seems to be universal acceptance of the fact that ecotourism was viable long before the 1980s in practice."[2] Writing in 1989, Karen Ziffer explains in *Ecotourism: The Uneasy Alliance*, that ecotourism aimed "to capture a portion of the enormous global tourism market by attracting visitors to natural areas and using the revenues to fund local conservation and fuel economic development."[3]

As early as in 1995, Herold Goodwin called eco-tourism "purposeful travel to natural areas to understand the culture and natural history of the environment taking care not to alter the integrity of the ecosystem, while producing economic opportunities that make the conservation of natural resources beneficial to local people."[4] Ecotourism in the Indian context has significant implications for nature and culture conservation, rural livelihoods and conservation education. Eco-tourism, being environment-friendly activity, aims at promoting environmental ethics and values and preserving nature in its uninterrupted form. The International Year of Eco-tourism 2002 instituted by the United Nations General Assembly offers an opportunity to review eco-tourism experiences world-wide for maximizing economic, social and environmental benefits from eco-tourism avoiding its shortcomings and negative impacts.

Tourism and Sustainability

Regardless of the level of development of any country, tourism is becoming one of the most important sectors of economic growth in the world that provides trading opportunities to all nations. Tourism Industry is a global industry characterized by some very specific features:

- Travel and tourism represent approximately 11 per cent of the world wide gross domestic product (GDP) (according to the tourism satellite account method of the World Travel & Tourism Council).
- It is a cross-sector industry that comprises many related economic sectors, such as culture, sports, and agriculture. All told, more than 30 different industrial components have been identified that serve travellers.
- This explains the industry's heterogeneity Its SME structure gives it its huge importance for regional development. For example, in the EU, there are around 1.3 million hotels and restaurants (9 percent of all enterprises). And 95 percent of them are very small (i.e., 1-9 employees).
- The supply and demand sides form a worldwide network in which production and distribution are based on co-operation.
- The product of the industry is perishable, complex, and emotional.
- A hotel bed not sold for one night represents lost income. The risk faced by suppliers can be alleviated if access to

information is available.

- The tourism product is a bundle of basic products aggregated by an intermediary To support the rather complex bundling process, products must have well-defined interfaces with respect to consumer needs, prices, and distribution channels.
- Vacations are emotional-experience structures that involve cognitive and sensory stimulations as well as affective responses to certain events.[5]

For many developing countries tourism is one of the dominant activities of their economies, while for others, particularly for some small economies, it is the only source of foreign currency and employment, and therefore constitutes the platform for their economic development. World Tourism Organization statistics indicate that the tourism industry will grow continuously and from 70 million international tourist movements in the year 1960, the number is estimated to be over 710 million in the year 2000. In the year 2010, the tourism sector witnessed substantial growth as compared to 2009. The Foreign Tourist Arrivals (FTA) in India during 2010 were 5.58 million as compared to the FTAs of 5.17 million during 2009, showing the growth of 8.1 per cent. The growth rate during 2010 was Rs 64889 crore as compared to Rs 54960 crore during 2009, registering a growth rate of 18.1 per cent.

The growth rate in Foreign Exchange earnings (FEE) from tourism during 2009 over 2008 was 8.3 per cent.[6] It is further estimated that the number of tourists worldwide has been registering substantial growth and it is expected that this number would touch 1.5 billion by the year 2020. International tourist arrivals grew by 5 per cent during the first two months. Growth was positive in whole world in all sub -regions in January and February with the exception of Middle East and North Africa.[7] Tourism contributes about 11 per cent of the world workforce and 10.2 per cent of the global gross domestic product. The dynamic growth of this industry is evident from the fact that a new job is added to this sector every 2.5 second. World Tourism Organization (WTO) reports that the tourism is one of the five top export categories and is the main source of foreign currency for at least 38 per cent of them. Himachal Pradesh received recognition as tourist destination in 19th century, when the British declared Simla as summer capital of India in 1864. In the year 1971, Himachal Pradesh became full fledged state and there after the investment was made to harness the fullest potential of the state for development of tourism. Now the mission of the state is :

> "To make tourism the prime engine of economic growth in the state by positioning it as a leading global destination by the year 2020."[8]

The tourism reached a significant level of development in this hill state in mid1980s and 90s due to Kashmir problem. In 1990 the tourist arrival in Himachal was 1.94 million, leading to a near sevenfold increase to 13.27 million in 2010, of which there were 454 thousand international tourists. The increase of 16.09 per cent of Indian tourist and 13.24 per cent of foreign tourist was reported in the year 2010. A 2011 census count put the State population at 6.85 million. The State is having two times of its population as tourist every year. To meet the demand of accommodation, the bed capacity of the State has been increased to 56023 in 2010 which was 10833 beds a decade back. Tourism contributes nearly 8 per cent of the State Domestic Product (SDP) which is roughly the same as horticulture sector which is main source of income in Himachal. The tourism industry of the State generates 47.5 employments from the investment of every ten lakh rupees, which is more than the traditional occupation of the State which is 44.7. The State Tourism policy proposes to increase SDP to 15 per cent by the year 2020 with careful planning and infrastructural development. While tourism is seen as a source of development, it is also associated with many negative effects, such as destruction of ecological system, loss of social and cultural heritage. In response to these concerns the terms surfaced in the tourism world are sustainable and ecotourism. The sustainable development claims to alleviate many problems of the conventional tourism development. The conceptual definition of sustainable tourism is given by WTO which states that "... applicable to all forms of tourism in all types of destinations, including mass tourism and the various niche tourism segments. Sustainability principles refer to the environmental, economic and socio-cultural aspects of tourism development, and a suitable balance must be established between these three dimensions to guarantee its long-term sustainability..."[9] Honey writes, "Ideally, if tourism is to become an industry truly grounded upon sustainable development, it must all be based on ecotourism principles and practices. But we are, of course, far from this reality. Therefore, a more attainable but still enormously important step is to promote worldwide adoption of sustainable tourism certification programs."[10]

Eco-Tourism in Himachal Pradesh

The guidelines were formulated by eco-tourism policy 1998 to ensure regulated growth of eco-tourism with its positive impacts of environmental protection and community development. The policy and guidelines are addressed to all state governments, industry associations and those involved in tourism development and preservation of environment and natural resources. The policy draws heavily on the definition provided by the United Nations World Tourism Organization (UNWTO) and enlists the key elements of ecotourism as being: natural environment as prime attraction, environment friendly visitors; activities that do not have a serious impact on the ecosystem and positive involvement of local community in maintaining ecological balance. The policy states that an elective approach, scientific planning, effective control and continuous monitoring are required for ecotourism development.[11]

The International Ecotourism Society (TIES) defines ecotourism as, "responsible travel to natural areas that conserves the environment and improves the welfare of local people". Nature-based tourism relies on a high diversity of tourism resources (landscapes, flagship species, ecosystems, outdoor activities relying on specific resources like water level in rivers for canoeing, etc.). These resources are highly variable in space, and will be affected by climate change in various ways. It is rather difficult to assess the magnitude of climate change impacts in nature based destinations, given this diversity of resources, compared for example to ski resorts, (relying principally on snow conditions), or coastal resorts (relying mainly on beach and bathing water conditions). Although ecosystems can be highly vulnerable to climate change impacts, probably there are good adaptation options in ecotourism, given the wide range of activities that can be developed and conducted in natural areas. Therefore, there are good possibilities to design effective adaptation strategies for ecotourism and nature-based destinations. Ecotourism had become a global catch phrase that the United Nations declared 2002 the International Year of Ecotourism, culminating with the Quebec Declaration on Ecotourism, affirming:

> ... that ecotourism embraces the principles of sustainable tourism, concerning the economic, social and environmental impacts of tourism. It also embraces the following specific principles which distinguish it from the wider concept of sustainable tourism:
>
> - Contributes actively to the conservation of natural and cultural heritage,
> - Includes local and indigenous communities in its planning, development and operation, and contributing to their well-being,
> - Interprets the natural and cultural heritage of the destination to visitors,
> - Lends itself better to independent travelers, as well as to organized tours for small size groups.[12]

Geographically diverse in nature, Himachal Pradesh known as Devbhoomi and Apple State of the country is paradise for the tourists round the year. The State is bestowed with matchless nature's splendor with its lush green valleys, snow covered Himalayan ranges, a serene environment and rich cultural heritage. To sustain the unique beauty and environment with global appeal the State is promoting eco-tourism activities with the sole objective of preserving the natural environment and promote community bases eco-tourism which is ecologically sustainable, financially viable, culturally acceptable and beneficial to the local community.

Mountain regions are important destinations of global tourism. Snow cover and pristine mountain landscapes are the principal attractions for tourism in these regions. The State is rich in natural and man-made heritage. Himachal Pradesh is one of the top five tourist destinations in the country. Much of the tourism related activities are concentrated in four major hill stations viz. Shimla, Manali, Dharamshala and Dalhousie. Shimla the capital city of the state tops the list with 2,48,5564 Indian and 12,7737 Foreign tourist arrival followed by district Kullu with the tourist arrival of 2,39,5990 Indian and 1,33,707 Foreign. There is no change in the trend as far as arrival of tourists is concerned in various districts of the state since time in report. The bulk of the tourist is not exposed to the country side, dense forest area and virgin natural beauty of the State. This lop-sided growth pattern is worrisome which has made the government to plan and develop the attractions for the tourists and to distribute the inflow of the tourist uniformly in various districts of the State. The central theme of eco-tourism policy (HP Eco-tourism Policy) was formulated by Himachal Pradesh Forest department in 2001. Forest Sector Policy & Strategy 2005 wherein it was stated: "Nature based tourism including wilderness tourism will be promoted in consonance with the eco-tourism policy of the State with an aim to maximize benefits for local communities...

- The government will encourage rural tourism for enhancing rural livelihoods.
- Dispersed tourism will be encouraged to decongest popular destinations and promote equitable benefits.
- Regulatory systems to minimize potential negative impacts of tourism to the forest sector will also be set up."

The above policy statement set the tone for revision of the Himachal Pradesh EcoTourism Policy, 2001. With this back drop the 'Revised Eco-Tourism Policy' was notified in 2005 by Government of Himachal Pradesh. The intent was to ensure that developing booming tourism in the state is environmentally benign, decentralized and that its benefits are equitably distributed—particularly to local rural households. In 2006, the instrument to carry it forward, the HP Ecotourism Society (EcoSoc) was made operative, through required facilitation provided by the HP Forest Department.[13]

After ten years of implementation of this policy there is no change in the distribution pattern of the tourists in the State, the trend of 2010 tourist inflow is same as that of the year 2006.[14] One of the core endeavors of this Policy is to create unique experiences of 'Unforgettable Himachal' by bringing the wilderness of Himachal closer to the tourists visiting the state with adequate safe guards and systems leading to the preservation of these natural resources. The State government has recently launched Home Stay Scheme-2008. The purpose of the scheme is to attract the tourists to lesser known and remote destinations of State. This scheme promotes the new tourism potential in rural areas or in natural habitat and homely atmosphere where domestic and foreign tourists are exposed to local culture, traditions and home cooked food. Till date, 338 Home Stay units have been registered in the State,with the capacity of 891 rooms. Kullu is forerunner with 75 units of Home Stay. This scheme is similar to 'Bed and Breakfast' scheme of ministry of tourism, Government of India. To boost the rural tourism another scheme known as 'Har Goan ki Kahani'(story of every village) has been launched by the government which aims at developing villages of historic importance as tourism villages by providing basic amenities which will acquaint the tourists will the rustic life of the hill State. Besides cataloguing rural folklore under Har Goan Ki Kahani efforts are being made to link up with MNREGA, job creating scheme for improving tourism infrastructure in rural area. The State government has taken initiative to construct and develop eco-parks near temples and religious locations to add new dimension to religious tourism in the hill State. The eco-parks will have all the facilities like offering prayers and meditation.

According to the plan of the government no commercial activities would be allowed in these parks,as they will be utilized purely for spiritual and religious activities. These parks will have plants and trees of various species, which are used for prayers, and various religious rituals.The State government is giving added priority to health tourism, develop health resorts and panchkarma. The State government has embarked upon an ambitious plan to launch water sports activities as tourist destination. The State government has invested Rs 76.37 crore while the private sector contributed Rs 70 crore to ply motorboats and strengthen quality water sports infrastructure in the man made water body. Various proposals of constructing ropeways are undertaken by the government. The ropeways would enable the tourists to use this mode for experiencing virgin locales of the hill State, which are not possible to explore by road route.

Eco-Tourism Policy: A Paradigm Shift Needed

Any policy is to be perceived differently from policy goals, and contains both a strategic statement and a settled course of action to be followed by an institution. The objective of a tourism policy is to provide tools for containing growth of tourism beyond viable, acceptable and sustainable natural, social and economic thresholds. Tourism policy should enable identification and mitigation of impacts. As far as eco-tourism sub sector is concerned, clear planning and control of the sector is a globally identified need. There seems to be only a thin line of difference between tourism and eco-tourism. Often, the difference is more in what you call it than in what you do. Any effort in the direction of policy formulation faces the following questions: who should be involved in policy making, what are the guiding principles, why do we pursue ecotourism, where should it take place and what are the expected outcomes. Expected outcomes of ecotourism depend on government's priorities: it could be conservation, poverty alleviation or generation of foreign exchange. Viewing ecotourism merely as an exclusive foreign exchange earner will end up in missing this route towards sustainability and discount its value as a conservation and livelihood tool. The tragedy of mass tourist-spots digging their own graves and the emerging global market for ethnic and unique experience gave rise to enterprises under the banner of eco-tourism (ET) in various parts of the world. Used as a tool to harvest consumer's surplus in the context of economic growth and environmental degradation, ET practices vary from wildlife and heritage to health and adventure. ET is generally perceived as 'high value low volume enterprise' depending on a few interested tourists with high willingness to pay. Developing countries are gradually realizing that ET can be a livelihood tool for rural communities and can also result in sustainable management of natural resources. The educational and cultural attributes attached to ecotourism adds value to the business and also make us think that it may not be the quantity of tourists but the quality, that we need to address first. Mainstream tourism is geared towards tourist satisfaction and ET on the other hand, has conservation (of nature and culture) and livelihoods (economic and educational benefits) as essential constituents. While it is obvious that tourism should at least be harmless to nature and society, ET needs to be pro-active towards all the four components mentioned above. Mass tourism could be based on pleasure, relaxation, religion or carnivals.

The process of policy formulation should be dynamic in nature reflecting the evolving understanding of the society. Policies may need periodic revisions based on emerging perspectives and techniques. Hence policy formulation benefits from guidelines brought out at different times, at different governance levels and by different agencies. The policy being recommended should find its origin in existing practices of the area, policies and guidelines both within and outside the country. Nevertheless it is realized that eco-tourism is a vast business domain having wide repercussions on the socio-ecological fabric of an economy. Therefore, it is time to develop the guidelines into clearer regulations, strategies and action plans. While guidelines can be national, policies need to reflect state-specific needs and imperatives of ET. Hence these recommendations provide space for regions and communities to innovate and to retain their ecological and cultural integrity. The only document available with regard to ecotourism policy at national level is the Ecotourism Policy and Guidelines 1998 which identifies key players in Ecotourism as: Government, Developers/operators and suppliers, Visitors, Host community, NGOs and Research Institutions. It also prescribes operational guideline. It lays out cardinal principles suggesting the importance of involvement of local communities, minimizing the conflicts between livelihoods and tourism, environmental and socio-cultural carrying capacities. It also perceives that ET should be part of integrated development of the area. It emphasizes the role of careful planning in infrastructure development and a detailed benefit cost analysis prior to implementation. It talks about standards, continuous monitoring and codes of conduct for visitors. The way to go ahead is to develop these guidelines into action plans, incorporating the missing components: institutional support, monitoring criteria, incentives and regulations.

The eco-tourism policy of the State has various loopholes and weaknesses. This policy fails to explain that it is not only natural systems which bears the brunt of impacts of unregulated and unplanned tourism but also is equally borne by people resources, especially the local communities, their right to decision making, right of access to local natural resources on which much of their livelihood depended on etc. The policy gives a notional idea that the core principle of the policy is that it is developed in close collaboration with the local communities and for their benefit or it is a policy that is by the people and for the people. The presumption of the policy was that the tourism generates wealth and employment, whereas experiences from most tourism ventures show that only marginal numbers of locals are employed by tourism industry. Most of them are employed at the lower rung of job category and people with traditional occupations get displaced due to restrictions imposed on harnessing of local natural resources with a view to promoting tourism. As per estimates, State is adding two times of its population every year, as tourist to the local population. The inflow of the tourists is maximum in the four major hill stations viz. Shimla, Manali, Dharamshala and Dalhousie.

While it accepts that there has been lopsided growth pattern resulting in these four identified places, it does not make any mention about any impacts of such lop-sided growth pattern of tourism. However there has been an underlying effort to build upon the negative experiences of tourism and therefore talk about regulating ecotourism activities in forest areas. The sanctity of eco-sensitive places has to be preserved in order to maintain the value of any tourist destination. The eco-sensitivity of snow covered areas which is main attraction of the tourists in the State should be preserved. The policy should include decisions regarding regulating tourists and vehicles in some eco-sensitive zones.

The policy states that "By involving the local communities, the policy would help improve their prosperity through increased livelihood opportunities. It would also ensure adequate economic returns to the State which would be ploughed back into the environmental system for its proper up keep and maintenance." The Policy while talking about creating community based ecotourism (CBET) does not prescribe or create communities' ownership and control on tourism development. It does not include any democratic decision making and prescribes a top down process. The decision making in tourism and the ownership and control on tourism is safely guarded and passed on to a Special Purpose Vehicle (SPV), created for anchoring the ecotourism activities in the state.

The eco-tourism projects being predominantly situated in forest lands are technically under forest department which has formulated ET policy in consultation with the tourism department of the State. Changing Role of Forest Department (FD) is of major concern that needs to be questioned. In India, the role of FD is made to regulate and restrict human interferences in the forest limits—a model carved upon the colonial principle of usurping control over forest and its resources from indigenous and local communities. Over the years, they have been restricting the indigenous and local communities' access to forest and its resources as well as have failed to stop activities like infrastructure developments like carving out major road and rail projects through the forests, saving forest land from submergence due to building of dams and also tourism. This has resulted in struggles and conflicts with local and indigenous communities who have claimed their rights over that of the FD.

The fact of matter is that only those forests which are virgin or free of human interference in the State remained thick and where their entry was allowed encroachment resulted in destruction of the whole forest. Allowing tourist activities means to develop infrastructure of course with minimum interference with nature. The policy does not vision and plan for such consequences.

In recent times, even passing of the Forest Rights Act (FRA) has not changed the situation. FDs in almost all states have refused to acknowledge FRA and grant the legitimate rights over forest and its resources to the forest dwelling communities. The HP Ecotourism Policy talks about granting the FD powers to control and expand eco-tourism in the state through the formation of the SPV and the same FD being involved in implementing CBET. The scheme seems to be intensifying the control of the FD of HP on forest and its resources, retain control over forests and its resources and now use the same as a source for earning revenue.

In regard to the last objective—To decongest the over-loaded tourist places so that the benefits of tourism are spread to rural areas. It will work in tandem with the Rural Tourism Scheme of the Department of Tourism. It is important to get details of all these projects. Crucial to understand how many of these projects are actually CBET in nature; how are they helping in preserving and protecting the natural heritage and flora and fauna of the state and have led to enhancement in livelihood of the local communities - the major visions of the policy, RTI needs to be applied. Ensure conducting periodic impact assessment studies, whether positive or negative with regard to each project covering—Environmental, Economic and Socio-cultural. It is critical to get more information on this aspect—how many studies have been conducted, at what time intervals, who has conducted them, what has been the process and methodology adopted, at which sites have these been conducted, how have the findings from these studies fed back into the system, etc.

The HP ESoI is an autonomous and independent body, with its main aim being to preserve and protect the natural, historical and cultural heritage of Himachal Pradesh; in order that it acts as a preferred destination for visitors and provides opportunities to promote CBET in Himachal Pradesh, particularly using latest approaches of Participatory Forestry Management, for sustainable development of the forests, thereby generating revenue for the State.

It has been a practice to draw expertise of specialists in any subject to make any processes work more efficiently. In that regard drawing expert knowledge of HP ESoI is understandable. However, what is incomprehensible is that if government did think about drawing knowledge from experts why they have not talked about direct engagement with local communities in planning and implementation of the CBETs. Being the local inhabitants they have maximum knowledge about the local ecosystems, the indigenous method of preserving it and also knowledge about the ground realities the various dynamics in existence in the society, the factors that can help avoid conflict with the local culture and practices etc. The experience from reviewing the ETP in relation to home stays has been the following—"Many rural tourism projects have the idea of homestays as a central part of the tourism product on offer. There are both opportunities and dilemmas related to homestays in a rural setting. On the one hand homestays allow for more decentralised benefits both in terms of economic benefits and in terms of varied and more authentic experiences for tourists. What is interesting is that the rural communities in the ETP seem to be demonstrating a preference for centralized accommodation option rather than the authentic homestay. Would the homestay option be the preferred choice if community members had an opportunity to economically benefit from a centralized accommodation option? It must be acknowledged that the jury is still out on this aspect. There are many social, cultural and economic reasons why homestays will not work or work in a limited manner. Culturally—"hospitality as a commodity"—the idea that one's guest pays for staying in one's home is difficult to accept. Also modes of interaction and the behavior of the tourist are criterion (some community members reported foreign tourists as being more at home than domestic tourists). Policy makers have been a vigorous promoter of the homestay idea—seeing it as an answer to the tourist accommodation deficit. This may work in urban areas - but a strong pursuit of this strategy in rural areas may not be advisable, without more feedback and research." The NGOs and community based organizations with good track record and reputation should be encouraged to take part in the activities related to ET especially for capacity building, promotion and evaluations.[15]

Conclusion

The growing concern for environment, economic and socio-cultural consequences of tourism development has given rise to the influential changes in the industry, which draws increasing attention of sustainable and eco- tourism which combine economic progress, environmental care, and socio-cultural awareness. Scheyvens contends that "even where ecotourism results in economic benefits for a community, it may result in damage to social and cultural systems thus undermining people's overall quality of life." To ascertain the net effect that ecotourism has on local communities, Scheyvens recommends, first, that local communities exert at least some control over proximate ecotourism operations, and that ecotourism's successful delivery of socioeconomic benefits be assessed by a thorough review of economic psychological, social, and political empowerment.

Himachal Pradesh is a favourite tourist destination in all seasons. Despite the fact that government is investing heavy in the industry of tourism, the State could not develop the capacity to empty the pockets of the high class tourists. According to the statistics released by the government State attracts only 0.2 per cent of high class tourists.[16] The concerted efforts are needed to make the tourism sustainable and eco-friendly.

REFERENCES

1. *Climate Change and Tourism—Responding to Global Challenges*, Published by the World Tourism Organization and the United Nations Environment Programme, 2008.
2. David Fennell, Ecotourism: An Introduction (New York, NY: Routledge, 2003) 65.
3. Karen Ziffer, Ecotourism: The Uneasy Alliance(Washington, DC: Conservation International, 1989), cited in "Ecotourism: Paradise Gained, or Paradise Lost?"
4. Relevance of OD Interventions in Ecotourism: An Empirical Study with Reference to Kerala. *Mr. C.D. Mathew and Dr. Kurian Josep in Conference on Tourism in India—Challenges Ahead, 15-17 May 2008, IIMK.*
5. Harmonise: A Step toward an Interoperable E-Tourism Marketplace Author(s): Oliver Fodor and Hannes Werthner Source: *International Journal of Electronic Commerce*, Vol. 9, No. 2 (Winter, 2004/2005), pp. 11-39.
6. Annual Report 2010-11, Ministry of Tourism, Government of India.
7. UNWTO World Tourism Barometer, Interim Update, April, 2011.
8. Tourism Policy 2005, Government of Himachal Pradesh, Shimla.
9. World Tourism Organization (WTO): 2004a, Sustainable Tourism (Martha Honey, Ecotourism & Certification: Setting Standards in Practice (Washington, DC: Island Press, 2002). Development Conceptual Definition, retrieved from the Web-site of the World Tourism Organization, http://www.world-tourism.org.

10. Martha Honey, Ecotourism & Certification: Setting Standards in Practice, Washington, DC: Island Press, 2002.
11. Eco-tourism in India, Policy and Guidelines, Ministry of Tourism, Government of India, 1998.
12. Quebec Declaration on Ecotourism," World Ecotourism Summit, accessed July 20, 2007 at www.world-tourism.org/sustainable/IYE/quebec/anglais/declaration.html.
13. Ecotourism in Himachal Pradesh—The Way Forward by Jasjit Singh Walia, Ecoclub issue, 93.
14. Notification of Department of Tourism & Civil Aviation, Govt of Himachal Pradesh, 2010.
15. Who Really Benefits from Tourism? EQUATIONS Critique on Tourism Working Paper Series section-1, 2010–2011.
16. Dainik Bhasker, Chandigarh, July 31, 2011 p. 3.

10

Introduction—Significance of Parliament, Constitutional Provisions & Tourism

S. Prabhakar

Today, India has earned the glory of being the largest working parliamentary democracy in the world. The founding fathers of the Constitution of India opted for a parliamentary form of Government in which Parliament is the supreme legislative body and the Executive is accountable to Parliament which exercises control over the formulation and implementation of both domestic and foreign policies. This is clearly mentioned in Clause (3) of Article 75 of the Constitution which proclaims that "the Council of Ministers shall be collectively responsible to the House of the People."

Parliament's main function is to legislate. Presently, due to coalition politics, Parliament is not able to contribute adequately in this sphere. Government has to take all its coalition partners with it if it wants to implement any scheme or programme. In the process, it faces many hurdles. Hence, avenues for revitalizing Parliament's contribution to democracy and nation building are far and wide. Certainly, Parliament and parliamentary debates can be made more vibrant by merely bringing before Parliament more important concerns of public for discussion and for finding solutions. Parliament's time can be used in a meaningful manner to highlight peoples' issues or concerns of farmers, and having threadbare discussions on issues involving education, trade, environment, business, communications, information technology, foreign policy, tourism, health, housing *et al.* More participation of Members in Parliamentary debates would bring out the finer elements of issues having impact on people.

Parliament wields enormous power in the governance of the country. The actions of government can be questioned and scrutinized by Parliament in its functioning. Parliament has been equipped with many constitutional provisions to take up issues concerning the policies, schemes, programmes and plans of the government. These provisions should be made to more use. Parliament should play an intensive and apex role in the ratification of International Treaties. At present, Executive ratifies the International Treaties. By changing this trend, we can certainly revitalize Parliament's contribution to democracy.

Parliament of India is the highest legislative body representing the people in implementing the provisions of Constitution and its goals. Indian Parliament has earned the glory of being the largest working parliamentary democracy in the world. The founding fathers of the Constitution of India opted for a parliamentary form of Government in which Parliament is the supreme legislative body and the Executive is accountable to Parliament which exercises control over the formulation and implementation of both domestic and foreign policies.

Tourism is the largest service industry with a contribution of 6.23 per cent of the GDP and 8.78 per cent of the total employment in India. Tourism is one of the major engines of economic growth. It leads to employment, and erases poverty eradication. It is one of the main sources of foreign exchange earners. Its role is strategic in nature. India has immense potential of tourism. There cannot be two opinions on this remark. To start visiting tourist places in India, it would take a lifetime and still there would be a lot of tourist destinations left out. Such is the vastness of tourism landscape of the country. Every State of the country is blessed with huge tourism potential. There may be many countries which are rich in one or two aspects but India is rich in every respect—be it breathtaking monuments, temples, hill resorts, palaces, landscapes, mountainous regions, dense forests, waterfalls, etc. It is for this reason that India has been voted as the 7th best destination in the world by the Conde Nast Readers' Travel Awards, 2010. It is by no means a mean achievement.

One cannot find such a variety of tourism in any other country of the world. We have every conceivable type of tourism —adventure tourism, pilgrim tourism, eco-tourism, rural tourism, cruise tourism, medical tourism, wellness tourism, heliport tourism, wildlife and forest tourism, tourism, Buddhist tourism, tribal cultural tourism, etc.

It is worthwhile to quote here what Max Muller said once. I quote:

> *"If we were to look over the whole world to find out the country most richly endowed with all the wealth, power and beauty which nature can bestowed—in some parts a veritable paradise on Earth—I should point to India.*
> *If I were asked under what sky the human mind has most fully developed some of its choicest gifts—I should point to India."*

Mark Twain, an American author, on India said:

> *"The one land that all men desire to see and having seen once, by even a glimpse, would not give the glimpse for all the shows of all the rest of the globe combined."*

Though there has been a decline in foreign visitors due to global slowdown, terrorist activities, H1N1 influenza pandemic, etc. there is no apprehension that foreign visitors would increase in the months ahead. With the tourism potential in our country, we could turn this trend. In fact, there has been an increase in Foreign Tourist Arrivals in 2010 as compared to 2009. We can further manifold the huge potential in the tourism sector if we develop our tourism infrastructure as we did before the start of the XIX Commonwealth Games in New Delhi.

We could earn Foreign Exchange Earnings during 2010 to the tune of Rs. 64,889 crore as compared to in 2009 when we could earn only Rs. 54,960 crore. We have huge potential in the tourism sector. There cannot be two opinions about that. Efforts are being made by different stakeholders to tap that. In all this, Parliament has a deciding role in steering through the tourism sector in the right direction.

Parliamentary Inputs on Tourism

Parliament displayed keen interest in India's tourism sector. Parliament's intervention in the form of seeking information from the Ministry of Tourism through Questions is one of the major avenues. Department Related Parliamentary Standing Committee and Consultative Committee for the Ministry of Tourism are the other areas where Executive is made accountable to Parliament. Other parliamentary devices like Matters Raised under Rule 377, Zero Hour, Half Hour Discussion, Demands for Grants of the Ministry, etc. too play a prominent role in bringing to the fore parliamentary inputs for the public at large. These are the avenues meant for the Members of Parliament to discuss in depth as to what Ministry of Tourism is implementing. Hence, it would not be an exaggeration if we say that Parliament has a definite role in the framing of tourism policy or tourism sector.

Apart from constitutional provisions, a number of opportunities exist for Members of Parliament to discuss the role of the Government in developing the tourism sector of the country. Parliament exercises budgetary control by debating the Demands for Grants of Ministry of Tourism.

In addition, Parliamentary initiatives and suggestions would help the Government to formulate various policy and programs. They are expected to affect vitally the broad orientation, detailed formulation, and implementation of tourism policy.

Apart from Parliament, we have a Ministry of Tourism, Parliamentary Standing Committee on Tourism and Consultative Committee on Tourism too plays its part in implementing the National Tourism Policy of 2002 and discussing the policy issues and various plans, schemes and programs of the Ministry of Tourism in detail, apart from other issues brought up before it from time to time. The key objectives of the National Tourism Policy are positioning and maintaining tourism development as a national priority activity; enhancing and maintaining the competitiveness of India as a tourism destination; improving India's existing tourism products and expanding these to meet new market requirements; creation of world class infrastructure; and developing sustained and effective marketing plans and programs. These objectives have been elaborated in the National Tourism Policy.[1]

Ministry of Tourism in the Government of India is the apex Ministry to overlook the tourism sector in the country. It has a major role in formulating policies and achieving stated objectives. Its initiatives have an impact on the tourism scene as a whole.

Ministry of Tourism

Ministry of Tourism is the nodal agency to formulate national policies and programs for the development and promotion of tourism. To fulfill this, the Ministry consults and collaborates with other stakeholders in the sector including various Central Ministries/agencies, the State Governments/Union Territories and the representatives of the private sector.[2]

Ministry's major functions are formulating policy matters, planning, regulation, extending cooperation and external assistance, taking care of infrastructure development, human resource development, publicity, marketing, etc.

The annual budgetary allocation for the Ministry of tourism was Rs. 1,500 crore for 2010-11. For 2009-10, it was Rs. 950 crore. It is certainly not a significant amount considering the status of tourism sector in the country. Though India's performance in tourism sector has shown a growth from 2.38 million in 2002 to 5.28 million in 2008 as regards foreign tourist arrivals, however, the numbers declined to 5.11 million in 2009 which is about 3.3 percent less than that of the previous year.[3] Foreign exchange earnings from tourism increased from Rs.15,064 crore in 2002 to Rs.54,960 crore in 2009.

Under the Ministry of Tourism, there is an Attached or Subordinate Office—India Tourism Development Corporation (ITDC), there are 6 Autonomous Bodies, Boards and Corporations; two Statutory Bodies and a Council—National Council for Hotel Management and Catering Technology.

The Ministry has in place a National Tourism Policy of 2003. The policy document seeks to enhance employment potential within the tourism sector and to foster economic integration through developing linkages with other sectors. It broadly attempts to—position tourism as a major engine of economic growth; harness the direct and multiplier effects of tourism for employment generation, economic development and providing impetus to rural tourism; focus on domestic tourism as a major driver of tourism growth; position India as a global brand to take advantage of the burgeoning global travel trade and the vast untapped potential of India as a destination; acknowledges the critical role of private sector with government working as a pro-active facilitator and catalyst; create and develop integrated tourism circuits based on India's unique civilization, heritage, and culture in partnership with States, private sector and other agencies; and ensure that the tourist to India gets physically invigorated, mentally rejuvenated, culturally enriched, spiritually elevated and "feel India from within".[4]

Ministry has enhanced focus on rural tourism. Rural tourism is providing a varied and vivid experience for visitors, both domestic and foreign. As per the newspaper report,[5] Ministry would carry out an audit of its Rural Tourism Projects to ensure that this important initiative is not lost. Union Tourism Minister, Subodh Kant Sahai has said that the key for development of tourism in future would be research, collaboration, innovation, public private partnership and sustainability.[6]

There is also a huge potential and a need to push Buddhist heritage sites. Andhra Pradesh has 140 sites of Buddhist importance including Amaravathi, one of the oldest Buddhist heritage sites in the country.[7] We can attract tourists from Japan, Sri Lanka and other Asian countries to these Buddhist sites and earn considerable foreign exchange.

One of the main activities of the Ministry of Tourism during the last year and before that was its preparedness for the XIX Commonwealth Games in the first fortnight of October, 2010.

Ministry has signed Memorandum of Understanding (MoU)/Agreement on Tourism Cooperation with 46 countries.[8] According to the Annual Report 2010-11,[9] in 2010, Foreign Tourist Arrivals in India were 5.58 as compared to 2009 when it was only 5.17 million. This shows a growth of 8.1 per cent.

Apart from the Ministry, Department-related Parliamentary Standing Committee on Tourism play a significant and decisive role in furthering the interests of tourism sector in the country. Its role cannot either be overlooked or brushed away. It has a definitive role and its role have been making an indelible impact on the overall tourism growth of the country.

Department-related Parliamentary Standing Committee on Tourism

In the Department-related Parliamentary Standing Committee on Tourism, discussion on demands for grants of the Ministry of Tourism, and other related issues concerning the national tourism policy of the country take place. As such, Parliamentary Standing Committee on Transport, Tourism and Culture plays a very major role in scrutinizing the Demands for Grants of the Ministry of Tourism, various activities of the Ministry and any other emerging issues from time to time.

It is a Parliamentary Committee serviced by Rajya Sabja Secretariat headed by Sitaram Yechury. It has 31 Members—10 from Rajya Sabha and 21 from Lok Sabha. In the Committee set up, discussions are more focused, as top officials of the Ministry of Tourism depose before these committees and the

Members of the Committees generally get all relevant information from the top officials then and there. Such information can be termed as authentic and valuable. It would not be out of place to state here the remarks of an expert on Indian foreign policy—"With the increasing time lost in the pandemonium inside the halls of Parliament, Committees seem to be the only escape buzz in which issues involved in Bills are discussed in detail, without any disruption."[10]

Members of Parliament thus get ample opportunities for expressing their views in the Committee to thoroughly examine and analyse national as well as emerging issues. The recommendations made in reports of the Committee are not mandatory for the Government to accept *in toto*. They are advisory in nature. But in the Committees, Members of Parliament take up pressing issues involving the tourism policy and sector and have healthy and threadbare discussions, which would have an impact on the Government's policies and decisions.

In its Report,[11] Department-Related Parliamentary Standing Committee on Transport, Tourism & Culture on Demands for Grants (2010-11) of Ministry of Tourism has observed that the tourism resources of India have the potential to generate significantly higher levels of demand from the domestic and international markets, and if exploited in a sustainable manner, it can prove to be an engine of growth for the economy. The Committee, therefore, recommends that the Government should provide more funds for promoting and tapping the vast and varied potential—modern and ancient.

Let me briefly analyze the recommendations of the Ministry on the Demands for Grants (2010-11) of the Ministry of Tourism.[12] It is stated that the Ministry does not provide a clear picture about actual performance/achievements during a particular year. It also remarked that domestic tourism is getting comparatively lesser importance by the Ministry, which leaves the most local tourism potential unexploited.[13]

The Report went on to state that there is a need for more

infrastructure development, apart from undertaking a review of target set for each and every projects and also there is a need for a more scientific approach.[14]

In its Report,[15] Department-Related Parliamentary Standing Committee on Transport, Tourism and Culture, while examining the action taken replies of the Ministry of tourism, noticed:

> "That to a large number of its recommendations, the Ministry had replied that it has forwarded the recommendations to the concerned agencies. The Committee was of the view that the Ministry of tourism should have obtained the responses of those agencies and provided to it for taking a view. By not doing so, the Ministry has not taken the Committee's recommendations as seriously as they deserved. It expressed its concern about inordinate delay in submitting action taken replies and also about not giving proper/complete replies."[16]

The above remarks of the Committee amply bring out the concern of Parliament and also brought to fore the measures to be taken by the Executive to act on the comments, recommendations and suggestions of the Legislature with due diligence.

Apart from the Department-related Parliamentary Standing Committee on Tourism, we also have a Consultative Committee of the Ministry of Tourism. Its existence serves a purpose.

Consultative Committee of the Ministry of Tourism

Consultative Committee for the Ministry of Tourism is chaired by the Minister for Tourism, Subodh Kant Sahai; the Co-chairperson is the Minister of State in Tourism, Sultan Ahmad. There are 14 Members from Lok Sabha and 4 from Rajya Sabha. There are a few permanent Special Invitees but they are not Members of the Consultative Committee. Since the beginning of 15th Lok Sabha, the Consultative Committee has met four times—on 6.11.2009 to discuss the general overview of tourism; on 9.3.2010 on tourism and Commonwealth Games; on 24.10.2010 on tourism in India with particular reference to ecotourism; and on 14.12.2010 on Swarna Jayanti Shahri Rozgar Yojana (SJSRY).

Apart from the Department-related Standing Committee on tourism, Parliament also has a Consultative Committee for the Ministry of Tourism which helps its Members to know first-hand information and details from the Minister of Tourism as well as briefings from the higher officials of the Ministry.

Parliament, moreover, can influence the formation of national tourism policy through its Consultative Committee on Tourism also. As its name indicates, it is expected to perform a purely consultative function. The meetings of the Consultative Committee do, however, serve one useful purpose. Since the proceedings of the meetings are confidential, Ministers can give details of international situation to the makers of India's foreign policy, which cannot be disclosed elsewhere.

The Consultative Committee of Parliament for the Ministry of Tourism is thus an important institutional link between Parliament and implementation of various schemes, policies, programmes and plans of the Ministry of Tourism. If it is allowed to work properly, this can be a useful instrument for Parliament to influence the Government's decision on issues relating to women empowerment. As its name indicates, it is expected to perform a purely consultative function. The meetings of the Consultative Committee do, however, serve one useful purpose. Since the proceedings of the meetings are confidential, Ministers can part with details and situations emanating on a certain policy or issue, which cannot be disclosed elsewhere. The Consultative Committee of Parliament on Tourism is thus an important institutional link between Parliament and Government.

The meetings of the Consultative Committee, of course, serve one useful purpose. Since the proceedings of the meetings are confidential, ministers can give details of international situations and India's foreign policy which cannot be disclosed elsewhere. Committee meetings thus serve to give all members of parliament who are interested an opportunity to hear all the facts and details which the Minister can give to the Committee but not on the floor of the House in the national interest. However, since the Committee's advice has no binding effect, the Government may not act in accordance with the Committee's recommendations. But over the years, we can see that many of the recommendations of the Committee have been accepted by the Government of the day.

Apart from the Committees, Parliamentary Debates bring forth the prevailing situation in the tourism sector and also provides an insight into various activities that are going on in the tourism scene of the country. Among the Parliamentary weapons or provisions, Parliamentary Debates. mostly in the form of questions, play an important role, as it touches the whole gamut of issues concerned the tourism sector.

Debates in the 15th Lok Sabha

Wide ranging issues relating to tourism sector have been debated in Lok Sabha during the 15th Lok Sabha. Till 10th December, 2010, 143 (19 Starred—oral and 124 Unstarred—written) questions have been asked which sought information from the Ministry of Tourism. Subject ranged from health tourism, special package for development of tourism, salary hike in tourism sector, tourism in North Eastern Region, cruise tourism, impact of Advisories on tourism, eco tourism, growth in tourism, space tourism, wildlife and forest tourism, Buddhist tourism, international cooperation in the tourism sector, promotion of rural tourism, UNDP assisted rural tourism projects, tourism policy, literature on tourism, report on tourism in the Commonwealth Games, schemes for promotion of eco-tourism, tourism infrastructure, medical tourism, beach tourism, showcasing tourism potential abroad, tourism in different States, code of conduct for safe tourism, tribal cultural tourism, assistance to tourism sector from Asian Development Bank, etc.

According to the reply given by the Ministry of Tourism,[17] the estimated number of foreign tourist arrivals (FTAs) in India during the last 6 years, that is, May-October, 2009, is 2.19

million, which is 2.4 per cent less than the FTAs during the corresponding period of 2008. The decline was ascribed to the H1N1 pandemic, global slowdown, etc. which was prevailing at that point in time.

Likewise, in Rajya Sabha, 221 questions (both Starred and Unstarred) were asked by Members in 2010 on wide ranging issues concerning tourism sector. For examples, proposals from different States, decline in foreign tourists, foreign tourists in India, medical tourism in India, allocation of funds to Maharashtra, tourism infrastructure in States, tourism potential in different States, funds for Incredible India programme, exploitation at tourist destinations, domestic tourists, spurt in foreign tourist arrivals, tourism infrastructure in the country, etc.

These interventions in Lok Sabha had brought to the fore the issue of nuclear non-proliferation. This debate has helped India in evolving a strategy to deal with the nuclear non-proliferation with the rest of the world. The Government on its part has come out with the factual information on the issues asked by the Members. Debates certainly throws light on the issues in vogue and helps Parliament to know as to what the Government is thinking on an issue and as to how it is going to resolve them. However, certain limitations do persists in the functioning of the parliamentary initiatives.

Limitations

Another pertinent point to be brought out is that only a miniscule portion of the policy aspect is scrutinized by the committees with the result majority of the important aspects of different ministries and departments are left out and never come in the domain of discussion and debate in the committees.

Though the recommendations of the Department-Related Parliamentary Standing Committee are not obligatory or mandatory on the part of Government to accept or implement, of late, a redeeming feature is that many of the recommendations of the Committee are accepted by the Government.

Due to huge business workload on Parliament and the

number of days of Session is limited to 80 or 85—of late, it has met even lesser number of days, particularly in 2008 and in 2006 and 2011, when States elections where held—serious and discernible discussion specifically on tourism fail to find a place in the agenda of the business of Parliament.

For instance, in the Monsoon Session of 15th Lok Sabha, Lok Sabha had 26 sittings spread over 136 hours and 10 minutes, out of which 45 hours were lost due to disruptions. This was cited by hon. Speaker, Meira Kumar: "Parliament is meant for debates and discussions; any matter permissible under the Constitution and Rules of Procedures can be discussed here. But the trend of disruption the proceedings days on end is alarming, and, if not checked, will ultimately lead to unforeseen circumstances."[18] Sittings of both the Houses during Monsoon Session were extended by 2 days. Both Houses sat late on several days to make up for the lost time—Lok Sabha worked for 94 per cent of the scheduled hours and Rajya Sabha for 100 per cent.[19]

Roadmap for Action

Parliament is bestowed by our Constitution with powers to oversee the functioning of the executive. This very purpose would be defeated if the sittings of Parliament are few and far between. Efforts should be made to evolve a consensus on not only having nearly 100 days of sitting but also to ensure that there will not be any stalling of parliamentary proceedings.

During the Winter Session of Parliament in 2010, Lok Sabha could transact business for a day only, that too, on the first day. It could not transact rest of the days of the Session because of lack of consensus on setting up of Joint Parliamentary Committee (JPC) between the Government and the Opposition parties. However, in the Budget Session of 2011, both Government and Opposition could reach an understanding concerning constituting Joint Parliamentary Committee on 2G Scam and the Session started functioning smoothly in the Budget Session of 2011.

Lok Sabha Speaker, Meira Kumar has expressed her concern and anguish over collapse of Question Hour as it would dent Parliament's image. In this direction, Lok Sabha Rules Committee has carried out an amendment in the rules to prevent collapse of Question hour. The Committee has also taken a series of decisions to ensure that the proceedings of the House were not stalled for some reason or the other.

Conclusion

Discussions in Parliament, without any iota of doubt, helped in finding out solutions. A general awareness is always created and a message goes out to the nation whenever parliamentary discussion takes place and the debate is telecast live in the Lok Sabha Television and highlights are shown in the national network and other prominent private channels. Debates in Parliament would undoubtedly help to know the issue in correct perspective. Editorials are written and a strong public stance is formed through all parliamentary inputs in the electronic and print media. Efforts should be made to make parliamentary debates and interventions more effective. There has invariably been consensus in Parliament on matters concerning the national interests.

After the 2008 Mumbai attacks, tourism industry is showing promise in terms of growth and with the vast improvement of infrastructure in the tourism sector, we could expect that tourism industry would flourish in the years to come and India would be treated as the most sought after destination by the foreign countries. We could see vast improvement in the infrastructure, tourism is bound to flourish as has been the case in 2010 when we could see substantial growth in the tourism sector as compared to 2009, particularly in regard to arrivals of Foreign Tourists.

Recent serial bomb blasts in Mumbai on 13th July, 2011 would certainly create a sort of panic among the tourists, particularly the foreign tourists visiting our country. Renewed an innovative efforts should be put in place to ensure that such dastardly acts by criminal elements are not repeated under any circumstances. There is nothing wrong in emulating the United States of America, which could ensure another terrorist attack after 9/11. India too should create a foolproof safety and security plan of action to ensure that such terrorists incidents do not recur in Indian soil, which would undoubtedly help to boost our growth in the tourist sector.

Though Government is responsible to Parliament, Parliament normally played only an advisory role. Parliament, of course, had an educative impact and discussions in Parliament have had the result of showing the world how Indians think. Parliament also educated people and helped in making tourism policy the way it should be framed.

Parliament has shown keen interest and has been able to influence policy outputs to a considerable extent whenever the Members sought information from the Government in Parliament. This has been highlighted in this paper. Hence, one can hardly deny the fact that Parliament contributes in its own ways to the Government's efforts to meet the challenges being faced by the tourism sector.

REFERENCES

1. National Tourism Policy, 2002, Department of Tourism, Ministry of Tourism, Government of India.
2. Annual Report, 2009-10, Ministry of Tourism, Government of India.
3. 154th Report of the Department-Related Parliamentary Standing Committee on Transport, Tourism & Culture on Demands for Grants (2010-11), Rajya Sabha Secretariat, New Delhi, April, 2010.
4. Document of National Tourism Policy, 2002, Ministry of Tourism, Government of India.
5. *The Pioneer*, New Delhi, dated 31st March, 2011.
6. Ibid.
7. *The Indian Express*, New Delhi, dated 20th May, 2011.
8. http://164.100.47.132/LssNew/psearch/OResult15.aspx?gref=95896, Retrieved on 2.14.2011.
9. Annual Report 2010-11, Ministry of Tourism, Government of India.
10. Interview with A.K. Ray, Professor of Political Science (Retd.), Jawaharlal Nehru University, in New Delhi on February 2, 2008. However, K. Natwar Singh, the former External Affairs Ministers and the the Rajya Sabha Member expressed the view in his interview on January 24, 2008 that "Committees have not

functioned as well as they should. There is a room for improvement."

11. 154th Report of the Department-Related Parliamentary Standing Committee on Transport, Tourism & Culture on Demands for Grants (2010-11), Rajya Sabha Secretariat, New Delhi, April, 2010.
12. 154th Report of the Department-Related Parliamentary Standing Committee on Transport, Tourism & Culture (Rajya Sabha Secretariat: April, 2010: New Delhi)

11

Tourism and Regional Cooperation in South Asia

Sudhir Kumar Singh

SAARC came into being in 1985 to promote regional cooperation within South Asia. After NAFTA it is one of the youngest regional organizations. In post-cold war international system, economic relationship has emerged as new pawn of the sustainability of good relations even between adversaries. It is true in the case of China-India relationship which has surpassed their bi-lateral trade with 60 billion $ in the FY of 2010-2011 and slated to touch 100 billion $ by 2015. It has been predicted that India and China will be able to sustain its preset pace of economic development which is around 8-9 per cent and unprecedented into the contemporary world due to turbulent contemporary global economy. Their economies are bound to aggravate in a phenomenon manner and that will be translated into enormous trade and commerce between China and India. Both countries are still considered as adversaries despite high profile bi-lateral trade because this bonhomie on trade front could not be emulate into strategic and political arena. There are many parallel example of this kind like India-Japan relationship and China-Pakistan relationship where despite less trade they have an excellent relationship on strategic and political arena.

Even the United States and China or Japan and China have enormous volume of trade but they don't have excellent strategic and political relationship. These adversaries have not been able to maintain a good relationship at strategic and political front despite maintaining good relationship on economic front merely because their interests are not converging on strategic and political front. Two and half millennia ago, the great Indian thinker, Kautilaya had stated in his seminal book, Arthsastra that commonality of interests is the basic determinant of foreign policy. His notion was that enemy's enemy is friend. Those tenets of foreign policy still prevail despite barrage of changes into context of the international system as the cardinal value of the international politics not in today context but in future too.

But one thing is perfect that the process of globalization, which has taken a new lease of life in post cold war scenario, has ensured that even adversaries countries will be engaged into economic relationship. They could maintain adversity into strategic and political arena but could cooperate on economic front. The above mentioned examples are candidly supporting these claims. But this newly emerged notion of globalization could not be replicated in the case of India-Pakistan relationship. Both since their inception have confronted with turbulent relationship. Both countries have minimum bi-lateral economic relationship despite enormous potential due to geographical proximity. Although SAARC was proposed by Bangladesh leader Zia-Ur-Rahman but all South Asian Countries namely India, Pakistan, Bangladesh, Sri Lanka, Nepal, Bhutan and Maldives became the members of the organization. Recently Afghanistan has also been included as the new member and there are many observers including China and United States, Iran etc. there are many theories for the regional cooperation but dominant one advocates for a better coordination at the regional level to maximize the benefits due to gamut of commonalities among regional countries. Regional trade are beneficial for surrounding countries mainly for two reasons, first fright cost is less of the commodities due to geographical proximity to the area and less time consumption is involved into the transfer of goods therefore even raw materials are easily exported/imported. But the biggest beneficiary is the common people because they get due price for their product and without much delay. It strengthens local level economy and thus strengthens the purchasing power capacity of the poorest of the poor. It also enhances people to people exchanges due to gamut of trade activities. These kinds of developments are positive for mitigating trust deficit among traditional adversaries like India and Pakistan or China and India or Japan and China or South and North Korea or United States and China. But it is more perfectly suited for regional countries like ASEAN which has 10 members and cooperating in an excellent manner. In the case of India and Pakistan it is extremely relevant because both countries are sharing barrage of similarities right from food habits to music. If one could locate the actual development which has taken place into the regional blocks since the inception of the idea, it is ample clear that SAARC remains at the bottom. Even NAFTA which came into being after SARRC has achieved excellent landmarks in the area. There are many other obstructive factors which have kept SAARC in this condition but adverse relationship between India and Pakistan have remained pivotal in this direction. One thing is also clear that regional cooperation like SAARC is meant for the economic and cultural cooperation and it has kept strategic relationship away from its ambit. Since its inception, bi-lateral relation between India and Pakistan has been at its lowest level despite many efforts made to normalize it. They have a common boundary and lived together for centuries. They could understand each other's languages and shares many similarities too. But the volume of bi-lateral trade between India and Pakistan despite the huge possibilities at present is at bare minimum. Official trade between the two countries is paltry and studies show bilateral trade can grow to $ 11 billion if steps are taken to streamline business relations. According to latest official data, bilateral trade between two traditional rivals stood at merely $ 1.8 billion in 2009-10.[1]

It is an open secret that without active cooperation between

India and Pakistan, SAARC is really unable to take off. However, it is a fact that in this era of globlisation that no country could ensure their all round sustainable development without involving themselves into regional cooperation. It is abnormally correct for India because India is seeking its place at the global table of governance and it would be push factor if India will engage its immediate neighbors. It is a lesson of history that government can optimize opportunities and enhance their capacity if they join hands and worked together for the elimination of common curse like poverty and illiteracy. SAARC is an umbrella organization of all South Asian countries, which is badly divided. Relations between different countries of the region have been characterized by mutual suspicion and trust deficit. The most striking feature of South Asia is the predominance of India by all counts. The largest country of the region and one of the fastest growing global economies despite worldwide recession, it has the potential to push the SAARC as one of most successful example of the regional cooperation. According to World Development Report, India occupies 78 per cent of the area, and accounts 73 per cent of the population and 80 per cent of the gross domestic product of South Asia. It is an open secret that South Asia is the home of half of the worlds poor. Twenty nine per cent Indians, 33 per cent of the Pakistanis, 42 per cent Nepalese, and of 50 per cent of Bangladeshis live below the poverty line. Equally important, India is at the core of the region, with the rest forming the periphery. Among themselves the SAARC countries have less intra regional economic, political as well strategic relations, which have hamper the prospects of the SAARC as a launching pad of the eradication of some of the existing curse from South Asia like poverty and illiteracy. India has to play a pivotal role if SAARC has to take off properly. India needs to understand that if South Asian region has to develop at par with at least South East Asian models, its role will be extremely important as an engine of growth within South Asia.

Tourism could play an important role besides other's to bring South Asian countries together. There is an ample space for that due to commonalties of many important things including language, culture and religion.

According to international agencies Tourism has become one of the world's largest and fastest growing industries. Over the period 1995-2005, international tourist arrivals grew at an average annual rate of 4.1 per cent, exceeding the 800 million mark in 2005. This outstanding performance can be attributed to several factors, including the following: rising levels of disposable income; improvements in transportation and the introduction of low-cost airline services; easier access to destinations by tourists from traditional source markets and the emergence of new source markets such as China and India; and the diversification of the industry with new market niches, such as cultural tourism, ecotourism and adventure tourism.

During the last 10-year period, the Asia-Pacific region outperformed the rest of the world, with increase in arrivals averaging 6.5 per cent annually, raising its global share of the tourist market from 15.3 per cent in 1995 to 19.2 per cent in 2005. By contrast, the two more mature regions, Europe and the Americas, saw their global shares decrease from 58.3 per cent to 54.8 per cent and from 20.2 per cent to 16.6 per cent respectively.

Tourism can be considered as one of the most remarkable socio-economic phenomena of the twentieth century. From an activity enjoyed by only a small group of relatively well-off people during the first half of the last century, it gradually became a mass phenomenon during the post-World War II period, particularly from the 1970s onwards.[3] It now reaches in increasingly larger number of people throughout the world and can be considered a vital dimension of global integration.[4]

South Asia is home to a solid one-third of the world's population. Some of the best brains that run the world have South Asian roots. The region is home to the highest and the second highest Mountain peaks of the world (Everest and K2). Most of the world's quality water resources are in the region with the river systems originating from the Himalayas. Some of world's best ocean resources (coral reefs of Maldives), beaches

(Coxes Bazaar), and mangrove areas (Sunderbans) are located in the region. Its biodiversity is unmatched (Sinharaja, Chitwan). Home to marvels such as the Taj Mahal, Ajanta, Sigiriya, Timpu, and Taxila, the heritage and cultures of the region date back thousands of years. For centuries, the region has been a hotspot for sea facing nations looking for spices and other riches. It was the playground of several colonial powers, and is now home to almost all of the world's religions. The cuisine of the region is exquisite, and its people are friendly and warm. The South Asian region has the key ingredients to delight its visitors.

Yet, with some 400 million people remaining below the poverty line and 71 million people affected by violence or its threat, most of South Asia remains conflict ridden. Poverty, health, child, and gender-related issues are pulling down the region's image.[5]

In 2007, the South Asian region received less than 1.1 per cent (9.7 million) of the 898 million visitors from around the world (UN World Tourism Organization 2008). In comparison, Europe received 53.5 per cent of the global arrivals, and the Asian region, including East and Southeast Asia, received 19.3 per cent. The volume of arrivals to the Asia Pacific region more than doubled between 2000 and 2007, from 85 million to 198 million (UNESCAP 2008). Within this growth scenario, regrettably, most of South Asia saw only marginal growth, with the exceptions of some significant growth to India and Maldives.

For several decades now, the region has promoted tourism. As far back as the early 1980s, the World Tourism Organization (now UNWTO) set up a Secretariat in Colombo for South Asian Tourism Promotion and attempted to promote the region. This initiative failed because of inadequate support and interest from the individual nations' state tourism organizations. In the 1990s, the SAARC Chambers of Commerce and Industry (SCCI) began a Nepal-based initiative to promote tourism to the region.[6] A special tourism committee was formed and several rounds of meetings were held. A promotional tagline "Magic That Is South Asia" was coined, and talk of a regional tourism year was initiated. It was thought that tourism would improve if private sector business and tourism stakeholders took the lead in moving regional tourism initiatives forward. Several South Asian tourism business and trade marts have been held since the 1990s.

Because of enormous proximity in variety of attractive points, South Asian countries could earn a huge amount from tourism sector. One thing is candidly clear that tourism sector is providing the bread to the most hapless sections of the society. In South Asian context it is abnormally correct. South Asia constitutes 1/5 of the global poor and governments throughout the region have not been able to provide basic amenities to this deprived section of the society.

For democracy it is the life blood to provide all kinds of amenities to the common people with exclusive arrangements for destitute. Kautilaya, the great Indian Philosopher has insisted in his famous book *Arthshastra* that a king must nurture their subject as a new born baby is nurtured by his/her mother. One could trace the origins of democracy and human rights from his writing. He was the prime minister of the greatest Indian empire called Mauryan Empire. We are aware about the fact that monarchy was not accountable for the people because merely it was of the opinion that it derives its legitimacy of rule from the almighty god therefore it is only accountable for god. In democracy, people are the custodian therefore the elected ruler must be accountable for the people and people are most benefited element by all theoretical frameworks. But in reality prevalence of chronic poverty across the globe particularly in less developed and developing countries exclusively in those countries which have adopted democracy as a mode of governance is a blatant denial of the fundamental rights of the common people. In many developing countries it is matter of governance but in majority of them lack of resources and rampant corruption is denying the basic tenets of democracy to the common people. Entire South Asia suited in this situation. Poverty as stated by Amartya Sen is the biggest denial of fundamental human rights and the prevalence of chronic poverty is rampant in South Asia. Since last few decades, South

Asia region is engulfed with worst kind of conflict and violence and needless to say that poverty is the root cause of conflict and violence. We cannot ensure peace and development in South Asia till we will not eliminate poverty.

It almost fits into the Indian context. India is a developing country and recently World Bank has announced that within next two years, India will be surpassing China in GDP growth.[7] Despite being a newly emerged country, India has done tremendous progress in all round development. Today after six decade of our independence, one of the biggest concerns remains and that is inclusion of the marginalized into the mainstreaming process of development. It is one of the most crucial factors, which sustains a kind of unrest in our society. Poverty is a great denial of democracy and human rights. It is true that since last few decades we have been able to upgrade the life standard of 300 million people. But according to the Planning Commission still around 35 per cent people lives below the poverty line. According to the 2011 census, India has 121 crore population and still existing gender gap vindicates the point that gender has been discriminated despite growing literacy and prosperity. Currently 11th Five Year Plan (2007-2012) is in operation. According to the Approach Paper of the 11th Plan "The 11th plan provides an opportunity to restructure policies to achieve a new vision of growth that would be much more broad based and inclusive, bringing about a faster reduction in poverty and helping bridge the divides that are currently the focus of so much attention.[8]

The sector of tourism would be a great panacea for the mitigation of the basic problems in South Asia like poverty and illiteracy. The fact is South Asian regions share common heritage and there are countless sites in these countries which attracts another country's people. Another important factor is it will mitigate the wrong impression of another country. It has the potential to cement the movement of peace throughout South Asia. Besides it will reduce the level of poverty across the region, which remains as the breeding grounds for all bloodshed. It will also strengthen South Asian region as an identity and they could search a common solution for their variety of common problem. Needless to say that it will promote democracy and human rights throughout the region therefore tourism as a sector could bring real peace in South Asia. We should not forget that in comparison with South East Asia, we are just earning a nominal resources from tourism although potential is much and if could be properly developed it could contest with the European income.

The promotion of intra tourism within SAARC countries will be a great facilitator for stability and peace within this region. The greatest obstacle is turbulent India-Pakistan relations. But some positive things are emerging. Despite the elimination of Al-Qaeda founder, Osama Bin Laden in May 2011, it is an open secret that tentacles of terror are still ruling the roost in Pakistan and in Afghanistan. Pakistan probably emerged as the real loser in it's own game to use terror as an instrument for the pursuance of its national interest. Pakistan has lost 35,000 people and 5,000 security forces while fighting with terror. But Pakistan must realize that there are elements within its system which has not only provided safe heaven to terror icon like Osama Bin Laden but still hosting many terror czars. Through people to people cooperation, Pakistan could mitigate the bad impression which has spread about its image. Remarkably there is hardly any huge protest by common people in Pakistan against the elimination of Osama Bin Laden. It vindicates the fact that common Pakistani has nothing to do with the terror groups and they want peace and development. While assuming the power Pakistani President Asif Ali Zardari had stated that his government will put burning issues including Kashmir into back and push commerce and trade to nurture the positive bi-lateral relationship with India. But due to Mumbai terror attack (2008) this spirit could not be promoted. After the elimination of Osama Bin Laden (May 2011) former Prime Minister and one of the most popular politicians of Pakistan, Nawaz Sharif has stated that Pakistan should forget to perceive India as an enemy no more. He has stated that if Pakistan has to cope with the prosperity which has been provided by the process of globalization, it has to nurture good relationship with India. It is one of the most positive statements made by the Pakistani leaders in recent years.

It is an open secret that Pakistan has to cope with the development at par with India to provide basic amenities to its poorest of the poor. In 1960's Pakistan was treated at par with South Korea in development. Today Pakistan is counted with the less developed countries of the world. It is also recognized as the breeding grounds for international terrorism.

Proper ambience needs to be created by Pakistan to provide basic amenities to its poorest of the poor, which constitutes almost 1/3 of its entire population. Tourism could be a great facilitator in this regard. Tourism has the potential to provide basic amenities to the poorest of the poor in some extent to the poorest of the poor to both India and Pakistan. Additionally it will serve the great purpose of the mitigation of rumor mongering machinery that India is a devil and will swallow Pakistan and vice-versa. Both countries have common cultural heritage and generations' memory. Language and music and many other things are common therefore it could be a push factor for the promotion of mutual trust between two of the most hostile countries of the globe. Both countries are confronting the problem of trust deficit and it needs to be eliminated. Being the big brother, it is Indian duty to pursue the matter. Already SAARC has provided the platform and subsequent SAARC summits have passed many resolutions for the promotion and protection of the cause. India has already done this with Nepal, Bhutan, Maldives and Sri Lanka and at some extent with Bangladesh. South Asia constitutes 1/5 of the global humanity and the same ratio of poor people also live in the region. Since millennia, this area has remained the cradles of civilization but due to non-cooperation among SAARC it has not been able to cope with the pace of development with developed countries.

There is an utmost need to build a South Asian identity based on diversity and a common history. In ancient times, India was called Golden Bird and majority of the present South Asian

Countries were provinces of that India. At the global level India has achieved a big place which it needs to sustain to further strengthen its global status. For this it must extent all possible relaxation under the rubric of SAARC to tourism sector in particular and rest issues in general. It is an open secret that till the atmosphere of mutual cooperation will not be established within SAARC, real progress on tourism seems to be an utopian idea. We have to cement a common identity within SAARC based on our millennia year old common heritage. Ultimately India will be the beneficiary due to its enormous economy and relative better infrastructure and edge on science and technology. Promotion of tourism sector will not only be able to promote the industry but will be a great facilitator of peace and stability within the region. It will promote common composite culture and music. For sustainable development, peace is badly required. Promotion of tourism within South Asia could be beneficial to all countries but the biggest beneficiaries will be India and Pakistan. They must seize this ample opportunity to eradicate all curses of humanity from this region.

The SAARC has provided ample space in this direction. The importance of tourism had been recognized since early days of SAARC. The Leaders during the Second Summit held at Bangalore in 1986 underlined that concrete steps should be taken to facilitate tourism in the region. A Technical Committee on Tourism was created in 1991. During the First Meeting of the Technical Committee on Tourism held in Colombo in October 1991, an Action Plan on Tourism was formulated. First Meeting of the SAARC Tourism Ministers was held in Colombo in September 1997. It adopted Colombo Resolution and approved a number of important activities. In 1999, the task of promoting tourism was assigned to the SAARC Chamber of Commerce & Industry (SCCI) Tourism Council.

The Twenty-fourth Session of the Council of Ministers (Islamabad, 2-3 January 2004) approved establishment of the Working Group on Tourism. The First Meeting was held in Colombo in August 2004. The Working Group on Tourism prepared Plan of Activities which includes promotion of SAARC as a common tourist destination, to encourage private sector in promoting regional cooperation in tourism, human resource development, promotion of South Asia identity through tourism, cultural and eco-tourism development. The Working Group was authorized to periodically review implementation of this Action Plan.

During the Thirteenth Summit (Dhaka, 12-13 November 2005), the Leaders stressed that continued efforts would be made by the Member States at all levels to promote people-to-people contact by facilitating travel among SAARC countries, promotion of youth exchanges in culture and sports, promotion of intra-SAARC tourism, establishment of linkages among professional bodies and through adoption of other concrete measures. They decided to launch 2006 as "South Asia Tourism Year." They directed their Ministers for Tourism to meet at an early date and elaborate a plan of activities to be undertaken during the year 2006.

The Tourism Ministers who met at Cox's Bazar (Bangladesh) in May 2006, adopted the *Cox's Bazar SAARC Action Plan on Tourism*. Second Meeting of the Working Group on Tourism, held in Colombo on 3-4 July 2006, recommended that for promoting SAARC as common tourist destination (i) national airlines may use SAARC logo on aircrafts and other promotional brochures; (ii) national airlines may also use SAARC flag with their own flag as well as national flags at their offices and (iii) the Head of Mission representing the Chair of SAARC will organize special events in celebration of SAARC Charter Day on 8 December, with focus on promoting tourism.

In the Fourteenth Summit the Heads of State or Government while noting the cultural and social ties among the SAARC countries, based on common history and geography, reiterated that the future of peoples of South Asia is interlinked. They stressed the importance of people-to-people contact as a key constituent in regional connectivity. They acknowledged the importance of intra-regional tourism and increased exchanges, particularly among the youth, civil society, and parliamentarians. They agreed to take measures to charge nationals of SAARC

Member States fees for entry into archeological and heritage sites as applicable to their own nationals.

The Heads of State or Government during the **Fifteenth Summit** underscored the vital contribution that tourism could afford to the economic development of the SAARC region. They agreed to make every effort to implement the comprehensive action plan adopted by the Second Ministerial Meeting held at Cox's Bazaar, Bangladesh. These efforts would include facilitating the movement of people through improved travel infrastructure and air, sea and land connectivity among the SAARC countries, collaboration in human resource development and the promotion of SAARC as a common destination through public-private partnerships and joint campaigns.

The Working Group in its Third Meeting held in Colombo in April 2009 reviewed the status of implementation of the Summit directives, SAARC Action Plan on tourism, and various decisions taken by the Ministerial and Working Group Meetings. It also finalized a list of activities to be undertaken during the year 2009-10 for tourism promotion among the SAARC countries.

In Thimpu Summit (29-30 April 2010). The Leaders underscored the need for promotion of tourism to enhance greater people-to people contacts in the region and called for the creation of tourism-friendly environment. They welcomed the offer of the Government of Nepal to host the Third SAARC Ministerial Meeting on Tourism in Kathmandu in 2011 which coincides with the Nepal Tourism Year 2011.

According to the latest report of the World Tourism Organization, international tourist arrival grew by close 5 per cent in first two months of 2011.[9] Asia and Pacific which had one of the fastest growth rate in 2010 have made significant progress but only maintained 6 per cent in first two months of 2011. While South Asia and South Asia steal the show by the average growth of 15 per cent each. Sri-Lanka maintained 34 per cent, while Nepal 13 per cent, India 11 per cent and the Maldives 13 per cent.[10] During the 2010, Asia-Pacific earns

$203 billion, which is 24 per cent of the global income from tourism. In terms of arrivals share, Asia Pacific received 204 million people during 2010, which is 22 per cent global arrival. The international tourist touched 919 billion $ in 2010 which was $ 851 billion in 2009. But interestingly it was $ 939 billion in 2008.

The above-mentioned data reveals that although Asia-Pacific has done tremendous progress in recent years but still is nowhere in comparison of Europe, which constitutes 50 per cent share both receipts and arrivals in 2010. Likewise South Asia nowhere existed in comparison with their South-East Asian counterparts and other sub-regions within Asia-Pacific. It insists that South Asia despite its enormous potential has not been able to utilize it properly therefore they need to maximize their benefits. The regional cooperation platform of SAARC could be of immense use for this purpose for South Asia. As we all know that 21st century is an opportunity and South Asia need to grab the situation and must implement real notion of democracy, good governance and human rights. Needless to say that tourism sector has been untapped in this unfortunate part of the globe despite many resolutions and efforts made by regional governments and SAARC. We need to garner all possible help to realize an ideal situation of this area to maximize the opportunity and make this area again as an abode of peace and international brotherhood.

REFERENCES

1. Surojit Gupta, Baby Steps to revive trade, *The Times of India,* New Delhi, April 1, 2011.
2. World Tourism Organization and World Travel and Tourism Council.
3. See UN (2001a). According to the World Tourism Organization (WTO), tourism is defined as "the activities of persons traveling to and staying in places outside their usual environment for not more than one consecutive year for leisure, business and other purposes not related to the exercise of an activity remunerated from within the place visited" (WTO, 2000).
4. See UN (1997: ch. X).
5. World Bank, South Asia Poverty Web reference, http://web.worldbank.org/WBSITE/EXTERNAL/COUNTRIES/SOUTHASIAEXT/0,content MDK:20969099- pagePK:146736-piPK:146830-theSitePK:223547,00.html.

6. See http://www.saarcchamber.com/.
7. *Times of India*, New Delhi, 13 January 2011.
8. Towards Faster and More Inclusive Growth; An Approach to the 11th Five Year Plan, Planning Commission, Government of India, New Delhi, 2006, p. 1.
9. World Tourism Organization [UNWTO] Report, Madrid, 2011.
10. Ibid.

12

Tourism Promotion and Marketing in Kerala: The Role of Educational Institutions

Suresh R.

Introduction

This paper is prepared on the basis of experience gained while carrying out a project on developing some micro sites by the Tourism club members of Sree Narayana College, Punalur, Kerala during the academic year 2007-08.[1] The major theme of this paper is that the educational institutions, especially higher educational institutions, can play a major role in the promotion and marketing tourism. The major findings of the study were incorporated in this paper.

Hypotheses includes

(i) Educational institutions have the infrastructure to identify and develop tourism products in each locality, especially micro sites, local festivals, local art forms etc.

(ii) It is essential that special schemes may be prepared by providing incentives to students and teachers involved in promotion and marketing of tourism.

(iii) All higher educational institutions are having contacts not only at the national level but also internationally. This connectivity would help these institutions to sell the tourism products without any amount of additional efforts or investment.

(iv) The information provided through educational institutions is more reliable and trust worthy.

(v) Better interaction between the tourism department and higher educational institutions are inevitable for tourism promotion and marketing.

This paper explores the potential role of educational institutions in developing and marketing tourism products.

What is Tourism?

Tourism has been defined as the totality of relationship and phenomenon arising from travel and stays of strangers, provided the stay does not imply the establishment of a permanent residence and is not concerned with a remunerated activity. The partakers in tourism are called tourists. A person visiting a country other than that which he resides for a period of at least 24 hours is a tourist.

The volume of tourists increased in the aftermath of World War I which paved the way for the exodus and family reunion latter. This necessitated a measurement for tourism. The major methods of measurement of tourism are governmental enumeration, accommodation registration, and the behavioral survey.

The influx of tourists to a nation is attributed to the basic components of tourism which are known as the A's of tourism. They are attraction, accessibility, and accommodation. Attraction is anything that creates an urge for a person to take part in tourism. It is largely the geographical difference of a place. Accessibility is the reachability of the place of attraction. And accommodation is a place of temporary residence. Though these are the basic components of tourism there are certain others which facilitate tourism. Thus tourism is the totality of relationship occurring from the three basic components. Behind this lies the motives of the people. Motives of the people are not only difficult to measure but also are dynamic.

Motivations for Tourism

The important motivations for tourism include **physical motives**, which prompt a person to physical rest and relaxation, sports and adventure. The **cultural motives**, tourists classified in this motivation enjoy the culture, heritage, architecture, music art, and the things related with that to experience tourism. The inter personal motives are those that retrace the origin of one's family. Therefore, tourists of this type visit relatives, friends and their native places. The status and prestige motivation is identified with the personal esteem of the individuals. Therefore, tourists of this category travel with business or professional interest and satisfy their ego.

Importance of Tourism

In a world where everything is turning to be mechanical tourism unleashes a spell of liveliness to the life. It is one area of the world which approaches the individuals rather than the individuals approaching it. It keeps the mind of people balanced by giving them refreshment from the day to day life.

Tourism promotes international understanding. It generates innumerable benefits, both in social and economic spheres. Today tourism is widely acclaimed as an important global industry offering immense employment opportunities, both direct and indirect. It earns the much-needed foreign exchange. Tourism is one of the biggest industries in the emerging global scenario. The globalization process has accelerated the movement of commodities and people across the world. The developments in the field of transport and communication enabled the fast growth of tourism industry.

Merits of Tourism

(i) Tourism is the best source of revitalization
(ii) It is available for all sections of the people
(iii) It is the best source of foreign exchange
(iv) It creates unity through socializations
(v) It promotes the culture of a country

(vi) It improves infrastructure
(vii) Regions get a face lift
(viii) Economy of a country improves
(ix) It helps settle the balance of payment
(x) It creates job opportunities
(xi) It initiates new ventures
(xii) It is one of the easiest business propositions.

Demerits of Tourism

(i) It promotes child labor
(ii) It promotes sex tourism
(iii) Lifestyles of the tribal people are affected
(iv) Ecological resources are depleted
(v) Wild life is adversely affected.

Though tourism has several merits and demerits it has been considered as smoke free industry. It is less polluting compared to other industries. Tourism promotion and marketing is very important component in the tourism industry. In tourism promotion the development of micro sites assumes great significance especially in the context of responsible tourism. Diversification of tourism products also demands new methods of tourism promotion and marketing.

Marketing Mix for Tourism

The marketing mix for any service industry is discussed as 8 Ps.[2] They are,

(i) Product
(ii) Process
(iii) Place and Time
(iv) Productivity and Quality
(v) Promotion and Education
(vi) People
(vii) Price and other user costs
(viii) Physical Evidence

It would be interesting to apply this marketing mix for service industry to the tourism industry.

(i) Product

The product in tourism is basically the experience and hospitality provided by the service provided. In general the experience has to be expressed in such a way that the tourists see a value in them.

(ii) Process

The process in tourism include, (a) trip planning and anticipation, (b) travel to the site/area, (c) recollection, (d) trip planning packages. The trip planning packages include, maps, attractions en route and on site, information regarding lodging, food, quality souvenirs and mementoes

(iii) Place and Time—Location and Accessibility

The place and time in tourism is providing directions and maps, providing estimates of travel time and distances from different market areas, recommending direct and scenic travel routes, identifying attractions and support facilities along different travel routes, and informing potential customers of alternative travel methods to the area such as airlines, rail and roads.

(iv) Productivity and Quality

This is similar to other service industries. The quality is assessed by time taken for a service, the promptness of the service, reliability and so on.

(v) Promotion and Education

Like other services, the promotion should address, the accurate and timely information helping to decide whether to visit target audience, the image to be created for the organization, objectives, budget, timing of campaign, media to be selected, and evaluation methods.

(vi) People

People are the centre for tourism. It is more a human intensive sector. For hospitality and guest relations it is very important to focus on people. It also plays a vital role in quality control, personal selling, and employee morale.

(vii) Price and Other User Costs

The price of the tourism services depend on business and target market objectives, cost of producing, delivering and promoting the product, willingness of the target, prices charged by competitors offering similar product/service to the same target markets, availability and prices of substitute products/services, and economic climate.

(viii) Physical Evidence

In tourism the physical evidence is basically depends on travel experience, stay, and comfort. Here, the core product is bed in case of stay.[3]

Today, tourism has been considered as an industry and the development of this industry is beneficial to all without much difference in regard to urban and rural, rich and poor, literate and illiterate. The diversification of tourism products with the involvement of people makes it one of the most attractive industries where all people can contribute and get benefited. Kerala being an industrially backward state in the production of manufactured goods, high density of population and higher rate of educated unemployed, tourism offers a best option for economic development. It is interesting to examine the initiatives taken by the Kerala government towards the promotion and marketing of tourism.

Kerala Tourism

Kerala is a green strip of land, in the South West corner of Indian peninsula. Its unique feature, culture and traditions, coupled with its varied demography have made Kerala one of the most popular tourist destinations in the world. Kerala offers a wide range of tourism possibilities especially in Nature Tourism, Back Water Tourism, Eco-tourism, Cultural Tourism and Health Tourism. Kerala, promoted as "God's Own Country" is blessed by nature with varied geographical features like beaches, hill stations, backwaters, national parks and wild life sanctuaries. The centuries old holistic medicine of Ayurveda, the unique boat races that is the largest team sport in the world, the ride through the winding waterways in a houseboat or the colourful and exotic festivals, Kerala offers a multitude of experience to the tourist.[4]

It is important to examine the various initiatives taken by the government of Kerala towards the promotion and marketing tourism.

Marketing Initiatives

Kerala Tourism is noted for its innovative and market focused campaigns.

(i) New initiative for the promotion of Monsoon Tourism.
(ii) New initiative for promoting Kerala as one of the best health tourism destinations in the World.[5]

Cultural Initiatives

The following are the Cultural Initiatives

(i) Onam week celebrations with great people participation.
(ii) Joint Initiative with Cultural Department to promote traditional arts and festivals.
(iii) Nishagandhi festival, the only one of its kind event that captures the spirit of the season was unfolded at the sprawling Kanakakunn palace grounds in Thiruvananthapuram city.
(iv) UTSAVAM—the Kerala Arts festival for the promotion of local cultural programme held in 42 venues across 14 districts of Kerala from 5th December 2009 to 28th February 2010.[6]

New Policy Initiatives

The new initiatives of Kerala Tourism during 2009-10 are as follows:

(i) New policy initiative on Responsible Tourism
(ii) Destination Management Committees to be formulated in every tourist destinations
(iii) Initiated schemes for promoting souvenir industry
(iv) District Tourism Promotion Council's reconstituted
(v) Initiated schemes for promoting Adventure Tourism
(vi) Initiated schemes for promoting Ethnic Food Tourism
(vii) Comprehensive development of Alappuzha heritage city
(viii) Comprehensive development of Kerala Kalamandalam
(ix) Development of Ashtamudi cruise circuit
(x) Kadinamkulam backwater project
(xi) Brining the merits of IT for the Tourism Industry in Kerala
(xii) A series of online initiative branded as **Login.Kerala** have been launched to promote Kerala on the internet
(xiii) Partnership with google
(xiv) A new print ad campaign and TV commercial is being produced to showcase the destinations in the generating markets.[7]

Responsible Tourism

Responsible tourism is a tourism management strategy embracing planning, management, product development and marketing to bring about positive economic, social, cultural and environmental impacts to the local community. Kerala tourism has been piloting the responsible tourism initiatives at 4 destinations, viz. Kovalam, Kumarakom, Thekkady and Wayanad with very active support of the local self governments, tourism industry, Kudumbasree, NGOs and the local community as a whole. The remarkable feature of Responsible Tourism is that it provides better living conditions to the local community, extra income generation, emergence of new entrepreneurs, micro enterprises and large area brought under cultivation.

Thrust Areas in Tourism Sector

The Department of Tourism has initiated various projects for the development of basic infrastructure at tourist destinations and improvement of tourism attractions at the destinations.

The following activities were initiated during 2009-10

(i) **My Village, Tourism Friendly Village:** Scheme launched to identify and develop unknown rural tourist destinations with participation of local bodies.

(ii) **Wake up to Malabar:** It is a comprehensive plan to promote North Kerala.

(iii) **Kerala Souvenirs:** A unique project launched for the design and development of capacity building.

(iv) **Let's Learn:** This unique human resource initiative is launched for skills development in the tourism and hospitality sector.

(v) **Grand Kerala Shopping Festival:** A bold initiatives to make Kerala the shopping hub in the country. It is an annual event being organized every year.

(vi) **Utsavam:** It is a year-long festival of traditional arts spread throughout the State—42 venues—805 programmes—more than 1000 artists.

(vii) **Dream Season Campaign:** Dream Season campaign launched to tackle seasonality.

(viii) **Monsoon Tourism:** Offering many packages by travel and tourism Industry.

(ix) **International Convention Centre** at Thiruvananthapuram is opened.

(x) **Home Stay:** Promotion and classification of home stay opportunities throughout Kerala.

(xi) **Vazhiyoram:** Vazhiyoram is a unique scheme for development of way side facilities through private participation.

(xii) **Tourism Conservation & Preservation Act:** Enacted to regulate tourism development, Management of Guest Houses, Residential Bungalows, Tourism Garage etc.[8]

Tourism as an upcoming Industry in Kerala

(i) Kerala is aiming to attract more and more investment in the Tourism industry.

(ii) Tourism is a high growth industry holding great potential and invited entrepreneurs to invest.

(iii) In the field of Health Tourism, Kerala is leaping to the top destination of the world. Kerala has world class medical infrastructure and can provide quality health care at about 10 percent of the costs in the US or UK.

(iv) A trust was given to the Malabar area, waterways from Manjeswaram to Kovalam, cleanliness and safety of tourism destinations, tourism festivals etc.

(v) Effort has been taken to meet the additional room requirements by encouraging Home stays and private investments at different levels.

(vi) The focus will be on the development of basic infrastructure in tourism destination and make them clean and safe as per international standards.

(vii) As part of promoting Domestic Tourism, Partnership meets were conducted in major cities viz. Bangalore, Chennai, Hyderabad Ahmedabad, Surat, Pune, Mumbai, Nagpur, Chandigarh, Indore, Kolkotta, New Delhi, Mumbai etc.

(viii) Kerala Tourism actively participated more than 17 National trade fairs.

(ix) In collaboration with Jet Airways, Kerala Tourism launched Jet2Kerala programme for arranging tickets in subsidized rates.

(x) Kerala Tourism installed more than 3350 LCD screens for viewing the greenery and beauty of Kerala in 20 major cities all over India.[9]

The government of Kerala has taken several initiatives towards the promotion and marketing of tourism. However, there is scope for further initiatives in this direction.

Tourists' Arrival in Kerala 2005-10[10]

Year	Foreign Tourists	Domestic Tourists	Income in Crores (Rupees)
2005-06	346409	5946423	NA
2006-07	428534	6271724	9126
2007-08	515808	6642941	11433
2008-09	598929	7591250	13130
2009-10	557258	7913537	13231

Role of Educational Institutions

Educational institutions are better equipped in the promotion and marketing tourism. At present the involvement of educational institutions in tourism activities is very less. At the college level there is tourism club, a voluntary organization, functioning mainly to create awareness among the youth about tourism. Tourism Clubs in Higher Secondary Schools and Colleges of Kerala has been constituted under the auspices of department of tourism, Government of Kerala as part of creating tourism awareness among the host community. The objective is to empower the student community as the Ambassadors of Kerala tourism, thereby creating massive awareness on the benefits of tourism among the families, societies and to open up career opportunities in tourism sector. As part of streamlining the activities of Tourism Clubs, department of tourism had entrusted KITTS (Kerala Institute of Tourism and Travel Studies) to co-ordinate and to strengthen the activities of tourism clubs of the state.[11]

Tourism Clubs work with the following objectives:

- (i) Generate more public attention towards tourism and its developmental efforts.
- (ii) Create awareness about the socio-economic relevance of tourism for the development of the State.
- (iii) Nullify and dilute the existing misconceptions and misguided apprehensions regarding the growth of tourism.
- (iv) Create platforms for more open expressions and exchange of ideas regarding tourism related activities.

(v) Impress upon the younger and upcoming generation, the importance and relevance of tourism in their career and thereby generate a positive attitude towards tourism.
(vi) Make the younger generation participate in the developmental activities of tourism.
(vii) Achieve professionalism in tourism.
(viii) Encourage travel mentality and promote national integration and international unity.
(ix) Create a rational approach towards tourism, environment and nature.
(x) Identify/locate potential tourist spots in the district.[12]

Though certain noble objectives were incorporated in the tourism club organizational documents, most of these objectives were not fully realized. This is mainly due to lack of interest shown while implementing the programme at the educational institutions. It is also because the lack of effective and constant monitoring of the programme. The activities of these club may be expanded to tourism promotion and marketing. Educational institutions are able to perform the following activities for tourism promotion and marketing.

1. To identify micro site, local festivals, local art forms and produce literature to market it.
2. To develop positive attitude towards tourism related activities among the children and youth.
3. To understand and appreciate divergent culture at the local, regional and international domain.
4. To undertake projects for the promotion and marketing tourism.
5. To conduct field survey on various aspects of tourism.
6. To minimize the negative impact of tourism on local culture.
7. Human resource development.

Advantages to the Tourism Industry

The involvement of educational institutions in tourism

promotion and marketing provides the following benefits to the tourism industry.

1. Cost effective—in promotion and marketing tourism.
2. Reliable and stable—information provided by educational institutions are reliable and continuous.
3. Tourist—friendly attitude can be created among the youth which in the long run is beneficial to the tourism industry.
4. Educational value in undertaking various projects on tourism. Students learn more about local culture and also through the interactions with foreign tourists other culture.
5. Educational institutions especially higher educational institutions have interactions with outside world. These contacts can very well be used for the marketing tourism products abroad.

Suggestions for promotion and marketing tourism through educational institutions

1. Tourism clubs to be organized at the primary, high school levels.
2. The existing tourism clubs at the College/higher secondary school level is to be strengthened. A yearly honorarium is to be given to the teacher coordinator, and visit to important tourist destinations may be arranged for club members. For tourism promotion and marketing special incentives may be given to tourism club members.
3. Each educational institution may be given at least one project to identify and promote micro sites, festivals, art forms in their locality.
4. Each college may be given major projects in the field of tourism promotion and marketing. Information given by reputed educational institutions are more reliable and acceptable. The collaboration between DTPC's (District Tourism Promotion Council) and educational institutions is to be strengthened. Representation may be given to tourism club coordinators in the executive council of the DTPC.

5. Annual tourism award be given to best school and college tourism clubs on the basis of their performance in tourism promotion and marketing.
6. Colleges may also develop a portal in their website about tourism, which disseminates data on various aspects of tourism. places, conveyance, accommodations, etc.
7. The district and state level camps of the Tourism Clubs is to be strengthened. A national level camp also may be organized with the involvement of the Union Ministry of Tourism.
8. Seminars, conferences and workshops on tourism promotion and marketing may be organized at colleges/ universities with the involvement of all stakeholders.

REFERENCES

1. The tourism club members of Sree Narayana College Punalur 2007-2008 under the supervision of Dr Suresh R, teacher coordinator of tourism club, visited five micro sites in and around Punalur and prepared a detailed book entitled *Punalur The Land of Hanging Beauty*. "Students of the Tourism Club of Punalur S.N. College have come out with a unique initiative to promote the tourism potential of Punalur and its periphery. They have prepared a 51-page booklet titled 'Punalur: The Land of Hanging Beauty,' giving detailed information on tourist attractions in the area." *The Hindu* (Thiruvananthapuram) dated 29 Dec 2008.
2. Kannan, Srinivasan, *Tourism Marketing: A Service Marketing Perspective*, MPRA Paper No. 14031, posted 12. March 2009 http://mpra.ub.uni-muenchen.de/ 14031 also see Kotler, Philip, Kotler, Kevin Lane, "Marketing Management", Printice Hall of India Private Limited, New Delhi, 2007 Batra, Rajeev, Myers, John G, Aaker, David A, "Advertising Management" Printice Hall of India Private Limited, New Delhi, 2007 Lovelock, Christopher, Wirtz, Jochen, Chatterjee, Jayanta, "Services Marketing People, Technology Strategy A South Asian Perspective", Peason Education Inc, Delhi, 2004.
3. Ibid.
4. *Economic Review 2010*, Kerala State Planning Board, Thiruvananthapuram.
5. Ibid.
6. Ibid.
7. Ibid.
8. Ibid.
9. Ibid.
10. *Economic Review* 2005-10, Kerala State Planning Board, Thiruvananthapuram.
11. www.keralatourism.org
12. *Guidelines on the programmes of Tourism Clubs,* The Department of Tourism, Government of Kerala has drafted a standard calendar for the activities of Tourism Clubs. The programmes of the Tourism Clubs are classified into: 1. Unit level programmes 2. District level programmes 3. State level programmes

1. Unit level programmes: Each college/school is considered a unit. Unit level programmes will be organised by the Teacher Coordinator/Student Coordinator in consultation with the DTPC. July-August A seminar or group discussion on the scope of Tourism in Kerala/India. Participation in the group discussion is open only to club members. All the students of the college shall be involved in the seminar. September-Octobe 1.Trekking/hiking/cycle rally to a nearby tourist destination. This programme is exclusively for members of the Tourism Club. 2. Celebrate World Tourism Day on September 27th. November-December Conduct a quiz programme viz., *Tourism Quiz*. All the members of the college/school shall be invited to participate in this programme. 1st and 2nd prize winners of the quiz competition will be selected for the district level tourism quiz. If winners are non-members, they will be given honorary membership of the Tourism Club. January-February *'Meet the Guest' programme.* This programme is designed to help the Club members interact with foreign tourists or tourists from other States who visit the concerned district. The programme must be arranged on a holiday exclusively for the members of Tourism Club. This is to prevent any kind of harassment to the invited tourists and to ensure proper interaction. The Teacher Coordinator of the institution shall be the supervisor of this programme. The invited tourists must be treated as distinguished guests. Finance The Department of Tourism will release the funds through the DTPCs of the district, subject to a maximum of Rs. 2500/-, per club per year. The break-up of the estimate is given below 1.Seminar or group discussion Rs. 500/- 2. Trekking/hiking/cycle rally to a nearby tourist destination Rs. 500/-3.Tourism quiz (unit level) Rs. 300/- 4. Meet the Guest programme Rs. 200/- 5. Identification of tourist spots Rs. 1000/- Total Rs. 2500.

2. District level programmes: The following district level programmes will be fully financed by the Department of Tourism. A. Two-day Tourism Camp Two-day tourism camp for selected members of Tourism Clubs will be conducted in an ideal tourist centre in the district. Each unit can sponsor a maximum of 5 active members.

3. State level programmes: State level programmes are also organized and financed by the Department of Tourism. A. State level tourism quiz A State level quiz competition based on tourism will be conducted by the Department of Tourism in association with KITTS. Winners of the district level quiz competition will be the participants. B. State level tourism camp for the Student Coordinators A major tourism camp will be conducted for the Unit Student Coordinators. The camp will be conducted in any of the known tourist centres of Kerala. The camp aims at strengthening the leadership quality of the participants and enlightening them on the organization and functioning of the Tourism Clubs. The Department of Tourism will provide second-class train fare (as per actuals), boarding and lodging. www.keralatourism.org

13

Assessment of Tourism Potential in Rural Murshidabad, West Bengal: An Empirical Study

N.C. Jana and Syfujjaman Tarafder

Introduction

Tourism is the outing of people usually for leisure, refreshment, recreation, health improvement and enjoying some adventure experience usually in the area beyond his or her place of residence. The Swiss Professor Hunziker and Kraf defined tourism as "the sum of the phenomena and relationship arising from the travel and stay of non-residence and are not connected with any earning activities."

The complex urban life in both the developed and developing countries encourages urban people to travel in relatively less complex rural areas for leisure and refreshments as rural areas are more pollution free, green and open spaces are available. From this point, tourism in rural areas started to develop. Today it is now an important sector of tourism, where both the government and private entrepreneurs are being interested to invest towards improving basic infrastructure as well as other associated recreational facilities for the tourists. A number of researches, although few, have been conducted for exploring the potentiality of rural tourism. It may be pointed out that in this context that the development of tourism in rural areas necessitates basic and higher infrastructural facilities. The present paper attempts to explore such areas in rural Murshidabad, where tourism can be developed.

The District of Murshidabad is very reach in history and heritage, unique art and culture, handicraft, most of which are scattered in its rural parts. Besides, maximum percentage of people (87.5%) lives in the rural areas. The western part of the district that is in the west of River Bhagirathi, fall in the *Rarh* area. The undulating plain with red soil and open countryside attract many people seeking fresh breath and to enjoy rural life style with their exclusive culture, religion, history and heritage.

Objectives of the Present Study

The present paper has the following objectives:

1. Exploring the areas of tourism in rural parts of Murshidabad District.
2. Categorization of tourism resources of rural Murshidabad.
3. Assessment of scope of rural people's involvement in the tourism sector and scope for investments in developing tourism infrastructures.
4. Assessment of potentiality of rural culture, handicrafts and foods as tourist attraction.

Database and Methodology

The present study is mainly based on secondary data collected from different sources like, Census Hand Book of Murshidabad District, 1961; Regional Tourism Office, Berhampore; Department of Tourism, Government of West Bengal; and different books, journals and magazines as well as an intensive field visit throughout the countryside of the district. This is a purely an empirical research.

Study Area

Murshidabad (geographically located within 23°43′30″ N and

24°50′20″ N latitude and 88°46′ E and 87°49′17″E longitude) (Map. 1) is very rich in history from the ancient time up to the modern British period in India, and a large number of remnants is found here and there throughout the district most of which in rural parts of the district. The blocks in the left bank of River Bhagirathi, known as Rarh, are rich in ancient and medieval history and almost has rural base.

Assessment of Tourism Potential in Rural Murshidabad

Tourism of Murshidabad is basically heritage tourism, though there are many spots of another importance. These are described below:

1. **Rural and Heritage Tourism**: Most of the tourism in Murshidabad is Heritage tourism based on historical sites. The 'Rarh area' of the district witnessed the change of history in a number of times and the remnants of different periods superimposed and make the 'Rarh' area important in history and heritage of Bengal as well as in the tourism map of the district.

   Besides, there are a number of heritage places where tourism activity is still not developed but have the potentialities to be developed as popular tourist spots. These are:

   - ***Lalbag-Murshidabad:*** There are number of heritage monuments scattered in the Lalbag area on both sides of the River Bhagirathi *Rural Heritage Tourism Circuit* can be developed along with the tourism of Murshidabad town in Motijhil, Khoshbag, Farhabag and Roshnibag on the left bank of Bhagirathi.
   - ***Rangamati-Karnasuvarna:*** The ancient capital of Gour Raj Sasanka. Here remains of three mounds of historical importance on the open Rarh area are found, which can be developed as popular tourist spot. This is the best area to develop *Rural Heritage Tourism* in the beautiful Rarh Bengal.
   - ***Berhampore-Cossimbazar:*** The heritage monuments here

are not still so popular though some visitors come here each year. There are many European Symmetries in this zone, which can attract large number of foreign tourists, especially from Europe if proper infrastructure is developed and advertised. The concept of *Grave Tourism* can be developed here.

- ***Rampara-Faridpur:*** This is the tomb of Mir Madan, the leading military commandants of Nawab Siraj-Ud-Doula in the Battle of Plassey. A rural tourism center can be developed centering the historic battlefield Plassey.
- ***Ajimganj-Jiaganj:*** This twin town is old where many old temples and buildings are found. The District Museum at Jiaganj town is also worth mentioning.
- ***Kiriteswari & Bhattamati:*** This is one Peeth of the 51 Sakti Peeths like Vrindaban, Varanasi, Amarnath, Puri, Nalhati, Bakreshwar etc. still awaited to be developed as popular religious tourist spot like others in India. Now people come here during 'mela' in the month of 'Paush' in Bengali calendar. This is an important place in the religious map of India.
- ***Kandi-Gokarna:*** Kandi Block is such a place where ancient settlements had been grown up and a number of ancient monuments are found. These are Kandi itself, Salar, Gokarna, Gobrahati, Jemo etc. which can be developed as a *Heritage Hub*. The beautiful rural background of the Rarh in this area may also help to develop *Rural Heritage Tourism.*
- ***Panchthupi:*** This is an important place in the heritage map of the district where the remains of '*Pala*' period is found and five 'stupas' from which the name of the village came, is found here. The present temple is said to be as one of the fives Buddhist 'stupas'
- ***Sagardighi-Mahipalnagar-Kherur-Monigram-Mirzapur:*** Sagardighi Block is important as many 'Pala' periods' remnants are found. It is another centre of history and heritage of the district. Covering the above places a rural

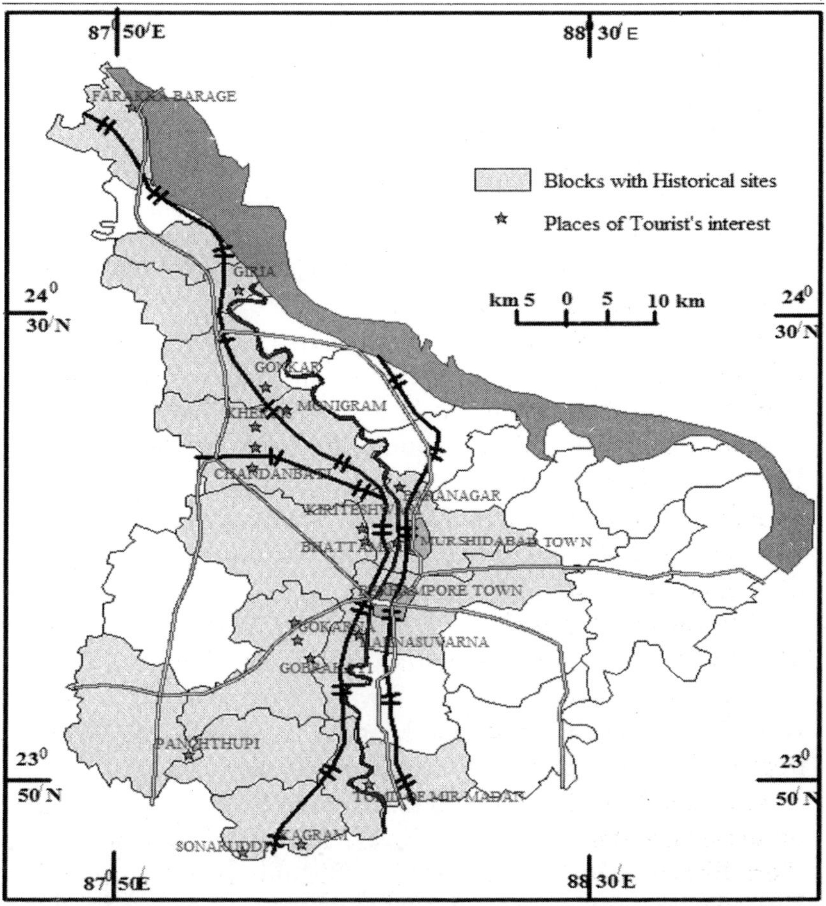
87°50'E
88°30'E
Blocks with Historical sites
Places of Tourist's interest
km 5 0 5 10 km
24°30'N
23°50'N
GIRIA

Map. 1

heritage tourism circuit can be developed. In the beautiful Monigram, tourist rest house can be developed and Mirzapur can be developed as *Art and Craft Village* based on silk weaving.

- *Aurangabad:* Nimtita Zamindari palace where Satyajit Ray did the shooting of *Jalsaghar* can attract the tourists.

Ecotourism: Ecotourism can be developed in the Subhash dweep, Farakka and at Bangshabati Bill. Bangshabati Bill, where '*Ahiron Pakhiralay*' is planned to be developed, is a natural wetland where large number of traveler birds comes each year. So it may attract the bird watcher as well as general visitors if proper management measures taken.

Religious Tourism: In Murshidabad District, successful religious tourism can be developed in the place of Kiriteawari Temple area in Nabagram Block, Radhmadhab Temple area in Murshidabad Block and Bishnupur Kali Temple at Cossimbazar, Pataleshwar Temple and Satighat at Cossimbazar.

Adventure and Sports Tourism: Small scale Adventure tourism like, 'Para Gliding,' 'Hang Gliding' *etc.* can be developed in Nilkuthi Mound.

Recreational Tourism: Recreational tourism can be developed basically in the natural bills and Marshes in the Berhampore and Murshidabad Towns. In the Bishnupur Bill, Kati Ganga in Berhampore and Motijhil in Murhidabad where popular water sports, fishing can be developed.

Cultural Tourism: Cultural tourism can be developed based on some important cultural festivals in Murshidabad. These are 'Bera Bhasan', 'Muharram', Mela at Bishnupur Kali bari and Kiriteshwari temple, 'Hazarduari Utsav' etc.

Scope for Rural People's Involvement

There is a vast scope for local people's involvement in the tourism activities in Murshidabad District if tourism industry is established in its full fledges. People can be involved in various sectors of tourism like (i) accommodation in hotels, (ii) in the restaurants, (iii) in the recreational parks, (iv) in the archaeological parks; (v) souvenir shops, (vi) in transportation sectors, (vii) travel agencies etc.

Besides, large percentage of people can be employed if community based rural tourism is developed in certain important areas like Baranagar Charbangla Temple Complex Area, Karnasuvarna area, Kiriteshwari- Bhattamati area, Kherur Monigram area etc.

Role of Government and Scope for Private Investments

The Government of West Bengal announced that, Murshidabad is a priority district in tourism according to *State Tourism Policy, 2008* (Tourism Department, Government of West Bengal).

The role of Government of West Bengal according to the Tourism Policy 2008 is drawing up and implementing tourism plans, policies and incentive schemes to facilitate vastly increased flow of investment to tourism projects in the state from private sectors, both domestic and foreign. The Department of Tourism will play the role of a facilitator in respect of investment by private sector. The State Government will mostly confine its effort to infrastructure development, publicity and dissemination of information and coordination of sectoral activities to create conditions conducive to private sector investment in tourism.

The Government of West Bengal may highlight the priority areas, where private investors can invest and also give advice to the private investors regarding the investment.

The Government may also promote home stay accommodation program with proper guide and financial assistance, extend consciousness program among local people and organizers about the sustainability and hospitality needs of tourism in the area and thus to accept tourists in open-mind and with care.

If all the above proposals are done, then there is large scope for private investment in the district of Murshidabad. Some infrastructures have already been developed by the private enterprises like, hotels and lodges, resorts for accommodation, recreational parks and restaurants *etc.* If the government helps in land acquisition in Murshidabad District and sites selection for establishment of tourist facilities like, hotels, resorts, facilities encouraging adventure tourists and sports tourists, various water sports in the bills, rivers and lakes such as in Motijhil, Bishnupur Bill, Banghabati bill at Ahiron and Katiganga then private investors may be encouraged to establish cottages in the central island of Motijhil lake for tourist accommodation and recreational parks as well as various water sports activities for tourists in the same.

Potentiality for Local Handicrafts, Foods, and Culture as Attractions to Tourists

Murshidabad has its own Culture, Arts and Handicrafts, Foods, which can be promoted in tourism markets. The State Government may promote local handicrafts and culture and then the producers of arts, handicrafts, and performer of culture can establish showcase for disseminating and marketing their products.

The important cultural festivals are:

- *Muharram*: Muharram is one of the most famous festivals of this part. During Mahuram a 10 days fair is held here. "*Matam Rat*" is one of the most surprising rituals of this festival. In this night pious Muslims walk through Bruning coal, sharp knives or swords. In the last day of Mahuram a procession is taken out from the Imambara. During these days the palace ground along with Imambara is decorated with lights- it is an unexplainable experience.
- *Bera Utsav*: The famous 'Bera festival' was the main festival among lots. In time of *Bera* Roshni Bag had been decorated with different types of lights, flowers *etc.* Large number of people gathered here to see the night of light. The River Bhagirathi was also got lighted. The '*Mehafil*' of music and dance was the great attraction of this festival.
- Folk songs like, *Fakiri*, *Murshidi* and folk dance like, *Ghora* Dance, etc.

- *Akklap:* Akklap is one kind of folk culture (singing with some instant lyric) can be an attraction of tourism. One can spend a night to see the cultural heritage of this part. Though it is a rare art but still one can enjoy by observing it.

The important handicrafts are:

- Murshidabad Silk
- Shola products
- Wood carving products
- Bell and Bras metals

Murshidbad is very rich in various types of mango. The delicious and scented mangoes of the district can attract tourists during the season of mango and tourist can taste these delicious mangoes in the mango orchards. There is large number of mango orchards in the countryside.

Recommended Measures

There are many areas in the rural parts of Murshidabad District, which are still to be explored because vast potentiality is there to develop them as successful rural and heritage tourism destination. In this regard some recommendations are:

1. Proper government initiatives should be taken to explore the potential rural tourism sites of Murshidabad District and should encourage the private entrepreneurs in developing basic needs of tourism infrastructures in the area under study.
2. Government should establish some basic infrastructures like, good transport link to the places giving some incentives to those private entrepreneurs who intends to establish tourism related infrastructures in these areas.
3. Government may take the role of coordinator and also provide financial assistance as well as advice to the private entrepreneurs.
4. Government should publicize these areas both in domestic

and international tourism markets to attract the tourists to the areas.

5. Government can establish Art and Craft Village and help in promoting local handicrafts by providing financial assistance to the artisans.
6. Government should develop a *Package Tour* in the areas of rural heritage tourism.

Conclusion

It may be concluded that the rural areas of Murshidabad has the vast potentiality for the development of rural heritage tourism. People are not so much aware to improve it at the commercial level. There are many areas of lacking but potentiality and prospects for countryside tourism are bright. Existing government plans are not sufficient and piecemeal type.

It may be mentioned that the district of Murshidabad is industrially backward with underdeveloped agriculture, where large percentage of population is unemployed and poverty-stricken. Keeping this in backdrop the district can be established as the prospective centre of tourist attraction towards boosting up the regional economy.

REFERENCES

1. Bandopadhtay, Bijay Kumar (2008): *Murshidabad Yuge Yuge*, Manthan, Murshidabad.
2. Bishai Murshidabad, *Jhar* (Murshidabad Namkaroner 300 Bachhar edition), February 2010, Murshidabad.
3. Bishai Murshidabad, *Jhar* (Third edition), December 2007, Murshidabad.
4. Canada Tourism Commission (2002): *Discovering Heritage Tourism: Practical Ideas for the Tourism Industry*, Canada.
5. Das, Sudhir Ranjan (1992): *Karnasuvarna Mahanagari*, West Bengal State Book Board, Calcutta.
6. Dhar, Prem Nath (2008): *Cultural and Heritage Tourism*, Kanishka Publishers, Distributers, New Delhi, pp. 37, 43, 186-187.
7. Dutta, Rangan (2007): "Next Weekend you can be at...Karnasuvarna", *The Telegraph - Metro* on Sunday 15th April 2007 (www.rangan-dutta.info).
8. O'Malley, L.S.S. (1914): *Bengal District Gazetteers: Murshidabad District*, Government of West Bengal, Calcutta, pp. 22, 129.
9. Repiso, Luciana Ines (2002): "Heritage, Tourism and Sustainability: An

Archaeological Park as a Tool for Local Sustainable Development", Faculty of Architecture, Urbanism and Design- National University of Cordoba, X5000JJP, Argentina.

10. Roy Supriyo, "Nana Aloi Murshidabad", *Pashchimbanga: Paryaton Sankha*, 28th September – 19th October, 2001, Tathya o Sanskriti Bibhag, Government of West Bengal, Kolkata.
11. Roy, Nikhil Nath (2009): *Murshidabader Itihash*, K.P.M., Calcutta.
12. www.culturalheritagetourism.com
13. www.murshidabad.net/tourism.html

Bibliography

Sustainable Development

Centre for Exploitation of Science and Technology (1991) *Industry and the Environment: A Strategic Overview*. CEST, London.

Daly, H. E. and Cobb, J.B. Jr. (1990) *For the Common Good. Redirecting the Economy Towards Community, the Environment and a Sustainable Future*. Green Print, London.

Dryzek, J.S. and Schlosberg, D. (1998) (eds) *Debating the Earth: The Environmental Politics Reader*. Oxford University Press, Oxford.

International Union for the conservation of Nature and Natural Resources (1980) *World Conservation Strategy. Living Resource Conservation for Sustainable Development*. IUCN, Gland.

Mannion, A.M. and Bowlby, S.R. (1992) (eds) *Environmental Issues in the 1990s*. Wiley, Chichester.

Meadows, D.H., Meadows, D.L. and Ronders, J. (1992) *Beyond The Limits—Global Collapse or a Sustainable Future*. Earthscan, London.

New Internationalist (1999) *The Radical Twentieth Century*. In A. Holden (2000) Environment and Tourism. Routledge, London.

Organisation for Economic Co-operation and Development (1980) *The Impact of Tourism on the Environment*. OECD, Paris.

O'Riordan, T. (1981) *Environmentalism*, 2nd edn. Pion, London.

Osborn, D. and Bigg, T. (1998) *Earth Summit II: Outcomes and Analysis*. Earthscan, London.

Pearce, D. G. (1995) *Blueprint 4: Capturing Global Environmental Value*. Earthscan, London.

Pearce, D. G., Markandya, A. and Barbier, E. (1989) *Blueprint for a Green Economy*. Earthscan, London.

Pearce, D. G. and Barbier, E. B. (2000) *Blueprint for a Sustainable Economy*. Earthscan, London.

Redclift, M. (1987) *Sustainable Development: Exploring the Contradictions*. Methuen, London.

Reid, D. (1995) *Sustainable Development: An Introductory Guide.* Earthscan, London.

World Commission on Environment and Development (WCED) (1987) *Our Common Future.* Oxford University Press, Oxford.

Tourism and the Environment

Brown, F. (1998) *Tourism Reassessed: Blessing or Blight?* Butterworth-Heinemann, Oxford.

Brown, F. and Hall, D. (eds) (1999) Case Studies of Tourism In Peripheral Areas. Bornholms Forskingscenter.

Burkart, A.J. and Medlik, S. (1981) *Tourism Past Present and Future.* Heinemann, London.

Burns, P. and Holden, A. (1995) *Tourism: A New Perspective.* Prentice-Hall, Hitchin.

Council of Europe (1996) *Tourism and the Environment: Towards a New Tourism Culture.*

Council of Europe (1997) *Tourism and the Environment.*

Davidson, R. and Maitland, R. (1997) *Tourism Destinations.* Hodder and Stoughton, London.

De Kadt, E. (ed) (1979) *Tourism: Passport to Development?* Oxford University Press, Oxford.

Diamantis, D. (1999) The Concept of Ecotourism: Evolution and Trends. *Current Issues in Tourism.* Volume 2.

Holden, A. (2000) *Environment and Tourism.* Routledge, London.

IUCN (1996) *Tourism, Ecotourism, and Protected Areas.* IUCN, Gland.

Mathieson, A. and Wall, G. (1982) *Tourism: Economic, Physical and Social Impacts.* Longman, New York.

McKercher, B. (1993) Some Fundamental Truths About Tourism: Understanding Tourism's Social and Environmental Impacts, *Journal of Sustainable Tourism*, 1 (1): 6-16.

Murphy, P. E. (1985) *Tourism: A Community Approach.* Methuen, New York.

O'Reilly (1986) Tourism Carrying Capacity: Concepts and Issues, *Tourism Management*, 8(2): 254-8.

Pearce, D. G. (1989) *Tourism Development*, 2nd edn. Longman Scientific and Technical, Harlow.

Singh, T.V. and Singh, S. (eds) (1999) *Tourism Development in Critical Environments*. Cognizant Communication Corporation, New York.

World Tourism Organisation (WTO) (1997) *Tourism 2020 Vision*. WTO, Madrid.

Sustainable Development and Tourism

Berry, S. and Ladkin, A. (1997) Sustainable Tourism: A Regional Perspective, *Tourism Management*, 18 (7): 433-440.

Bramwell, B. and Lane, B. (2000) *Tourism Collaboration and Partnerships. Politics, Practice and Sustainability*. Channel View Publications, Clevedon.

Bramwell, B. and Lane, B. (1993) Sustainable Tourism: An Evolving Global Approach, *Journal of Sustainable Tourism*, 1(1): 1-5.

Bramwell, B. (1996) in W. Bramwell, I. Henry, G. Jackson, A. G. Prat, G. Richards and J. van der Straaten (eds) *Sustainable Tourism Management: Principles and Practice*. Tilbury University Press, Tilbury, 147-170.

Brent Ritchie, J.R. (2000) The Competitive Destination: A Sustainability Perspective, *Tourism Management*, 21 (2000): 1-7.

Buhalis, D. (1999) Information Technology as a Strategic Tool for Sustainable Tourism Development, *The Courier*, EU, July 1999.

Butler, R.W. (1980) The concept of a tourist area cycle of evolution: Implications for management of resources, *Canadian Geographer*, 24(1): 5-12.

Butler, R.W. (1991) Tourism, Environment, and Sustainable Development, *Environmental Conservation*, 18 (3): 201-209.

Butler, R. W. (1998) Sustainable tourism-looking backwards in order to progress? In C.M. Hall and A. Lew (eds) *Sustainable Tourism: A Geographic Perspective*. Addison Wesley Longman, Harlow, 25-48.

Cater, E. (1994) Environmental Contradictions in Sustainable Tourism, *The Geographical Journal*, 161 (1): 21-28.

Cater, E. and Lowman, G. (1994) *Ecotourism: A Sustainable Option*? Wiley.

Ceballos-Lascurain, H. (1987) The future of ecotourism. In Diamantis, D. and Ladkin, A. (1999) The Links Between Sustainable Tourism and Ecotourism: A definitional and operational perspective, *The Journal of Tourism Studies*, 10 (2): 35-46.

Clarke, J. (1997) A Framework of Approaches to Sustainable Tourism, *Journal of Sustainable Tourism*, 5 (3): 224-233.

Cronin, L. (1990) A Strategy for Tourism and Sustainable Development, *World Leisure and Recreation,* 32 (3): 12-18.

Collins, A. (1999) Tourism Development and Natural Capital, *Annals of Tourism Research*, 26 (1): 98-109.

Curtin, S. and Busby, G. (1999) Sustainable Destination Development: the Tour Operator Perspective, *International Journal of Tourism Research*, 1:135-147.

Diamantis, D. and Ladkin, B. (1999) The Links Between Sustainable Tourism and Ecotourism: A definitional and operational perspective, *The Journal of Tourism Studies,* 10 (2): 35-46.

Dovers, S.R. and Handmer, J.W. (1993) Contradictions in Sustainability, *Environmental Conservation*, 20 (3): 217-222.

Dymond, S. J. (1997) Indicators of Sustainable Tourism in New Zealand: a Local Government Perspective, *Journal of Sustainable Tourism*, 5 (4): 279-293.

Eber, S. (1992) *Beyond the Green Horizon*. Tourism Concern/WWF.

Farrell, B.H. (1999) Conventional or Sustainable Tourism? No Room for Choice, *Tourism Management*, 20 (1999): 189-191.

France, L. (ed) (1997) *The Earthscan Reader in Sustainable Tourism*. Earthscan, London.

Garrod, B. and Fyall, A. (1998) Beyond the Rhetoric of Sustainable Tourism? Tourism Management, 19 (3): 199-212.

Hall, C.M. (1998) Historical antecedents of sustainable development and ecotourism: new labels on old bottles? In C.M. Hall and A. Lew (eds) *Sustainable Tourism: A Geographical Perspective*. Addison Wesley Longman, Harlow, 13-24.

Hall, C.M. and Lew, A. (eds) (1998) *Sustainable Tourism: A Geographical Perspective*. Addison Wesley Longman, Harlow.

Harris, R. and Leiper, N. (1995) *Sustainable Tourism: An Australian Perspective*. Butterworth-Heinemann, Oxford.

Harrison, L. (1996) *Practicing Responsible Tourism: International Case Studies.* Wiley.

Hawkes, S. et al (1993) *The Greening of Tourism: A Casebook of Environmental Good Practice*. Simon Fraser University.

Holden, A. (2000) *Environment and Tourism*. Routledge, London.

Hughes, G. (1996) Tourism and the Environment: a Sustainable Partnership? *Scottish Geographical Magazine*, 112 (2): 107-113.

Hunter, C.J. (1995) On the need to re-conceptualise sustainable tourism development, *Journal of Sustainable Tourism*, 3 (3): 155-165.

Hunter, C. (1995) Key concepts for tourism and the environment. In C. Hunter and H. Green, *Tourism and the Environment: A Sustainable Relationship*? Routledge, London, 52-92.

Hunter, C. (1997) Sustainable tourism as an adaptive paradigm, *Annals of Tourism Research*, 24 (4): 850-867.

Hunter, C. and Green, H. (1995) *Tourism and the Environment: A Sustainable Relationship?* Routledge, London.

Inskeep, E. (1991) *Tourism Planning: An Integrated and Sustainable Development Approach*. Van Nostrand Reinhold, New York.

MacLellan, L.R. (1997) The Tourism and Environment Debate: from Idealism to Cynicism. In Foley, M., Lennon, J. and Maxwell, G. (eds) *Hospitality, Tourism and Leisure Management*, Cassell, London.

MacLellan, L.R. (1997) The Effectiveness of Sustainable Tourism Policies in Scotland. In Stabler, M. J. (ed) *Tourism and Sustainability: Principles to Practice*, CAB International, Oxford.

McKercher, L.R. (1993) The Unrecognised Threat to Tourism: Can tourism Survive Sustainability? *Tourism Management*, April: 131-136.

Manning, T. (1999) Indicators of Tourism Sustainability, *Tourism Management*, 20 (1999): 179-181.

Martin, C. (1995) Charter for Sustainable Tourism. In L. France (ed) (1997) *The Earthscan Reader in Sustainable Tourism*. Earthscan, London.

Moscardo, G. (1998) Interpretation and Sustainable Tourism: Functions, Examples and Principles, *The Journal of Tourism Studies*, 9 (1): 2-13.

Mowforth, M. and Munt, I. (1998) *Tourism and Sustainability: New Tourism in the Third World*. Routledge, London.

Muller, H. (1994) The Thorny Path to Sustainable Development, *Journal of Sustainable Tourism*, 2 (3): 131-136.

Page, S.J. and Thorn, K.J. (1997) Towards Sustainable Tourism Planning in New Zealand: Public Sector Planning Responses, *Journal of Sustainable Tourism*, 5 (1): 59-77.

Priestly, G.K. *et al* (1996) *Sustainable Tourism: European Experiences*. CAB International.

Ryan, C. (1999) Issues of Sustainability on Tourism (editorial), *Tourism Management*, 20 (1999): 177.

Sharpley, R. (2000) Tourism and Sustainable Development: Exploring the Theoretical Divide, *Journal of Sustainable Tourism*, 8(1): 1-15.

Shipp, D. (2001) Loving them to Death? EUROPARC Federation.

Sindiga, I. (1999) Alternative Tourism and Sustainable Development in Kenya, *Journal of Sustainable Tourism*, 7 (2): 108-127.

Stabler, M.J. (ed) (1997) Tourism and Sustainability: Principles to Practice. CAB International, Oxford.

Tourism Society (undated) *Tourism: Development in Balance with the Environment.*

Twinning-Ward, L. (1999) Towards Sustainable Tourism Development: Observations from a Distance, Tourism Management, 20 (1999): 187-188.

Weaver, D. (2001) Sustainable Tourism: Is it Sustainable? In B. Faulkner, E. Laws and G. Moscardo (eds) *Tourism in the 21st Century*. Continuum, London, 300-311.

Welford, R. (1997) *Hijacking Environmentalism: Corporate Responses to Sustainable Development.* Earthscan, London.

Sustainable Tourism Documents (codes, guidelines, principles)

APEC (1997) *Tourism and Environmental Good Practice in APEC Member Economies.* APEC.

BMU (1998) *Proposal of Global Guidelines for Tourism and Biodiversity to the CBD/COP IV.* BMU, Bratislava.

CCA (1975) *Code of Ethics for Tourists.* CCA, Penang.

CCA (1980) *Manila Declaration.* CCA, Manila.

Commission on Sustainable Development (1999) *Working Programme for Sustainable Tourism.* CSD.

DNH et al (1995) *Sustainable Rural Tourism: Advisory Booklet.*

Ecotourism Society (1993) *Ecotourism Guidelines.*

ECTWT, TEN, WCC (1986) *The Bad Boll Statement.* ECTWT, TEN, WCC, Bad Boll.

ECTWT (1993) *Mission Statement on Third World Tourism.* ECTWT, Hong Kong.

ECTWT (2001) *Open Letter from the conference "Mission Perspective in Tourism".* ECTWT, Penang.

EEC (1998) *A European Community Strategy to Support Sustainable Tourism Development.* [Com (1998) 563 Final].

ESCAP (1993) Management of Sustainable Tourism Development. ESCAP.

EU, UNEP, GEF, WTO, IUCN, DFV, DNR, DRV, Forum U&E (1997) Berlin Declaration. Berlin.

Federation of Nature and Natural Parks of Europe (1997) *The European Charter for Sustainable Tourism.*

Forum Development & Environment (1998) *Position Paper Tourism and Sustainable Development to the CSD-7.* Forum Development & Environment.

German NGO Forum Development & Environment (2000) *Statement "Tourism & Biodiversity".*

Global Reporting (2000) *Sustainability Reporting Guidelines from the Global Reporting Initiative.*

Local Government Association (1998) *Tourism - Towards Sustainability.*

Mediterranean States (1997) *Calvia Declaration on Tourism and Sustainable Development in the Mediterranean.*

New Forest District Council (2000) *Our Future Together: Tourism and Visitor Management Plan.*

RDC/ETB (1992) *The Green Light: Guide to Sustainable Tourism Development.*

TEN (1984) *TEN Declaration.* TEN, Stuttgart.

TEN, ECTWT (1998) *Position Paper on the Global Code of Ethics.* TEN, ECTWT, Stuttgart.

Tourism Concern (1992) *Beyond the Green Horizon: Principles for Sustainable Tourism.* WWF.

Tour Operators Initiative for Sustainable Tourism (2000) Statement of Commitment.

UK NGOs (1999) Position Paper on Tourism, Poverty and Sustainable Development to CSD-7.

UNEP (1995) *Environmental Codes of Conduct for Tourism.*

UNEP (2000) *Principles for the Implementation of Sustainable Tourism.* UNEP.

UNEP (undated) *Sustainable Tourism: Bridging the Gap.*

WTO (1980) *Manila Declaration on World Tourism.* WTO, Manila.

WTO (1985) *Tourism Bill of Rights and Tourist Code.* WTO, Sofia.

WTO, UNEP, IUCN (1992) *Guidelines: Development of national Parks and Protected Areas For Tourism.* WTO, UNEP.

WTO (1993) *Sustainable Tourism Development: Guide for Local Planners.* WTO.

WTO, UNESCO, UNEP (1995) *Charter for Sustainable Tourism.* WTO, UNESCO, UNEP, Lanzarote.

WTO (1996) *Practical Guide to the Development and Use of Indicators of Sustainable Tourism*. WTO.

WTO (1997) Manila Declaration on the Social Impact of Tourism. WTO, Manila.

WTO (1997) *Male Declaration on Sustainable Tourism Development*. WTO, Male.

WTO (1998) *Guide for Local Authorities on Developing Sustainable Tourism*. WTO.

WTO (1999) *Global Code of Ethics for Tourism*. WTO.

WTO (2000) *Tourism: An Effective Tool for Sustainable Development in the New Millennium*.

WTTC/WTO/Earth Council (1995) *Towards Environmentally Sustainable Development*.

WTTC, WTO/OMT, Earth Council (1998) *Agenda 21 for the Travel and Tourism Industry*.

WWF (2000) *Position Paper on Tourism*.

WWF-UK/Synergy (2000) *Global Reporting Guidelines and Certification: An Analysis*.

WWF (2001) *International Guidelines for Community-Based Ecotourism Development*. WWF.

Tourism and the Environment in Scotland

A and M Training and Development (1997) *Review of Wildlife Tourism in Scotland*, Inverness: Tourism and the Environment Task Force.

Arnott, J. (1993) Issues Facing Scotland. In Fladmark, J. M. (ed), *Heritage*. Donhead Publishing, London: 63-76.

Barron, S. (1992) Conservation Agency for Scotland, *The Planner*, April, 10-11.

Bryden, D. (1995) Tourism and the Environment - Maintaining the Balance. In Proceedings of Association for the Protection of Rural Scotland (APRS) conference, *Tourism and Recreation: A Sustainable Approach for Rural Areas*, APRS, Edinburgh: 1-6.

Buie, E. (1996) Making Tracks on Cairngorms, *Herald*, 30/01/96: 1:5.

Butler, R.W. (1985) Evolution of Tourism in the Scottish Highlands, *Annals of Tourism Research*, 18 (1): 26-40.

Caffyn, A. (1997) *Developing Sustainable Tourism in the Trossachs, Scotland*. Paper presented at the ATLAS Conference - Tourism, Leisure and Community Development - September 1997.

Cairngorms Partnership (1997) *Managing the Cairngorms: The*

Cairngorms Partnership Management Strategy, The Cairngorms Partnership, Grantownon-Spey.

Countryside Commission for Scotland (1990) *The Mountain Areas of Scotland.* CCS, Edinburgh.

Crabtree, J. R., Leat, P. M. K., Santarossa, J. and Thomson, K. J. (1994) The Economic Impact of Wildlife Sites in Scotland, *Journal of Rural Studies,* 10: 61-72.

Crabtree, R., Appleton, Z., Thomson, K., Slee, W., Chalmers, N. and Copus, A. (1992) *The Economics of Countryside Access in Scotland,* SAC Economic Report No. 37, SAC, Aberdeen.

Cramb, A. (1996) *Who Owns Scotland Now: the Use and Abuse of Private Land.* Mainstream Publishing, London.

Crofts, R. (1995) *The Environment: Who Cares*? Scottish Natural Heritage, Perth.

Dargie, T. D. C. and Briggs, D. J. (1992) *State of the Scottish Environment 1991.* Scottish Wildlife and Countryside Link, Perth.

Dargie, T., Aitken, R., and Tantram, D. (1994) *Trossachs Tourism Management Programme: Environmental Monitoring.* Highlands and Islands Enterprise, Inverness.

Edwards, T., Pennington, N. and Starrett, M. (1993) The Scottish Parks System: A Strategy for Conservation and Enjoyment. In Fladmark, J. M. (ed), *Heritage,* Donhead Publishing, London, 141-151.

Getz, D. (1994) Residents Attitudes Towards Tourism. A Longitudinal Study in Spey Valley, Scotland, *Tourism Management,* 15 (4): 247-258.

Halhead, V. (1987) *Employment in Nature Conservation and Related Activities in Highland Region.* Nature Conservancy Council, Edinburgh.

Hall, D. (1998) *Rural Tourism Management: Sustainable Options.* Scottish Agricultural College.

Highlands and Islands Enterprise (1992) *The Way Forward. A Strategy for Tourism in the Highlands and Islands of Scotland.* Highlands and Islands Enterprise, Inverness.

Highland Regional Council, Scottish Natural Heritage (1994) *An Interpretative Strategy for the Highland Region.* HRC, Inverness.

Holden, A. (1998) The Use of Visitor Understanding in Skiing Management and Development Decisions at the Cairngorm Mountains, Scotland, *Tourism Management,* 19 (2): 145-152.

Holden, A. (1999) High Impact Tourism: A Suitable Component of

Sustainable Policy? The Case of Downhill Skiing Development at Cairngorm, Scotland, *Journal of Sustainable Tourism*, 7 (2): 97-107.

Hughes, G. (1995) The Cultural Construction of Sustainable Tourism, *Tourism Management*, 16 (1): 49-59.

Huxley, T. (1993) Where the Shoe Hurts: The Ecological Impact of Tourism. In Fladmark, J. M. (ed), *Heritage*. Donhead Publishing, London.

Independent Northern Consultants (1995) *Assessment of the Direct Employment Impact of Environmental Activity in the Highlands and Islands. A Report for HIE and Scottish Natural Heritage*. HIE, Inverness.

Littlejohn, D. and Goulding, P. (1994) *Scotland, EIU International Tourism Reports*, 2: 63-81.

Mackay, D. (1995) *Scotland's Rural Land Use Agencies*. Scottish Cultural Press, Aberdeen.

MacLellan, L. R. (1993) *Tourism and Scottish Mountain Environments: Values and Public Policy, Proceedings of Conference: Values and the Environment*. University of Surrey, September.

Minch Partnership (1995) *The Minch Project: General Information*. Minch Partnership, Stornoway.

Morrison, D. (1995) *Wildlife Tourism in the Minch: Distribution, Impact and Development Opportunities*. Minch Project, Stornoway.

Ross, A., Rowan-Robinson, J. and Walton, W. (1995) Sustainable Development in Scotland: The Role of Scottish Natural Heritage, *Land Use Policy*, 12 (3): 237-252.

Royal Society for the Protection of Birds (1995) *Nature Conservation, Employment and local Economies: A Review of Studies in Scotland*, Briefing Paper for Scottish Tourist Board. RSPB, Edinburgh.

Scott, M. (1992) *What Future for the Cairngorms? Ecos*, 13 (2): 16-23.

Scottish Natural Heritage (1992) *Working with Scotland's People to Care for Our Natural Heritage: Mission Statement and Promotional Brochure*. Scottish Natural Heritage, Edinburgh.

Scottish Natural Heritage (1993) *Sustainable Development and the Natural Heritage. The Scottish Natural Heritage Approach*. Scottish Natural Heritage, Perth.

Scottish Office (1993) *Common Sense and Sustainability: A Partnership for the Cairngorms*, The Report of the Cairngorms Working Party, March. HMSO, London.

Scottish Tourist Board (1993) *British Tourism in the Highlands and Islands, 1992*. Scottish Tourist Board, Edinburgh.

Scottish Tourism Coordinating Group (1992) *Tourism and the Scottish Environment: A Sustainable Partnership*. Scottish Tourist Board, Edinburgh.

Scottish Wildlife and Countryside Link (1997) *Protecting Scotland's Finest Landscapes: A call for Action on National Parks for Scotland.* Scottish Wildlife and Countryside Link, Perth.

Smout, C. (1993) *The Highlands and the Roots of Green Consciousness, 1750-1990*, Occasional Paper No. 1. Scottish Natural Heritage, Perth.

The Tourism and Environment Task Force (1993) *Tourism and the Scottish Environment, Tourism Management Initiative: Guidelines for the Development of Tourism Management Programmes.* Scottish Tourist Board, Edinburgh.

The Tourism and Environment Task Force (1993) *Going Green: Guidelines for the Scottish Tourism Industry.* Scottish Tourist Board, Edinburgh.

The Tourism and Environment Task Force (1996) *Action Plan 1996-1999.* Highlands and Islands Enterprise, Inverness.

The Tourism and Environment Task Force (1997) *Review of Wildlife Tourism in Scotland.* Highlands and Islands Enterprise, Inverness.

Wightman, A. (1994) *The Greening of Rural Development.* Scottish Wildlife and Countryside Link, Perth.

Wightman, A. (1996) *Scotland's Mountains: An Agenda for Sustainable Development.* Scottish Wildlife and Countryside Link, Perth.

Scotland and National Parks

Bishop, K., Green, M. and Phillips, A. (1998) Models of National Parks, *Scottish Natural Heritage* Review No. 105. Scottish Natural Heritage, Perth.

Cherry, G. (1975) *Environmental Planning 1939-1969, National Parks and recreation in the countryside*, Vol. 2. HMSO, London.

Clough, B. (1998) National Parks for Scotland: A New Opportunity for Land Management, *The Scottish Planner*, 61: 6-7.

Clough, B. (1998) National Parks Proposal Unveiled, *The Scottish Planner*, 65: 5.

Countryside Commission for Scotland (1990) *The Mountain Areas of Scotland.* Countryside Commission for Scotland, Edinburgh.

Crabtree, J. R. (1991) National Park designation in Scotland, *Land Use Policy*, 8 (3): 241-252.

Crofts, R. (1999) Tailor-made solutions for Scotland, Editorial in *Scotland's Natural Heritage, The Magazine for Scottish Natural Heritage*, No. 14 (2).

Dickinson, G. (1991) National Parks - Scottish Needs and Spanish Experience, *Scottish Geographical Magazine*, 107 (2): 124-129.

Dower, M., Buller, H. and Asamer-Handler, M. (1998) The socio-economic benefits of National Parks: A Review Prepared for Scottish Natural Heritage, *Natural Heritage Review*, No. 104. Scottish Natural Heritage, Perth.

Ferguson, M. P. (1988) National Parks for Scotland? *Scottish Geographical Magazine*, 104 (1): 36-40.

Foster, J. (1982) A Park System and Scenic Conservation in Scotland. Countryside Commission for Scotland, Perth.

Garner, G. (1989) National Parks for Scotland? The Designation Debate, *Ecos*, 10 (3): 13-16.

Giongo, F. et al (2001) *A Study of Visitor Management in the World's National Parks and Protected Areas*. Colorado State University.

Govan, H., Inglis, A., Pretty, J., Harrison, M. and Wightman, A. (1998) Best Practice in Community Participation for National Parks, *Natural Heritage Review*, No. 107. Scottish Natural Heritage, Perth.

MacEwan, A. and MacEwan, M. (1982) *National Parks: Conservation or Cosmetics*? Allen and Unwin, London.

Moir, J. (1991) National Parks: North of the Border, *Planning Outlook*, 34 (2): 61-67.

North Yorkshire Moors National Park (1993) *A Landscape for Visitors: Sustainable Tourism in the National Park*.

Packer, N. (1998) Shared Authority for National Parks, *Planning*, 8.

Poustie, M. (1999) National Parks for Scotland: A Consultation Paper, *Environmental Law and Management*, 11: 40-44.

Scottish Council for National Parks (undated) National Parks in Scotland? Twenty Questions, Publicity Leaflet. Scottish Council for National Parks, Dunbartonshire.

Scottish Natural Heritage (1998) *National Parks for Scotland: A Consultation Paper*. Scottish Natural Heritage, Perth.

Scottish Natural Heritage (1999) *National Parks for Scotland. Report on the Process of Consultation*. Scottish Natural Heritage, Perth.

Scottish Natural Heritage (1999) *National Parks for Scotland. Conference Proceedings: Developing Proposals for National Parks*. Scottish Natural Heritage, Perth.

Scottish Natural Heritage (1999) *National Parks for Scotland. Scottish Natural Heritage's Advice to Government.* Scottish Natural Heritage, Perth.

Scottish Wildlife and Countryside Link (1997) *Protecting Scotland's Finest Landscapes: A call for Action on National Parks for Scotland.* Scottish Wildlife and countryside Link, Perth.

Scottish Wildlife and Countryside Link (1997) Protecting Scotland's Finest Landscapes, *Conference Proceedings, Session 1, Time for Action on National Parks*, Stirling, 17th September 1997. Scottish Wildlife and Countryside Link, Perth.

Scottish Wildlife and Countryside Link (1998) Protecting Scotland's Finest Landscapes. *Conference Proceedings, Session 2, National Parks—The Opportunities*, Inverness, 16th March 1998. Scottish Wildlife and Countryside Link, Perth.

Wightman, A. (1996) *Scotland's Mountains: An Agenda for Sustainable Development.* Scottish Wildlife and Countryside Link, Perth.

Index